Jesus and His Parables

Jesus and His Parables

INTERPRETING THE PARABLES OF JESUS TODAY

Edited by
V. GEORGE SHILLINGTON

With a Foreword by
SEÁN FREYNE

T&T CLARK
EDINBURGH

T&T CLARK LTD
59 GEORGE STREET
EDINBURGH EH2 2LQ
SCOTLAND

Copyright © T&T Clark Ltd, 1997

First published 1997

ISBN 0 567 08596 1

British Library Cataloguing-in-Publication Data
A catalogue record for this book is available from the British Library

Typeset by Waverley Typesetters, Galashiels
Printed and bound in Great Britain by Bell & Bain Ltd, Glasgow

To
WALLACE *and* WESLEY
. . . themselves twin parables

Contents

Contributors

MARY ANN BEAVIS, Ph.D., Lecturer in the Faculty of Theology and in the Institute of Urban Studies, University of Winnipeg, Canada. Her publications include articles on parable interpretation in the *Catholic Biblical Quarterly* (1990) and the *Journal of Biblical Literature* (1992).

MICHAEL FARRIS, Ph.D., D.Min., Minister-at-large in the Presbyterian Church in Canada and Editor of Inter-Word, a publication on the Internet for church leaders; part-time Lecturer at Concord College, University of Winnipeg, Canada.

SEÁN FREYNE, Ph.D., Professor of New Testament at Trinity College, Dublin, Ireland. Professor Freyne's benchmark work is *Galilee, Jesus and the Gospels*, Fortress (1988).

J. IAN H. McDONALD, Ph.D., Reader in Christian Ethics and New Testament Studies, New College, University of Edinburgh, Scotland, UK. His earlier work on the good Samaritan, published in the *Scottish Journal of Theology* (1996) was a forerunner to his chapter in the present collection.

J. C. O'NEILL, Ph.D., Professor Emeritus, New Testament, New College, University of Edinburgh, Scotland, UK. Professor O'Neill is particularly interested in the question of Jesus' Messiahship. Recent work includes *Who Did Jesus Think He Was?* Brill (1995).

DONALD PETERS, M.A., Principal of the Mennonite Brethren Collegiate Institute, Winnipeg, Canada, and volunteer with the Mennonite Central Committee.

RICHARD L. ROHRBAUGH, Ph.D., Professor of Religious Studies (Mediterranean Studies), Lewis and Clark College, Portland, Oregon, USA. Professor Rohrbaugh is best known for his social-scientific analysis of New Testament texts.

V. GEORGE SHILLINGTON, Ph.D., Professor of Biblical and Theological Studies, Concord College, University of Winnipeg, Canada. His most recent publication is a commentary on *2 Corinthians*, Herald Press (1997).

WILLARD M. SWARTLEY, Ph.D., Professor of New Testament Studies and Dean at Associated Mennonite Biblical Seminaries, Elkhart, Indiana, USA. Recent publications include *Israel's Scripture Traditions and the Synoptic Gospels: Story Shaping Story*, Hendrickson (1994).

PAUL TRUDINGER, Th.D., Ph.D., Adjunct Professor of Theology, Faculty of Theology, University of Winnipeg, Canada. He has written numerous articles on Gospel literature.

JOEL R. WOHLGEMUT, M.A. in New Testament Studies (McMaster University, Hamilton); currently studying medicine.

Foreword

When I accepted the editor's kind invitation to write a foreword to this collection of essays on the parables of Jesus, I
had envisaged a piece that would situate the essays within the
context of contemporary parable studies. However, the fine
introduction by the editor has made that task redundant. I find
myself cast in the role of being one of the first readers of this
very fine collection, which deserves a wide readership. My
reflections take the form of musings as to how the collection
as a whole measures up to some of what I consider to be the
most significant developments in parable studies since Adolph
Jülicher challenged the hitherto dominant allegorical approach
to their interpretation.

In the intervening period interpreters of the parables have
responded to the various methodological shifts that have
been occurring within their discipline generally. Indeed, it
could be said that parable studies have often blazed the trail in
these very developments. Despite the varying results from such
a variety of approaches—historical, literary and social scientific—
it is true to say that the parables of Jesus continue to fascinate
and challenge the interpretative ingenuity of their hearers/
readers. In that respect, the present collection does not
disappoint as a variety of approaches are adopted to individual
parables yielding a rich harvest of insights from many different
perspectives.

In this century, the studies of Joachim Jeremias and Charles
H. Dodd have been highly influential and one can see their
continuing importance in almost all of these contributions,
even when they have both been criticised for imposing later
theological categories onto the message of Jesus. Jeremias
was greatly respected for his knowledge of the Jewish literary
sources contemporary with Jesus. The recognition that Jesus

participated in a wider parable-telling tradition has only heightened interest in his particular use of the form and how, by comparison with others, it seems to give expression to his distinctive 'voice'.

Our knowledge of the Jewish world of Jesus is today greatly enhanced, even since Jeremias' time, not just by the publication of many more of the Dead Sea Scrolls than were available to him, but also by the mass of archaeological data which, when properly interpreted, can illumine the daily life of Galilee in considerable detail. Furthermore, our understanding of the Rabbinic sources has been considerably nuanced through the literary and historical studies of Jacob Neusner and his students. Stereotypes of Pharisees or Jews, which smacked more of the Reformation split between law and gospel rather than the varieties of Judaism that coexisted in the first century, have been exposed by the work of E. P. Sanders. Jesus the teller of parables is no longer to be seen over against his own tradition but must be located firmly within it, even as he brings his creative insights to bear on that inheritance, stretching back to the Israelite prophets. Happily, *Jesus and His Parables* is conscious of these developments even when Jeremias' basic approach of locating Jesus within the social, cultural and religious world of his day is firmly adhered to.

Dodd's insight that the parables are essentially meta-phorical has been developed considerably in recent scholar-ship, mainly in the light of French philosopher Paul Ricoeur's treatment of 'the rule of metaphor.' One of the most important aspects of modern parable study is the awareness that the parables are intended to shock and stimulate us into active exploration of their possible meanings through their—at first sight—unlikely comparisons, amoral plots and unexpected outcomes. The notion of example stories illustrating well-established truths can no longer be sustained. Yet the parables are not simple metaphors, but rather extended narratives in which likenesses can only be perceived through the negation of literal meanings by an awareness of the strangeness of the plots. Dodd's other contribution, that as parables of the kingdom they reflect 'a realised eschatology,' cannot be sustained. Here again Ricouer's explorations of the relationship between time and narrative have contributed to a more nuanced understanding of the temporality of the kingdom as proclaimed by Jesus.

A striking aspect of this collection is the fact that five of the ten parables chosen come from Luke's special material. With regard to these parables John Drury makes the provocative, even 'parabolic,' statement that if the special Lukan parables are parables of the historical Jesus, then a good case can be made for Jesus as author of the third gospel! Drury's remark does strike a cautionary note to the assumptions of Jeremias, Dodd and others that with the parables in particular we have reached bedrock Jesus tradition. At the same time Drury also compels us to remember that the parables come to us within larger texts in which the main character, Jesus, is himself portrayed as a storyteller of power and imagination. Undoubtedly, this was based on a particular memory of Jesus, deeply rooted in the tradition, yet the assumption that Jesus told parables and the Evangelists allegorised them, as a way of separating Jesus from later tradition, is open to question on purely historical grounds. The present, post-modern climate can too readily lead to a modernisation of Jesus the teller of parables, which needs to be resisted. I am happy to report that for this reader at least, the contributors to *Jesus and His Parables* have admirably avoided any such temptation. Indeed the awareness of the different cultural codes operative in the first-century Mediterranean world—explicit in some of the contributions and implicit in the others—ensures that no such anachronistic treatment of Jesus is likely to occur.

The question of interpreting the parables of Jesus, either inside or outside the Gospels (it surely must be both) does highlight the situation of the modern interpreter. The Irish writer Seán O'Faolain reminds us that as a genre the short story calls for attentive and intelligent readers. The condensation of the various elements which the genre demands means that every word is crucial, a vital clue to the understanding of the whole. While scholars equipped with historical and literary skills are best placed to pick up all the subtle nuances of these stories and restore them to their original freshness, it is also encouraging to report that the parables of Jesus are today often read with new and exciting insights within the context of basic communities. As they struggle to interpret their lives in the light of the gospel in situations of apparent despair, where the temptation to apathy is all too real, *Jesus and His Parables* is for them also. The editor and contributors are to be congratulated for responding so creatively to the challenge.

SEÁN FREYNE
Trinity College
Dublin

Preface

Of all the fascinating kinds of 'snapshots' from the ministry of Jesus, none has attracted more attention in recent times than the parables, and that with good reason. Unlike an actual snapshot, *a parable speaks*. Its meaning is as much in echo and code as in plain speech. The challenge for the interpreter of this 'talking photo' is to break the code by listening sensitively to the echo and the plain speech. This quality of the parables of Jesus continues to elicit new insights from interpreters, yielding cumulative results in our understanding of Jesus of history and faith.

Parables can be sorted and grouped variously. In this book the four-fold grouping follows the surface structure of the parables, which in turn seems to reflect the structure of life from which the parables arose in the mind and ministry of Jesus in Roman-occupied Palestine of the Second Temple of Judaism. The four dimensions are: The Temple, The Land, The Economy, and The People. Given the Palestinian Jewish setting of the parables, one might think that a most obvious dimension would be the Law. Quite right, the Law as such undergirds all of the parables in one way or another. But in the society where Jesus lives it comes to play in the religious service of the Temple, in agrarian peasant life on the land, in a stratified economy, and in the communal lives of the people. The parables of Jesus are 'kingdom trajectories' out of these dimensions of life in Roman occupied Palestine, particularly Galilee.

The ten writers, all well qualified academically but from different walks of life, were free to listen to the echoes and to decipher the codes from their own place, using their own chosen hermeneutical method. The result is a striking collage of parable interpretations focusing Jesus in his time, among his people, obliquely pointing to the 'other' rule of God for the world.

To all of the contributors I offer my sincere thanks for a job well done. Without their co-operation, coupled with their skilful handling of the text before them, the aim of the book could not have been reached. Concord College also deserves a vote of thanks for granting salaried time to devote to the writing and editing of these chapters. And not to be forgotten, my wife Grace, who is at the moment preparing dinner without my help for the birthday of our son, makes glad my heart by her endless encouragement.

VGS
Winnipeg
January 1997

1

Engaging with the Parables

V. GEORGE SHILLINGTON

The significant number of works on the parables of Jesus, rather than making another book on the subject superfluous, bears witness to the provocative power of the parables to evoke new insights and interpretations. The nuances in the interpretations in the present collection prove the point. Like their Galilean architect, the parables of Jesus are positively elusive. They keep inviting their readers back to peer through their literary window once more for some further clue to the mystery of the Galilean figure who first spoke these teasers, of the audience who first heard them, and of the bloody execution of this peasant Jewish teller of parables from Lower Galilee. On the one hand, the parables can function as literary 'windows on the world of Jesus,' to use the title of Bruce Malina's book,[1] but on the other, they are encrypted images of a new reality that call the received world of Jesus' time and place into question. Jesus of the Gospels signals the breakthrough of a new reality by announcing the advent of 'the kingdom of God,'[2] a highly charged phrase in Roman-occupied Jewish Palestine.

---

[1] Bruce J. Malina, *Windows on the World of Jesus: Time Travel to Ancient Judea* (Louisville: Westminster/John Knox, 1993).

[2] *hê basileia tou theou*, e.g. Mark 1:15. Appearing frequently in the Synoptic Gospels, the term (kingdom of God/heaven) is deeply imprinted on the tradition of Jesus, and was doubtless minted in the preaching of Jesus himself. Even so, the frequent use of the phrase to introduce parables, particularly those in the Gospel of Matthew, may be due to the inclination of the Evangelist.

Purpose and Method of the Book

The book has two principal purposes. The first is to offer fresh
glimpses into the thought and life and vision of the historical
figure of Jesus. If the parables of Jesus constitute 'a particularly
firm historical foundation,'[3] as Jeremias has argued, and if
they are drawn from the 'common life'[4] of the society in which
the teller of parables lived, as Dodd has proposed, then the
ongoing interpretation of the parables serves to illuminate the
character and mission of the one who told these tales in the
environs of Lower Galilee, and who was eventually sentenced to
death by crucifixion in Jerusalem. The mosaic of parable
interpretations represented in the chapters that follow reflects
the many enigmatic profiles of the Galilean Jewish visionary who
still 'comes to us as One unknown,'[5] whose word and act together
translated into life-giving memory in the community of his
followers. The memory energised a mission that pulsed its
way out of Jewish Palestine into the Mediterranean world and
beyond. The cluster of parable interpretations in these pages
respects the collective memory of Jesus enshrined in the Gospels,
but it also points behind the scripted memory in the Gospels to
the one who uttered the parables in the particular setting of
Palestinian Jewish society.

Linked with this purpose of viewing the figure of Jesus afresh
through a new reading of his parables is the aim of testing
interpretive possibilities relative to the narrative parables. As a
way of framing provocative thought and vision, the narrative
parable is distinctive, and merits serious investigation and lively
experimentation. Such is the character of the ensuing chapters
dealing with many of the well-known narrative parables of Jesus
in the Synoptic Gospels.[6] The originality and variety of these
parables of Jesus, both in form and content, elicit more than

[3] J. Jeremias, *The Parables of Jesus*, 8th ed., trans. S. H. Hooke (London: SCM,
1972): 11; based on *Die Gleichnisse Jesu*, 8th ed. (Göttingen: Vandenhoeck &
Ruprecht, 1970).
[4] C. H. Dodd, *The Parables of the Kingdom* (New York: Scribner's, 1961): 5.
[5] Albert Schweitzer, *The Quest of the Historical Jesus: A Critical Study of its Progress
from Reimarus to Wrede*, translated from *Von Reimarus zu Wrede* (1906) by
W. Montgomery (New York: Macmillan, 1961): 403.
[6] With parallels in non-canonical gospels, such as the Gospel of Thomas, judged
and incorporated where appropriate.

one approach, more than one person's understanding from one place.[7] Reading a parable through the eyes of an educated female in an Anglo-American culture, for example, would likely elicit a different response than reading it through the consciousness of an educated male in the same social setting. Even among educated male interpreters the social location varies, depending on the kinds of cultural influences they encountered along the way.

Moreover, the second principal purpose of the book is to expose in one volume different approaches to the interpretation of the narrative parables of Jesus. Another way of carrying out the experiment, of course, might have been to invite the same number of different interpreters to engage a single provocative parable, such as the good Samaritan or the labourers in the vineyard, and thus to compare independent approaches and outcomes using only one referent.[8] But this method would have truncated the other principal purpose, to illuminate the literary mosaic that signifies the historic figure of Jesus. By having different interpreters engage different parables, both purposes can be accomplished with reasonable success. The hope is that this collection of interpretations of the best known narrative parables of Jesus will serve students of gospel literature in their search for the meaning and mission of the historical Jesus, and will also function as a guide for instructors and leaders in religion more generally.

The book does not attempt to classify or categorise the parables under formal labels[9] such as parables of advent, action, and reversal, much less under interpretive conclusions.[10] Rather,

---

[7] The critical value of citing social location in the *reading* of biblical texts, not merely for locating scripted social codes, is now coming into its own, as evidenced in the important collection of essays edited by Fernando F. Segovia and Mary Ann Tolbert, *Reading from this Place: Social Location and Biblical Interpretation in Global Perspective* (Minneapolis: Fortress Press, 1995): 'Real readers lie behind all models of interpretation and all reading strategies, all recreations of meaning from texts and all reconstructions of history; . . . all such readers are themselves regarded as variously positioned and engaged in their own respective social locations.' (From the opening chapter by F. F. Segovia, 'Cultural Studies and Contemporary Biblical Criticism:' 7.)

[8] Cf. J. D. Crossan, 'Thirteen Ways of Looking at a Parable,' in *In Parables: The Challenge of the Historical Jesus?* (Sonoma: Polebridge Press, 1992): 118–120.

[9] E.g. Crossan, *In Parables*: 37–117.

[10] E.g. Jeremias, *Parables*: 115–229.

the four classifications at the beginning of each section reflect explicit elements in the narrative structure of the parables themselves, which in turn resonate with the particular setting of Second Temple Palestinian Judaism within which Jesus lived: Parables of the Temple, Parables of the Land, Parables of the Economy, and Parables of the People. *Foundational to all of these four dimensions is the Jewish Law* that governed the social-religious lives of the Jewish inhabitants of Roman-occupied Palestine.

The parables of Jesus, like Jesus himself, reside within two contexts, both of which are considered in each of the interpretations in the four sections of the book: their context within the gospel literature, and their context within the setting of Jesus in Jewish Palestine before the revolt of 66–70 CE.

Jesus' Parables in the Gospels

'In his identity, words, and deeds Jesus of Nazareth provides the possibility and promise of ministry in his name,'[11] so writes Paul J. Achtemeier. But one is led to ask immediately, who exactly is Jesus of Nazareth? Are his identity, words, and deeds prominently displayed in neutral documents for all to read with one accord? Not so. While the person of Jesus constitutes the central character and principal concern of the Gospels, the historical figure of Jesus of Nazareth stands within, and thus also chronologically behind, the Gospels. These kinds of questions continue to haunt historical Jesus research, the same ones that fed into the recent 'Jesus 2000' debate on the Internet in 1996, with John Dominic Crossan and Marcus Borg on one side and Luke Johnson on the other. Johnson challenged the method of the Jesus Seminar (of which Crossan and Borg are members) in its quest for the 'real Jesus' behind the various Gospels. Johnson argued, instead, that the real Jesus is the one depicted in the church's Gospels and Epistles, whose character is that of Messiah of God. 'The "real Jesus" is first of all the powerful, resurrected Lord whose transforming Spirit is active in the community.'[12] Johnson's statement is one of faith, the church's faith in Jesus, and as such

---

[11] Paul J. Achtemeier, 'The Ministry of Jesus in the Synoptic Gospels,' *Interpretation*, 35 (1981): 157.

[12] L. T. Johnson, *The Real Jesus: The Misguided Quest for the Historical Jesus and the Truth of the Traditional Gospels* (HarperSanFrancisco, 1996): 166.

merits the profile he gives it in his book. Still, one is left with nagging questions concerning the figure that existed before the Evangelists incorporated traditional Jesus material in the shape of their respective Gospels for their communities of faith: Was Jesus' audience different from those of the Evangelists? What religious, social, and political situation attended Jesus in Palestine as compared to that which attended the Gospel writers? How did Jesus view himself in his own world of Jewish Palestine? What did he think of the particular way of life within the borders of the holy land occupied by Romans? These kinds of questions arise from the Synoptic Fact of three Gospels that carry similar, yet different, data about the one figure of Jesus.

Each of the three Synoptic Gospels, where the parables are found, manifests its own distinctive tone and texture and thrust (not to mention the Greek language, which Jesus probably did not use to tell his parables). As 'gospels' these documents, whether the canonical four of the New Testament or the extra-canonical ones, all have an audience and a purpose. In the Greco-Roman period the noun *euaggelion* ('gospel') normally 'means simply "news," "message" and particularly in Christian usage "preaching;" the verb should then be translated as "to bring a message," or "to preach."'[13] All of this to say that the Gospels in which Jesus and his parables appear are evangelical tracts intended to *preach the news* of Jesus' messiahship. Like any good preachers, the Evangelists used the available material from the tradition of Jesus to persuade their audiences. Consequently, the data from the Jesus tradition was gathered, shaped and interpreted by the particular Evangelist to achieve the end for which that gospel document was designed. This phenomenon is well illustrated by Matthew's and Luke's use of Q, 'a collection of sayings and discourses . . . attributed to Jesus,'[14] in their respective Gospels. Matthew brings many of the sayings from Q together in one place in the context of the Sermon on the Mount (chs 5–7), whereas Luke has some in his Sermon on the Plain (6:20–49) and others in different contexts in his

---

[13] Helmut Koester, *Ancient Christian Gospels: Their History and Development* (London: SCM Press, 1990): 2.

[14] Norman Perrin and Dennis C. Duling, *The New Testament: An Introduction. Proclamation and Parenesis, Myth and History*, 2nd ed. (San Diego: Harcourt Brace Jovanovich, 1982): 106.

Gospel.[15] The point is, each of the Evangelists drapes the sayings of Jesus in a context suited to the purpose of that particular Gospel.

In some cases a parable of Jesus manifests allegorical elements intertwined in its structure, as in Matthew's rendition of the parable of the marriage banquet put on by a king for his son (Matt. 22:2–14; par. Luke 14:16–24; Thomas 64). Some of the invited guests in Matthew's version treat the servants shamefully and kill them, thus incurring the wrath of the king, who promptly kills the murderers and burns their city. Matthew's parable of Jesus echoes the events surrounding the destruction of the city of Jerusalem in 70 CE, as well as a messianic faith of the church that confessed Jesus as Son of God and the church as the eschatological bride of Christ. The parallel parable in the Gospel of Luke and the Gospel of Thomas has none of these Matthean elements. In such instances a reconstruction of the parable of Jesus is required using literary and historical analysis.

In some instances the Evangelist (or the tradition, or both) tacks on interpretive elements to the parable, making the attachment part of the parable proper. The parable of the labourers in the vineyard is a case in point (Matt. 20:1–16). The closing line of the parable, 'the last shall be first and the first last' (v. 16, cf. Mark 10:31), comes out of the Markan context (Mark 10) into which Matthew placed the parable of the labourers in the vineyard. But this axiomatic closure to the parable fits better with Matthew's church positioning itself against such principal forces as post-70 Judaism at Jamnia,[16] than it does with the chiastic structure of the parable in the mouth of Jesus in Lower Galilee in the early thirties.

At no point is the evangelical interest in the parables of Jesus more pronounced than in the allegorical interpretation of the parable of the sower in Mark 4 (par. Matt. 13; Luke 8). The interpretation is set off from the parable proper by a

---

[15] On the complexity of the problem of Q in Matthew and Luke see H. D. Betz, 'The Sermon on the Mount and Q: Some Aspects of the Problem,' in *Gospel Origins and Christian Beginnings: In Honor of James M. Robinson*, ed. J. E. Goehring, et al. (Sonoma: Polebridge Press, 1990): 19–34.

[16] Demonstrated in W. D. Davies, *The Setting of the Sermon on the Mount* (Cambridge: The University Press, 1964): 256–315.

transitional explanation about the nature and purpose of parables: to the outsiders the parables are confusing puzzles, but 'to you' insiders (the church) the secret of the kingdom of God is revealed. Then follows the allegorical explanation of the various elements of the preceding narrative parable, which corresponds to the experience of the church in its post-Easter missionary endeavours. As a parable of Jesus in Jewish Palestine, however, the story is charged differently. Jesus told the tale on Jewish holy land, which was occupied by a foreign power, exploited by merchants, and failing to support the disenfranchised Jewish inhabitants.

In short, the parables of Jesus as we have them in the gospel literature carry two interpretive contexts: a secondary explicit context in the particular Gospel in which they appear, and a primary implicit context in the life and thought and culture of Jesus in Second Temple Jewish Palestine. To engage the parables in their primary context is the express interest of the chapters that follow.[17]

Jewish Palestinian Environment

Several important elements about the figure of Jesus have emerged on solid ground from the critical scrutiny of biblical scholars over the last century.[18] Outstanding among these is that Jesus carried out his ministry in Lower Galilee within the religious environment of Palestinian Judaism at the time of the Second Temple when the land and people were occupied by the Romans. Whatever else may be said of his place in the matrix of

[17] Some of the writers are less committed to the enterprise than others, believing that a sure and certain reconstruction is speculative at best; these writers prefer to engage the parable of Jesus at the level of the Gospel in which it appears.

[18] E. P. Sanders lists eight such elements as follows: '1. Jesus was baptized by John the Baptist. 2. Jesus was a Galilean who preached and healed. 3. Jesus called disciples and spoke of there being twelve. 4. Jesus confined his activity to Israel. 5. Jesus engaged in a controversy about the temple. 6. Jesus was crucified outside Jerusalem by the Roman authorities. 7. After his death Jesus' followers continued as an identifiable movement. 8. At least some Jews persecuted at least parts of the new movement (Gal. 1:13, 22; Phil. 3.6), and it appears that this persecution endured at least to a time near the end of Paul's career (2 Cor. 11:24; Gal. 5:11; 6:12; cf. Matt. 23:34; 10:17),' in *Jesus and Judaism* (Philadelphia: Fortress Press, 1985): 11.

Mediterranean life,[19] Jesus' place within Jewish religious, social, and political life in Second-Temple Palestine stands as the primary context for engaging the parables he told.

The Temple

A certain tension appears to have existed between the Jewish populace of Galilee and the elite religious custodians of religious Temple service in Jerusalem, as Seán Freyne has argued.[20] While the Jewish people of Palestine generally would have affirmed the central symbols of their traditional faith that welded them together as a people,[21] they could, at the same time, protest against a system and its functionaries that placed a burden on their situation in life.[22] The Jewish covenanters at Qumran are a classic example of such a protest attitude in their sharp critique of the Temple and its High Priest.[23] Jesus is also reported in the Gospels as having spoken against the Temple (Mark 14:58; cf. 13:1–2). A verbal attack on the Temple of God would have been considered blasphemy by the teachers of the Law, since the Law requires the service of the central shrine of Jerusalem for the salvation and security of the people (Deut. 12). The charge against Jesus in Mark 14, even though reported as false, seems to have had some basis in fact. All four canonical Gospels preserve

[19] E.g. J. D. Crossan's view that Jesus was of Mediterranean peasant class, and taught out of the life-style and mind-set of Jewish Cynicism. *The Historical Jesus: The Life of a Mediterranean Jewish Peasant* (HarperSanFrancisco, 1991): 421–22.

[20] 'The complex set of social and religious tensions within which Galilean life was lived in the first century was indeed fertile soil for the emergence of an alternative view of Jewish faith and practice; on the one hand this was deeply attached to and respectful of the central symbols of that faith, and yet, on the other hand it was constantly being drawn to break out of a narrow definition of the meaning of those symbols and to recognize their universal importance in religious terms.' Seán Freyne, *Galilee, Jesus and the Gospels: Literary Approaches and Historical Investigations* (Philadelphia: Fortress Press, 1988): 270 (argued in 135–268).

[21] See e.g. Alan F. Segal, *Rebecca's Children: Judaism and Christianity in the Roman Period* (Cambridge: Harvard University Press, 1986): 38–67.

[22] On the question of peasant turmoil and protest in the first century see especially Crossan's chapter, 'Rebel and Revolutionary,' in *The Historical Jesus*: 207–24.

[23] Freyne, *Galilee*: 224, and note 8. See also Richard A. Horsley, *Jesus and the Spiral of Violence: Popular Jewish Resistance in Roman Palestine* (San Francisco: Harper & Row, 1987): 18.

a memory of a saying of Jesus about the destruction of the Temple, and all four likewise record a symbolic act of judgement on the Temple system.

Jesus entered the Temple in Jerusalem shortly before his trial and execution in that city, and overturned the tables of the money-changers in the court of the Gentiles (Mark 11:15–19), signifying either an 'action against a corrupt priestly oligarchy,'[24] or the destruction of the existing system of Temple religion.[25] The Temple taxed its devotees for the maintenance of the buildings and the support of the priests, while offering them little in the way of practical help in the struggles of their lives, especially their peasant-village lives in Galilee where Jesus lived, preached, healed, and exorcised demons. Two parables in particular reflect Jesus' negative attitude towards the Temple and its priestly service: the Pharisee and the Toll Collector (Luke 18:10–14b) and the good Samaritan (Luke 10:30–36). Both of these parables implicitly indict the Temple service as ineffective in giving life to victims in the land and forgiveness to sinners within the system's jurisdiction.

The Land

If the Temple constituted one in a cluster of central symbols in Palestinian Jewish thought and life, then another is the land on which the Temple stood. W. D. Davies[26] and Walter Breuggemann[27] have both demonstrated the central importance of the theology of the land in First-Temple Israel and in Second-Temple Judaism. 'The land is a promised land. . . . The legend of the promise entered so deeply into the experience of the Jews that it acquired its own reality.'[28] The land on which Jesus lived and told his parables to the people was God's gift to Israel. The

---

[24] John J. Rousseau and Rami Arav, *Jesus and His World: An Archaeological and Cultural Dictionary* (Minneapolis: Fortress Press, 1995): 296.

[25] So Sanders, *Jesus and Judaism*: 63–76.

[26] W. D. Davies, *The Gospel and the Land: Early Christianity and Jewish Territorial Doctrine* (Berkeley: University of California Press, 1974): 15–74.

[27] Walter Brueggemann, *The Land: Place as Gift, Promise, and Challenge in Biblical Faith* (Philadelphia: Fortress Press, 1977): 1–14; 184–196. See also Norman C. Habel, *The Land is Mine: Six Biblical Land Ideologies* (Minneapolis: Fortress Press, 1995): 17–158.

[28] Davies, *The Gospel and the Land*: 15, 19.

land was to be treated with respect, as in a seventh year Sabbath for the soil. And the elect people who occupied the land in trust, the Jewish people, were not to lose their inheritance indefinitely. If a member incurred a debt that caused the person (or family) to lose their portion in the land of promise, the debt was to be forgiven in the year of jubilee and the land returned to its original trustee (Lev. 25). But in the time of Jesus the debt law had fallen into disuse; peasants had lost their plot that sustained life to elite city dwellers; the elite rich were permitted to retain their foreclosures of land without censure from the authorities; and landless peasants were forced into destitution on the land promised them by the Law.[29]

In the place where Jesus told his metaphoric stories in Galilee many disenfranchised people had their hopes in God's gift of life on the promised land dashed. The land had lost its power to sustain the life of people for whom it was intended. There is strong indication that Jesus viewed the current situation on the land of promise with great displeasure. The life-supporting land had come under the tyranny of Roman occupation and Jewish religious impotence.

His metaphor of the *fertiliser of the land* in Matthew 5:13 (*halas tēs gēs*, mistakenly translated 'the salt of the earth;' cf. Luke 14:34–35) is a two-edged sword. On the one hand, the land requires the life-giving agency of Jesus' disciples. But on the other hand, the same land-fertilisers could lose their life-giving potency, as their Jewish counterparts had lost theirs, in which case they would be fit for nothing except to become a barren footpath for humans and horses to trample under their feet.

In Palestine at the time of Jesus, the land that promised life for the people of God had become for many a sterile place overrun by Roman soldiers and bandits, and used by elite land-lords to generate a surplus for their sumptuous city life at the expense of the dispossessed poor of the villages. A number of Jesus' parables provoke questions about the state of affairs in the land of promise where the life of many landless peasants had become non-sustainable. The parable of the rich fool (Luke 12:16b–20) warns against hoarding a surplus of crops selfishly. The self-centred farmer will lose his life the very night he thinks

[29] Brueggemann, *The Land*: 167–75. Cf. Crossan, *Historical Jesus*: 124–224.

he has it made! The parable of the sower (Mark 4:3b–8) creates an image of a sizeable proportion of waste land, and thorns and rocks and thieving birds and scorching sun, with only one portion producing abundantly. A strange and shocking picture of the holy land of promise it is, but one to which many a Jewish peasant could no doubt give his own version.

The Economy

It is difficult to separate out the land from the economy in Jewish Palestine, since the economy of an agrarian society was land based. But there is more than a hint that Jesus was keenly aware of an economic net in which his people were caught since the kingship of Herod I.

> Under Herod I (37–4 B.C.) much of the land had been administered as the king's own estate. Subsequently his lands were sold off and this led to the increase of large estates often with absentee landlords (see Matt. 21:33–41). Archaeological evidence shows the existence of such estates with a central settlement and dependent villages.[30]

Lenski's graphic representation of the relationship among classes in agrarian societies depicts a pyramid structure of social reality.[31] The ruler sits at the very top, with a thin population line of a governing class directly below him. Next to the governing class are grouped merchants, retainers, and priests. Below them fits a large block of peasants, and at the bottom another large number of unclean and expendables. Power and privilege reside with the few who control the life of the populous classes economically subservient to the smaller elite. It is quite likely that Jesus experienced such a social and economic structure first hand, and spoke of a new reality, the rule of God, in which expendables are blessed while the powerful, rich, ruling class fall under divine judgement.

Allusions to the economic situation in Jewish Palestine crop up in various *pericopae* in the Synoptic Gospels and the Gospel

---

[30] John Riches, *The World of Jesus: First Century Judaism in Crisis* (Cambridge: University Press, 1990): 24.
[31] G. E. Lenski, *Power and Privilege: A Theory of Social Stratification* (New York: McGraw-Hill, 1966): 284.

of Thomas, but especially so in Luke. A rich ruling class member will have great difficulty comprehending the rule of God. One of this class is said to have asked Jesus how to attain eternal life, God's kind of life. Answer: sell all that you own and distribute it to the destitute, and then you will find heaven's treasure instead. The man walked away from the answer, because he was very rich. Then follows the tragically ironic image of a camel trying to go through the eye of a needle. It is easier for that to happen than for a rich person to come under the rule of God and experience the new reality that Jesus brings (Luke 18:18–25; Mark 10:23–27).

A number of parables script the economic situation of the people of agrarian Jewish Palestine. The parable of the talents/pounds portrays a rich merchant who praises his servant-retainers for 100 percent profit they earned while he was absent from the scene. The servant in Matthew who fails to invest his one talent is summarily expelled into the outer darkness. Is Jesus extolling the goodness of the merchant or the courage of the one-talent man? This is one of the paradoxical puzzles of that parable. The parable of the labourers in the vineyard likewise points to an economic situation in Jewish Palestine. In that story the householder gives one denarius to everyone, and chastises the hard workers who fail to see his generous side that will not let the destitute end the day in hunger. Is this the way of rich householders? Or is the story a spoof on householders who take advantage of a large unemployed workforce in the land of promise? Whatever way the answers go for either of these parables, the questions the stories evoke contain in themselves a protest against an existing economic system.

The People

Until recently, much of the secondary literature about the people in Palestine at the time of Jesus focused on the four schools, or philosophies, in Roman-occupied Jewish Palestine: Sadducees, an aristocratic priestly group that ran the Temple service; Pharisees, an educated class of teachers of the Law in charge of synagogue worship; Essenes, a group of ascetics who distinguished themselves by withdrawing from mainstream religious and political life; and Zealots, a self-styled political group inclined to revolution. These four are prominent in the secondary literature mainly because of their elitist political/ religious power (the priestly Sadducees), or their erudition in matters of the Law (Pharisees), or their group statement about devotion to the Covenant against the corrupt state of Temple religion in Jewish Palestine (Essenes), or their militant political profile in resisting Roman domination (Zealots). But there were also bandits, such as Barabbas from the trial narratives of the Gospels, and prophets, such as John the Baptist, tenant farmers who tended the land of rich absentee land owners, a mass of peasant farmers living at a subsistence level, labourers who had either lost their land or were otherwise forced out of the family, and still others without work of any kind, living on the edge of destitution and death. In such a society, as Richard Horsley attests, 'the wealthy and powerful tend to use and abuse their power in ways that are detrimental and unfair to the peasants, and the peasant-producers build up hostilities and resentments which make the powerful anxious lest the poor strike back at them.'[32] But the socially and politically powerful continued to maintain their position, working through retainers (servants) and overseers to keep the lower classes in their subservient place. The Jewish priestly authorities in Jerusalem were either powerless to do anything to alleviate the situation of the peasant population in Galilee, occupied as Palestine was by the higher power of imperial Rome, or the Jewish authorities simply closed their eyes to the mass of impoverished people where Jesus ministered. 'The imperial situation in which the Palestinian Jewish people were living entailed tension and conflict,'[33] which led inexorably to an 'escalating spiral of violence in Roman-dominated Jewish Palestine.'[34]

Jesus incorporates these occupied Jewish people of Second-Temple Palestine into the script of his narrative parables—along with their political, religious, economic overlords—and then shockingly turns the accepted rule of Palestinian life on its head in favour of a new rule and a new reality: the rule of God. In one

---

[32] Richard A. Horsley, with John S. Hanson, *Bandits, Prophets and Messiahs: Popular Movements in the time of Jesus* (San Francisco: Harper & Row, 1985): 2.

[33] Horsley, *Jesus and the Spiral of Violence*: 19.

[34] Ibid.: 29.

parable, tenants are entrusted with a newly planted vineyard belonging to an absentee landlord. They protest violently at having to pay the absentee landlord from the meagre crop of a new vineyard. In another parable, a young son leaves his village home in hope of a better life in a far-away city. He fails in his adventure and brings shame to his home and village. The father, who should have disowned his wastrel son by normal standards, welcomes him home and throws a party for him.

The parables of Jesus strangely, and perhaps with more than a touch of ironic humour,[35] are about the kinds of people living in the villages of Lower Galilee, about their socio-economic situation, about the land that promised life to all of the covenant people, and about the Temple intended to meditate between God and his people. To interpret the parables in categories other than their scripted speech violates the integrity of their speaker and robs the parables of their paradoxical power to effect change.

Stories as Parables

'Parable' in the mouth of Jesus may not be as difficult to discern as the myriad technical studies of the form would imply. Comparable forms of speech were already in wide use in the Hebrew tradition, as well as in the Greco-Roman world.[36] Jesus would surely have known the use of the form of communication, if not from the Greek and Latin schools, then certainly from the Hebrew Bible. Nathan's 'catching' story to King David after the Bathsheba affair, about the poor man's lamb that a rich man stole for his own use, is a classic case in point (2 Sam. 12:1–6). This kind of story Jesus would have known from his Hebrew Bible and Jewish tradition. Of the many points that could be made about 'the parable' as a medium of communication in the ministry of Jesus, three must suffice to serve the purpose of the book.

[35] David M. Granskou, *Preaching on the Parables* (Philadelphia: Fortress Press, 1972): 46–53.
[36] Mary Ann Beavis, 'Parable and Fable,' *Catholic Biblical Quarterly*, 52 (1990): 473–94. Beavis contends that Aesopic fables provide an apt context for the interpretation of the parables of Jesus. The Evangelists, if not Jesus, attached a 'moral' to the parable story, e.g. 'the last shall be first' or 'many are called but few are chosen.'

Form

There is a risk of becoming too technical in attempting to understand the parables of Jesus, as Granskou counsels: 'No interpretation of the parables of Jesus can achieve true technical
competence until it rises above that which is merely technical to
the level of that which is genuinely human.'[37] Hence the discussion above that attempted to locate the parables of Jesus in
the life-world of the Jewish people of Lower Galilee in Roman-
occupied Palestine at the time of the Second Temple. At the
same time, critical attention to this particular form of communication is needed if responsible interpretation is to take
place. It could be argued, of course, that the first audience would
not have puzzled over the technical form. They would have been
familiar with such fabulous stories, and would have drawn
moralistic conclusions from Jesus' parables, as Aesop's audience
did from his fables.[38] Yet the 'parable' in the mouth of Jesus goes
beyond a simple tale with an obvious moral to it. The parables
of Jesus are open-ended, puzzling, perplexing, perhaps in a
certain way even empty and silent. 'We are frightened by the
lonely silences within the parables . . . We want them to tell us
exactly what to do and they refuse to answer.'[39] The parable does
not inform; it incites. It is a call to act, not precise instructions
on how to act. Hearers have to have 'ears to hear' the parable
(Mark 4:9, 23; 7:16). Parables give a sense of direction without a
detailed map. They create a different world from the accepted
world, a tantalising new world not unlike the old world, yet
radically unlike it. C. H. Dodd's definition of 'parable,' quoted
repeatedly, still has much to commend it: 'the parable is a
metaphor or simile drawn from nature or common life, arresting the hearer by its vividness or strangeness, and leaving the
mind in sufficient doubt about its precise application to tease
it into active thought.'[40] Four words in particular in this definition capture the genius of the 'parable' form of communication
in the speech of Jesus: metaphor, arresting, strangeness, and
tease.

[37] Granskou, *Preaching*: 7.
[38] Beavis, 'Parable and Fable:' 493–96.
[39] Crossan, *In Parables*: 80
[40] C. H. Dodd, *The Parables of the Kingdom*, rev. ed. (New York: Scribner's, 1961):
5. (Italics mine.)

As *metaphor*, the parable of Jesus projects an image of a new reality using recognisable elements from the existing reality. Metaphor signals more than it describes;[41] it hints from behind an illuminated curtain, rather than performing in the spotlight on centre stage. The metaphor creates an image of the reality to which it points, and thus also in the imaginative sense the reality itself. The parable is *arresting* on the one hand because it is familiar, and on the other because it is so unfamiliar. Both of these, the familiar and the unfamiliar, interact throughout the structured movement of the narrative parables. For example, priests are well known to Jewish people, as are Levites and Samaritans. But Samaritans are not known to be so lavishly good in Jewish thinking. Rich vineyard owners and day labourers are well known, but vineyard owners are not known to go to a marketplace and ensure that everyone there is hired at full salary. Rich farmers have a good life and are known to live longer than the destitute, but the rich farmer in the parable dies on the very night he lays his plans to store his surplus. The *strangeness* in the parables of Jesus comes not so much from their unfamiliar elements, but from the particular twist given to both the familiar and the unfamiliar. The two collide. The familiar world (what I have called the received world) cracks under the impact of the unfamiliar. Part of the strangeness in a parable of Jesus is in seeing the received world cracked open, and a glimpsing of a new world through the cracks. Prodigals can come home again; Samaritans can be loving and be loved; the land can produce enough for all; wealthy householders distribute their profits, etc. In this sense, the parables of Jesus *tease* the mind of the audience to think differently about life. Hence, the stories are *parabolai* in the Palestinian tradition of *meshalim* from the Hebrew Bible. The narrative plot of 'parable' in the Jesus tradition does not lead simply and irresistibly to a 'moral of the story,' even though moral maxims have been attached, however unsuitably, to some of the parables (see note 36 above). Etymologically, the *parabolē* is a comparison, something thrown alongside. Yet the narrative structure of Jesus'

---

[41] On the signalling aspect see especially Susan Wittig, 'Meaning and Modes of Significance: Toward a Semiotic of the Parable,' in *Semiology and Parables: Exploration of the Possibilities Offered by Structuralism for Exegesis* ed. Daniel Patte (Pittsburg: The Pickwick Press, 1976): 319–40.

parables is not straight illustration; it is tinged with riddle. Parables invoke questions without giving answers. The audience answers. But their answers are not univocal. Audiences divide in their response to 'parable' from within their own horizon. Consider the possible responses to the parable of the good Samaritan, for example. Jewish people of Jerusalem would 'choke on the irony' of being served by a 'despised half-breed' Samaritan.[42] Samaritans in the audience, on the other hand, might respond differently to a parable in which they fare very well, an issue Ian McDonald picks up in his interpretation in chapter 3. The idea of multiple responses leads to the next point.

Polyvalence

'A parable saying should never return empty,'[43] says Herman Hendrickx astutely. Nor should its meaning be sought strictly in the intention of the teller of the parable, but also (and perhaps more so) in the effects of the telling of the parable. The plural, 'effects,' is deliberate. There is no single effect created in the telling of an open-ended parable, not even within a relatively homogeneous audience, much less a heterogeneous one. The parable form creates an impression of approval, only to be checked by another impression of disapproval. The house-holder who pays the one-hour workers a full day's wage evokes approval at first blush, until the all-day workers make their case. Where is justice in all of this goodness? It is in the char-acter of a parable of Jesus, as in an artist's painting or a poet's poem, to evoke mixed responses, and therefore also polyvalent interpretations.[44] Multiple interpretations should not be an

---

[42] Robert W. Funk, *Parables and Presence: Forms of the New Testament Tradition* (Philadelphia: Fortress Press, 1982): 33.

[43] Herman Hendrickx, *The Parables of Jesus: Studies in The Synoptic Gospels* (London: Geoffrey Chapman, 1986): 12.

[44] John Dominic Crossan's theory of polyvalence in parable interpretation helps explain the propensity of the church to allegorise the parables as it did: 'Polyvalent narration at its most self-conscious level is lucid allegory, that is, a paradox formed into narrative so that it precludes canonical interpretation and becomes a metaphor for the hermeneutical multiplicity it engenders,' in *Cliffs of Fall: Paradox and Polyvalence in the Parables of Jesus* (New York: Seabury/Crossroad, 1980): 102.

embarrassment to scholarship. Parables as parables evoke multiple responses and therefore multiple interpretations.[45]

Polyvalency in interpretation should not be confused with flights of fancy, nor yet with the notion that truth is relative. Parables of Jesus point to the 'not-yet' of the new reality, which Jesus calls the kingdom of God. In this sense a parable creates distance from that other reality, as much as it makes connection; it alienates as much as it invites.[46] Interpretation occurs in the tension between the feeling of distance and the feeling of connection, like standing in a room 'with two mirrors facing each other and you in the middle.'[47] The result is polyvalence. But the parable itself remains, always beckoning its audience back for another listen, another look.

Provocation

If 'parable is narrative paradox, paradox formed into story,'[48] then the parables of Jesus carry provocative power more than they do moral education. The parable invites the audience to step inside an alternate world from where they stand in the received world. The step is taken in the mind, in creative imagination. Participants in the plot fill in the gaps, envision the possibilities, and in this sense become co-creators of the parable. Once inside the parable plot, the participant is caught in the narrative interplay, with no escaping the repercussions of answering the question inherent in the parable.

Jesus invests his parables with this kind of provocative power. Consider the parable of the two debtors recorded in Luke 7:41–42, set in the home of a Pharisee called Simon. Simon is offended by the extravagant display of devotion from a woman known to be a 'a sinner.' Jesus then tells the parable: 'A certain creditor had two debtors; one owed him five hundred denarii, and the other fifty. When they could not pay, he cancelled the debts of

---

[45] This issue of multiple interpretations is taken up positively by Mary Ann Tolbert, *Perspectives on the Parables: An Approach to Multiple Interpretations* (Philadelphia: Fortress Press, 1979): 15–31, 67–91.

[46] This draws on the insight of Hendrickx that 'a good parable should create distance, provoke, and appeal,' *Parables*: 10.

[47] Crossan, *Cliffs*: 103.

[48] John Dominic Crossan, 'Parable, Allegory, and Paradox,' in idem. *Semiology and Parables*: 248.

both of them. Now which of them will love him more?' Whether the question is stated or not, it stands in the story. The participant feels it, answers it, and is provoked to affirm the other realm to which the parable points obliquely. The parables of Jesus are provocative.

What Provoked Jesus' Execution?

In 1984 Ellis Rivkin published a book under the title *What Crucified Jesus?* Both in his title and in his argument, Rivkin shifts the blame for Jesus' crucifixion from persons to the situation of the time and place. He writes in his conclusion:

> Should our focus shift from casting blame on persons to casting blame on the time, the place, and the situation, we may be able to view the issue in a new light . . . It emerges with great clarity, both from Josephus and from the Gospels, that the culprit is not the Jews, but the Roman imperial system.[49]

The merit of Rivkin's point is that it focuses on a system rather than on a people. The Roman imperial system, imposed on Jewish Palestine, and intertwined with the system of Judaism, could not tolerate the provocative power of Jesus' speech and action. He had become identified with a peoples' movement in Galilee, had twelve disciple-missionaries, healed the sick, drew crowds, and as such he posed a threat to the security of the system in which Palestinian Judaism was forced to live. The Jewish religious system itself did not escape critique from Jesus. His action in overturning the tables of the money-changers in the Temple court was subversive to the Jewish Temple system, and no less so his parable of the Samaritan who lavishes love on the roadside victim while the Temple priest and Levite obey their system and pass by the victim. The parable of the Pharisee and the Toll Collector praying at the Temple carries the same provocative challenge to the system of Judaism, interfaced as it was with the system of imperial Rome.[50]

The issue is not in the *name* of the system, but what the system—any system—does to the people forced to live within its

---

[49] Ellis Rivkin, *What Crucified Jesus?* (Nashville: Abingdon Press, 1984): 74.
[50] Rome appointed the procurator, who appointed the high priest.

bounds. Jesus stands in for God. He speaks of God's rule that alleviates the oppressed. He provokes his audience to think about a new reality ordained of God, blesses the poor who have fallen outside the system, and forgives the Toll Collector and the prostitute who have fallen prey to the wiles of the system. Jesus himself in the end felt the full weight of the system of imperial Roman occupation of Jewish Palestine. As Helmut Koester puts it, he was 'Jesus the victim,' whose person and action and preaching 'implied a complete reversal of all political, social, and religious values that were held sacred and holy in the world of ancient Judaism as well as in the Roman system of realised eschatology.'[51] In his trial in Jerusalem before the Roman and Jewish powers, Jesus was not defending his own honour, much less a philosophy he espoused. The systemic powers called Jesus to account because, in parable and practice, he had challenged the system that oppressed the peasant Jewish people with whom he lived and worked, and thus he *became* a victim with the victimised. Hence an even more fitting epitaph might read: 'Jesus the victim for victims.'

The question remains never completely answered: What provoked the execution of Jesus by Roman crucifixion in Jewish Palestine? The parables Jesus told do not answer completely, neither are they completely silent on the matter. The parables of Jesus *effectively* subvert the 'world dominated by the strong,'[52] and point paradoxically to a new world in which God's will is done on earth as it is in heaven (Matt. 6:10).

---

[51] Helmut Koester, 'Jesus the Victim,' *Journal of Biblical Literature*, 3 (1992): 14.
[52] William R. Herzog II, *Parables as Subversive Speech: Jesus as Pedagogue of the Oppressed* (Louisville: Westminster/John Knox, 1994): 258.

Parables of the Temple

If you busy yourselves with the service of the Temple, I shall bless you as in the beginning; . . . thus thou dost learn that there is no service more beloved of the Holy One, blessed be He, than the Temple service. (From *The Fathers According to Rabbi Nathan*, 1955)

2

A Tale of Two Taxations
(Luke 18:10–14b)

The Parable of the Pharisee and the Toll Collector

MICHAEL FARRIS

The Text in Translation

Two men went up to the temple to pray, one a Pharisee and the other a toll collector. The Pharisee, standing by himself, was praying thus, 'God, I thank you that I am not like other people: thieves, rogues, adulterers, or even like this tax collector. I fast twice a week; I give a tenth of all my income.' But the toll collector, standing far off, would not even look up to heaven, but was beating his breast and saying, 'God, be merciful to me, a sinner.'[1]

Before taking on the two protagonists of the tale it is important to recognise a third character, the Temple. The location for any story is full of meaning, and the setting of the parable in sacred precincts is particularly potent. The Temple is a player too in the parable, with a role at least as important as the well-known figures of Pharisee and toll collector.

What part does the Temple play in the parable? The Jerusalem Temple, of course, is the concrete embodiment of Jewish identity and tradition just as Westminster, or the Capitol or the Kremlin

---

[1] The Lukan framing of the parable needs to be noted. '[Jesus] told this parable to some who trusted in themselves and regarded others with contempt . . . for all who exalt themselves will be humbled, but all who humble themselves will be exalted' (Luke 18:9, 14b). For Luke, the parable has become a fairly straightforward moral lesson about humility versus arrogance. But as a painting should be studied apart from its frame, so too should this parable be studied apart from Luke's interpretive frame.

embody the nations in which they stand. The Temple stood for the primary system by which Israel knew its God and fulfilled its sacred obligations.[2] What happened, or what failed to happen in its precincts, was inextricably linked to the history and future of the Jewish people. Thus the outcome of the parable will say something not only about the Pharisee and toll collector[3] but also about the institution in whose shadow the drama unfolds.

For dramatic purposes, the Temple setting heightens the action in the parable. Each man goes up to the Temple, to God's House, before he returns to his own (v. 14a). By implication, God is party to the parable. The same interchange between Pharisee and toll collector would hardly be the same out on the road to Emmaus! The Temple setting for the parable is a shorthand for telling the listener that this is a story not only about how two men pray but also about how God acts.

Less obvious, but critical to the parable, the Temple is an *institution* in every nuance of that word. It was not only a venerable place of worship; it was an economy unto itself, second only to the Roman system. It employed thousands to keep its sacrificial system running and its precincts in repair. Its treasury held huge wealth and it served as a central bank for rich and poor alike.[4] In short, the Temple was an institution of immense economic power, influence—and need. This last point deserves some attention. Temple funds came sometimes from generous benefactors but, in the main, its economy was sustained by the regular collection of tithes and taxes from the faithful.

The requirements for the faithful were enumerated by the Torah in a code as complex as any modern income tax guide. There were three major taxes: (1) the annual 'wave offering,' or first fruits set at from 1 to 3 percent of the produce; (2) the annual first 10 percent tithe, provided to support the priests

---

[2] See Shillington, 'The Temple,' in chapter 1 above, pp. 8–9.

[3] The usual term Tax Collector or Publican is a misnomer for *telōnēs*. The toll collector was a lesser official in the Roman taxation system. John R. Donahue, 'Tax Collectors and Sinners: an Attempt at Identification,' *Catholic Biblical Quarterly* 33 (1971): 39–61.

[4] Macc. 3:4–12; Josephus, *Wars* VI:282. Mishnah *Shekelim* reflects the considerable complexity of the Temple tax system and the many projects it financed.

and Levites; and (3) a *second* tithe, used for different purposes during the six-year cycle between sabbatical years. Thus the total religious obligation owing on agricultural produce could be as much as 23 percent.[5] The cost of true piety was steep at the best of times. In times of hardship, it could be crushing.[6]

Here is a key point for the parable. To fulfil one's Temple obligations and tithes was a mark of faithfulness The Pharisee embodied a tradition that, by definition, paid its tithes scrupulously. Thus his final words, 'I tithe everything I own,' resonate rather strongly within the very walls which he helps maintain. He is a true Temple-taxpayer. One should expect the Temple to be a most hospitable location for his prayer.

The same cannot be said for the toll collector. His vocation operated in direct competition to the Temple taxation system. He collected funds on behalf of another powerful institution, the Roman imperial system. His place on the Temple mount was suspect quite apart from any sins he may have committed. He came there as an interloper, a competitor, and a paid supporter of another economy. One will not expect the Temple to smile kindly on any of his requests.

Nor should we expect Jesus' hearers to view the toll collector with any sympathy. If the cost of true piety was steep, the cost of living in a Roman-occupied land was steeper still. The poll tax and the land tax were the primary taxes demanded by the Romans. To these could be added various land transfer taxes, export and import duties and a tax on houses in Jerusalem.[7] Their administration was farmed out to a bureaucracy whose goals were not only the collection of revenue but also the maximisation of it. The general population understandably despised those who collaborated with Roman taxation. The 'toll collector' (*telōnēs*) of the parable was but a minor official in a corrupt, oppressive system. As the mere collector of tolls at some town gate or public highway, there was no hiding from the contempt of his own people that day when he went up to pray.

[5] Marcus Borg, 'Conflict, Holiness and Politics in the Teaching of Jesus,' *Studies in the Bible and Early Christianity* 5 (New York: Edwin Mellon): 32, cited in William R. Herzog II, *Parables as Subversive Speech: Jesus as Pedagogue of the Oppressed* (Louisville: Westminster/John Knox, 1994): 181.

[6] Herzog, *Parables*: 53–73.

[7] Josephus, *Wars* XIX.vi.3.

The setting for the parable is now quite different. Quite beyond Luke's tidy moral instruction which introduces the story (Luke 18:9, 14b), the parable now carries with it a whole system of social tensions, conflicting interests and religious assumptions. These are the subject-matter of the parable and the 'stuff' of its drama, all of it conveyed in the few words, 'Two men went up to the Temple to pray, one a Pharisee and the other a toll collector.' Expectations have already been established and a social script has been invoked for what *should* happen.

But modern readers have to recognise and set aside a script of their own about what 'should' happen in the parable, specifically to Pharisees; set aside the common jaundice against them as hypocritical, rigid and unbelieving. The common modern picture of Pharisees is not at all helpful for understanding this parable. To frame the Pharisee as a 'bad guy' in whatever form quite derails the direction of the parable.

Pharisees were considered to be models of piety and proper Jewish observance. According to the contemporary Jewish historian Josephus they were widely respected by the common people for their good deeds and zeal for Torah.[8] They were leaders among their people and the common people looked up to them. There may have been 'bad' Pharisees but for the purposes of the parable, this Pharisee who goes up to the Temple to pray is a model of Jewish faithfulness.

The first step then, in dealing with the Pharisee, is to take what he says seriously. There is nothing 'wrong' with his prayer. An example of prayer from the Talmud is quite similar.

> I thank thee, O Lord, my God that thou hast given me my lot with those who sit at the street corners; for I am early to work on the words of the Torah, and they are early to work to things of no moment. I weary myself, and they weary themselves. But I weary myself and profit thereby, and they weary themselves to no profit. I run, and they run; I run towards the life of the age to come, and they run towards the pit of destruction (b. Berakot 28b).[9]

[8] Josephus, *Ant.* XIII.ix.6; xiv.5; XVIII.i.3–4.
[9] The Babylonian Talmud comes from many years after Jesus but a contemporary Qumran source confirms similar prayers. 'I praise thee, O Lord, that thou hast not allowed my lot to fall among the worthless community, nor assigned me a part in the circle of the secret ones' (1QH 7.34).

It *was* appropriate to thank God for a righteous life. Taken in its own terms, the Pharisee's prayer is not self-righteous or arrogant; it properly thanked God as the true author of righteousness. Jesus' hearers would have respected the prayer and surely would emulate it if they could. In fact, the parable requires that the Pharisee be taken at face value in order for the parable to communicate its disturbing conclusion.

The Pharisee truly was, in his own words, 'not like other people.' He had the discipline to study Torah and to follow its instruction scrupulously. He basked in the esteem of religious people and had the economic wherewithal to fulfil his religious obligations well past what was legally required. He surely was well-off financially, having risen somehow above the agrarian cycle of subsistence farming in Judea. Anyone who can fast twice weekly must be well fed. Anyone who can tithe all that he owns had some income to spare. In these ways too he was not 'like other people' and, of course, thankful for it.

The claim that he was 'not like other people' was likely a source of envy rather than anger. His thanksgiving for not being like other people, a claim which so jars modern egalitarian ideals, was quite justified. No one would have condemned it.[10]

Specifically, he says that he is not a thief, rogue or adulterer. That truth too we must take as a given. These terms are but stock phrases for the grosser forms of sin which any observant Jew must have avoided. Not too much should be read into the specifics of the transgressions nor need they be applied to the Temple crowd or even the wretched toll collector.[11] Structurally, the list is shorthand for one half of the Pharisee's righteousness. There are two parts to it:

Negative: What he *does not* (swindling, hypocrisy, adultery)

Positive: What he *does* (fasts twice a week, pays tithes on everything)

One can assume that those standing in the Temple were likewise not the 'thieves, rogues, or adulterers' the Pharisee decries. The issue is not the list of obvious sins; it is the extra deeds of special righteousness. What sets the Pharisee apart from the crowd on

---

[10] Luke's editorial frame (v. 9) implicitly condemns the attitude but this was a later concern when Church and Pharisee were in spiritual competition.

[11] The puzzling phrase *ē kai hōs* ('or even like this toll collector') seems to distance the toll collector from the list of sins rather than to connect him.

this day is not what he avoids but what he does without fail. He supports the Temple far beyond the basics. And it is precisely at this moment we meet the toll collector. He is the foil for the Pharisee's true claim. 'I thank you that I am not like other people, thieves, rogues, adulterers, *or even like this toll collector.* I fast twice a week and pay tithes on everything I own.' At one level, the phrase is a tidy transition to the next character in the parable. But, at a deeper level, the named differences are significant. The highlight of the Pharisee's self-definition was his fasting and Temple support. Why are these details so important to the parable?

The Pharisee fasts *twice a week.* The Torah only enjoined regular fasting for the Day of Atonement (Lev. 16:29–31; 23:27, 29, 32; Num. 29:7). Other fasts were for occasions of national importance (Neh. 9:1, Esther 9:31, Zech. 8:19).[12] The Pharisee fasts twice a week, far exceeding the demands of Jewish law. The Scriptures depicted fasting as an act of mourning, penitence or intercession. However, there was little if anything for which the Pharisee had to be penitent or mournful in his life as described in verses 11b–12.

The twice-weekly fast may have been an act of intercession for the people.[13] Perhaps the fasts were an act of contrition on behalf of the same people who were not like the Pharisee: the swindlers, hypocrites, and adulterers. This conclusion is not certain but gains some support from the second element in the Pharisee's claim: he tithes everything he owns.

Once again, the Torah has a clear stipulation about tithing of agricultural produce, seed, grain, wine, oil and the first born of every herd and flock (Deut. 14:22–23). These tithes were to be paid by the producer but often were not. Such untithed produce was therefore unclean and those who ate it became impure.[14] To make sure of personal purity, the Pharisee tithed everything he owned, even that which presumably he had not himself produced. It was an act of piety not only on his own behalf but also on behalf of the fellow Jews who had somehow failed to

---

[12] Joachim Jeremais, *The Parables of Jesus,* 2nd rev. ed. (New York: Scribner's, 1972): 140.

[13] Ibid.

[14] Mishnah *Demai* makes it clear that such untithed produce was widespread and demonstrates a highly developed code to protect the observant.

live up to their Torah obligations. Perhaps both acts of supererogation by the Pharisee were not an act of personal protection but an act of intercession on behalf of the people. In any event, even taken by themselves, the fasting and scrupulous tithing were acts of recognised religious worth to those who heard the parable. The Pharisee is a figure to be admired and his religion to be emulated as much as possible. According to all expectations, his piety should put him in a right standing with God.

Even the two men's posture in the Temple court underlines this expectation. Each man knew where he stood before God. The Pharisee stood off 'by himself' prominently while the toll collector 'stood far off' in a place of shame.[15] In contrast to how the Pharisee expects to be heard, the toll collector standing far off on the margin of the Temple court expects very little for his prayer. He cannot even lift his eyes up to heaven, the proper attitude of prayer, and can only cry out, 'God be merciful to me, the sinner!'

Some care must be taken here not to make the toll collector into the original Protestant, being justified by faith alone. He is not. He is still a member of a hated order, expressing penitence falling far short of Jewish norms. One of the reasons that toll collectors were considered so far beyond the pale of redemption was that they could not make restitution for their extorted gains.[16] Compare, for example, the toll collector's chest beating with the much more satisfactory repentance of Zacchaeus, a *chief* toll collector in the next chapter (Luke 19:1–10). He gives half what he has to the poor and repays fourfold all he defrauded from the public. Even the Pharisee would approve of that kind of penitence!

But what of the toll collector standing in the Temple court with only a plea for mercy to offer? Again, we must recognise the expectation that this was not enough. No one would want to have stood in his place. No one would have expected his prayer to find favour.

---

[15] The phrase 'by himself' (*pros heatōn*) can describe the mode of prayer or the place of standing. The comparison to the toll collector standing 'afar off' later makes it probable that the Pharisee was standing 'by himself,' that is, prominently.

[16] Donahue 'Toll Collectors:' 53ff.

'Have mercy on me, the sinner!' cries the toll collector, and he too must be taken seriously. So must the timing of his plea at the hour of daily sacrifice. Within the precincts of the Temple, the call is no generalised plea for divine forbearance; it invokes the language of atonement. The verb *hilasthēti* in this context means 'make an atonement for me.'[17] But how can there be an atonement for '*the* sinner'? The definite article here is not hyperbole to convey the depths of remorse. Not only did a toll collector defraud people and associate with Gentiles—sin enough—but also his very vocation robbed the Temple of its dues, by forcing the faithful to pay taxes rather than tithes, thus supporting the hated Roman occupation rather than the sacrificial system. He is *the* sinner. But he is also '*the* sinner' because he forced his fellow Jews into impurity through failure to pay their tithes. His sin was not his alone. It involved the nation. The irony of such a man asking for atonement through the Temple should not be missed.

Now, with all expectations laid out for Pharisee, toll collector and Temple, it is time for *parable*: 'This man [the toll collector] went down to his house justified rather than the other' (v. 14a). There should be a moment of speechlessness here, not an explanation.

Expectations have been reversed, assumptions toppled and a whole world of how things work has been brought into question—if the parable is true. It has caught the hearer by surprise by taking hold of a worldview and turning it upside down so that, before the hearer knows it, a new world is disclosed to imagination—at least for an instant.

What kind of world is disclosed in that moment? One where the Temple sacrifice fails its own proponent and is effective for an opponent against all expectations. It is not a rejection of the Temple system as some have suggested; it is a vision of how the Temple sacrifice should be efficacious—even for the sinner whose job it is to undermine it. And, of course, such a vision implicitly indicts the Temple system of the time. The Temple was not at all for 'the sinner.' It was for those without sin and

---

[17] Kenneth E. Bailey, *Through Peasant Eyes: Poet and Peasant and a Literary-Cultural Approach to the Parables of Jesus*. Combined ed. (Grand Rapids: Eerdmans, 1983): 154.

specifically for those with the wherewithal to pay their taxes. It was not the centre of boundless salvation as God intended.

The parable reaffirms the Temple as the place of God's saving action, but questions what it has become. The parable does not reject the Temple; it exposes its corruption and opens a vision for its reform. In a sense, the parable is the same as the so-called 'cleansing of the Temple' (Luke 19: 45–46, par.) but in narrative form.

The parable may therefore not be about the individual piety of two men. It may well deal with the great institutions represented by Pharisee and toll collector, and about the two taxations they required. The Temple as institution required the Pharisee and those like him to support its enormous economy, while it excluded those who could not pay its taxes. But more important, the Temple required the ideology of tithing and tax paying which the Pharisee promoted with zeal. It also required ostracism of those who failed in their obligations for whatever reason. Those who failed were called *am-ha-aretz*, or 'people of the land,' a title which implied that such persons were no longer God's people.[18] Thus, the pressure on people to pay their Temple dues in addition to Roman taxes was immense. But the physical duress of the Roman sword was not any more threatening than the internalised spiritual coercion of Torah teaching. The teaching was not evil, but the new economic order of double taxation made it difficult to fulfil, especially for the poor. Their choice lay only between not paying the tithe and living under powerful ostracism, or paying the tax and foregoing the necessities of life. For many Judeans and Galileans their own faith presented them with an utterly winless choice.[19]

The story of the widow paying her tax is a useful example of the situation (Luke 21:1–4). Jesus observed the rich paying their Temple tax and then saw a widow drop in two copper coins. He tells his disciples that she has paid more than all the others because she 'put in all she had to live on' (21:4). But Jesus is not highlighting her generosity; he pities her predicament. This woman believes she must provide for the Temple before the basics of life. The situation was a sad one, sadder still because she had internalised a worldview that

[18] See Misnah *Demai*, note 14 above
[19] Herzog, *Parables*: 173–93, has a truly brilliant analysis in this regard.

truly believed Temple tithes were more important than life itself.

Perhaps we have some clue here as to why Jesus chose 'parable' to teach about Temple. His aim was not merely the preaching of the right facts but of opening up a new way of seeing, thinking and speaking for his hearers. What needed to be challenged was a worldview that placed those who paid Temple tithes in prominence and shamed those who did not support the system. The dramatic reversal of the parable, for a moment at least, opens up the possibility of a new reality and asks the hearer for a decision. Is it possible? Do I want it? Will I commit myself to it? Dan Otto Via insists that parable is not simply a communication, but an event in the consciousness of the hearer.

> The judgement . . . evoked by the parables entails a far-reaching decision, for the pre-understanding of the hearers is challenged, and they must decide between their old understanding and the new one that confronts them in the parable. While Jesus' parables placed the hearers inescapably in the situation of decision, Jesus could not determine how people would decide. Those who refused his word made a decision and hardened in their old existence. Those who accepted his new understanding were carried across the disunity of decision and challenge and into a new situation of unity and adjustment.[20]

How did this parable of Pharisee and toll collector place people 'inescapably in the situation of decision'? It did so by invoking the deeply held assumptions about Pharisees, toll collectors and Temple, by heightening them dramatically, then suddenly by dissolving them all with the utterly surprising turn at the end. Doing so unleashed

> a barrage of questions. On what basis? By whose word? How could God speak outside of official channels? If the toll collector is justified by a mercy as unpredictable and outrageous as this, then who could not be included? And if toll collectors and sinners are justified in the very precincts

[20] Dan Otto Via, *The Parables: Their Literary and Existential Dimension* (Philadelphia: Fortress Press, 1967): 54.
[21] Herzog, *Parables*: 192–93.

of the Temple itself, then how is one to evaluate a Temple priesthood and its scribes who declare that nothing of the kind is possible?[21]

Here too is the danger inherent in parable, and in the freedom it leaves to the hearer. Having seen the old order exposed and the possibility of the new revealed, hearers with vested interest might be inclined to grasp the old world even more tightly and resist whoever would disturb again its sanctity. Supporters of the current Temple system would have rejected violently Jesus' vision of boundless salvation within the Temple system. Even the common people who otherwise heard Jesus gladly may have found the suggestion too much that a despised toll collector could make it into God's favour. Thus a link is forged between parables of this sort and the eventual fate of Jesus in Jewish Palestine.[22]

Some heard the parable of Pharisee and toll collector, and other parables like it, and understood full well the kind of world it proposed, where religious elites no longer held sway and where the likes of the toll collector walked away with God's favour. The new world of such parables was hardly good news to power brokers within the system of Roman occupation of Jewish life, so they conspired together to crucify the teller of parables. Silencing seemed the only way to deal with someone whose 'simple' story threatened to undo the structured world.

[22] J. D. Crossan, *The Dark Interval: Towards a Theology of Story* (Niles, Ill.: Argus Communications, 1975): 124.

3

Alien Grace

(Luke 10:30–36)

The Parable of the Good Samaritan

J. IAN H. McDONALD

The Text in Translation

A man was going down from Jerusalem to Jericho, and fell
into the hands of robbers, who stripped him, beat him, and
went away, leaving him half dead. Now by chance a priest
was going down that road; and when he saw him, he passed
by on the other side. So likewise a Levite, when he came to
the place and saw him, passed by on the other side. But a
Samaritan while traveling came near him; and when he saw
him, he was moved with pity. He went to him and bandaged
his wounds, having poured oil and wine on them. Then he
put him on his own animal, brought him to an inn, and took
care of him. The next day he took out two denarii, gave them
to the innkeeper, and said, 'Take care of him; and when I
come back, I will repay you whatever more you spend.' Which
of these three, do you think, was neighbour to the man who
fell into the hands of the robbers?

Come with me to Chartres Cathedral. Let us enter by the Royal
Portal, passing the North and South towers, and for a moment
absorb the magnificence of the Nave. As we wonder at the
marvels of its stained glass, the third window catches our
attention on the South Aisle on our right. The lower half, above
the presentation panels (it was presented by the shoemakers),
depicts sequentially and dramatically the story of the good
Samaritan. Here are the robbers in action, the hapless victim,
the priest and Levite passing by, the good Samaritan and the
innkeeper: a graphic portrayal of the story Jesus told. The upper

35

half presents the stories of Adam and Eve, Creation and Fall from Genesis 2–4. The window as a whole invites us to understand the specific story of the parable in the light of the universal symbols of Creation, Fall and Salvation, and thus find the parable transparent upon the human situation. The man going down from Jerusalem is leaving paradise, 'Salem' or 'shalom.' Such is our human lot as children of Adam, making our journey through a dangerous world. The thieves represent the onset of temptations, which rob us of our immortality. Priest and Levite show the inability of the Old Testament to heal wounded humanity. Help comes from the Samaritan who embodies Christ. Hostile as the world is, there is a centre of refuge: the inn symbolising the Church, as the innkeeper symbolises the apostle. The promised return of the Samaritan is the Second Coming of the Lord. In the uppermost panel, Christ, the Redeemer, has got the whole world in his hand and dispenses blessing.[1]

What can we say, in brief, about this medieval masterpiece? It is, in fact, only one of a number of such iconic representations. Others are found, for example, in Bourges and Sens cathedrals. As an interpretation, it is relatively sophisticated, approximating to the process which modern literary critics term 'intertextuality.' Allegory it most certainly is, but it should not be dismissed on that score. Today, some argue cogently that all 'parable' involves an element of allegory. Its context is the worship, faith and spiritual needs of the medieval church. And it completely involves the interpreter or beholder in the story, even as it sets him or her in the security of the Church as the mediator of salvation.[2]

The interpretive tradition it reflects was popular in the *glossa ordinaria*, or standard medieval commentaries on the Bible, and can be traced through the sermons of Anselm and the Venerable Bede, and the works of Augustine, Origen and Clement of Alexandria, to Irenaeus in the second century. The fact that earlier instances of the allegory are more restrained than later suggests or supports the notion of the progressive

[1] Cf. M. Miller, *Chartres Cathedral* (Pitkin, 1985): 68–71.
[2] For a brief consideration of allegory, cf. the articles by A. Louth and A. J. Bjordalen, in *A Dictionary of Biblical Interpretation*, ed. R. J. Coggins and J. L. Houlden (London: SCM Press; Philadelphia: Trinity, 1990): 12–16.

allegorisation of a passage that was not originally an allegory. Such was the vigour with which scholars such as Jülicher, Dodd and Jeremias attacked the allegorical interpretation of parables that it takes an active determination of the will to set aside their disapprobation and look more constructively at what is virtually the unanimous interpretive approach of the Fathers. Is there, after all is said and done, an intrinsic connection between this interpretation and Jesus' approach in his socio-historical context in Second-Temple Palestinian Judaism? Dodd, following Jülicher, thought not. Allegorical reading springs from a mis-understanding of parables as a veiling of the truth from the uninitiated, and arose after the death of Jesus to explain in particular the rejection of Jesus by his own people and the mysterious outworking of the purpose of God. 'The probability is that the parables could have been taken for allegorical mystifications only in a non-Jewish environment.'[3]

Dodd overstated his argument. The Old Testament is no stranger to allegory. The Messianic, or Christological, interpre-tation of the Old Testament employed allegory as one of its main strategies, as Paul himself testifies. Matthew, the most rabbinic of the Synoptists, uses allegory more than Mark and much more than Luke. To quote Michael Goulder, 'the rabbinic—and for that matter Old Testament—parables have about the same order of allegory as Matthew.'[4] Nevertheless, Dodd's view would not have received the credence it enjoys had it not possessed a fair degree of plausibility. It is true, as we suggested above, that the context of patristic and medieval interpretation is that of the interpreter and his community. In terms of the first context of the parable, there is no doubt that Jerusalem was the earthly, not the heavenly, city; that priest and Levite were religious figures serving in the Second Temple; and that the Samaritan, like inn and innkeeper, was precisely what was claimed. But the Fathers did not for a moment deny the literal or historical dimension, even if they were determined to advance beyond it. Didymus the Blind, much of whose work has come to light in more recent times, 'seems to work with a clear methodology: first constructing

---

[3] C. H. Dodd, *The Parables of the Kingdom*, 1st ed. (London: Nisbet, 1935): 15; cf. J. Jeremias, *The Parables of Jesus*, 1st ed. (London: SCM Press, 1954): 52–70.

[4] M. D. Goulder, *Midrash and Lection in Matthew* (London: SPCK, 1985): 57.

the letter of the text, examining its logic and structure, and enquiring into its "earthly" or historical reference; then enquiring whether the text has a figurative meaning, and if so what its reference is in the spiritual world.'[5] The Fathers, like the designer of the Chartres window, believed that they were interpreting the story of the good Samaritan for their day. They were enlarging upon its interpretation, but not telling a different story. They were pushing the metaphor to its limits. The question is therefore about the *connection between the versions*, about their faithfulness to the movement or tenor of the story which must be respected and reflected in any valid interpretation.

Stated otherwise, allegorical interpretation is sometimes likened to imposing a transparency with an intricate design upon the relatively unsophisticated outline of the parable. But for this to work, there must be a basic compatibility of outline or structure. One cannot superimpose a transparency of Australia on an outline of Africa and expect to make sense. But one can superimpose a detailed physical or contoured slide of Australia on a political outline of the same land-mass and make excellent sense. The critical issue is the coherence or convergence of the two models. Parable and allegory do not belong to different worlds or genres of literature. Both depend on narrative and analogy.

The critical question is, therefore: Are the Fathers faithful to the tenor of the story? To borrow the categories of narratology, the first axis of the story communicates the advent of the victim. He is at the receiving end of the violence of the robbers, the perpetrators of the crime. The sympathies of the hearers are with the victim. Help is urgently needed. The story then moves to the second axis, that of volition. The Temple figures of priest and Levite are, paradoxically, opponents of the victim in that they decline to help him. Servants of the Temple are supposed to serve their constituents in need. The focus then falls on the true helper figure who handsomely demonstrates the power of neighbour love.

B. Gerhardsson has observed that 'it is a fact that is given less attention than it deserves that *the early church fathers all interpreted*

---

[5] Frances Young, 'Alexandrian Interpretation', in *A Dictionary of Biblical Interpretation*: 11; cf. M. Simonetti, *Biblical Interpretation in the Early Church* (Edinburgh: T&T Clark, 1994): 6–14.

this parable Christologically.'[6] The battle-weary critic is inclined
to respond: 'Well, they would, wouldn't they?' They had a
dogmatic understanding of the parable, which arose within
the church context but was foreign to Jesus' purpose. But
there is a more fundamental, structural point. In order to elicit
the Christological point, they had to recognise the basic
movement or tenor of the story itself. This presupposes the
attack on the victim. They identified with the very human
victim, and invited their hearers to do likewise. The crux of
the story turns on the helper, in contrast to the non-helpers of
the Temple service. The helper figure, in all his strangeness,
acts with total compassion and generosity. He expresses grace.
It is on the basis of this structure that a Christological
interpretation can be built. 'Go and do likewise' is an invitation
to the *imitatio Christi*, to act towards others in the spirit of the
Covenant of grace. Is it not the case, then, that the allegorical
interpretation, in its own peculiar way, identifies the basic logic
of the parable?

Before we investigate this question further, it may be pointed
out that if the parable is understood in this way, it is brought
into line with other motifs which appear to characterise Jesus'
teaching. Prominent among these is the motif of the (good)
shepherd. Without a shepherd, the people perish. They become
prey to thieves and robbers. Their own religious leaders, who
are described as false shepherds, lead them astray. The shepherd
seeks out and saves the lost. The good shepherd cares for his
sheep and is prepared to lay down his life for them. The Fourth
Gospel identifies him with Jesus. The whole theme is deeply
embedded in the Scriptures. John 10:1–16 has been described
as a 'messianic midrash' on Ezekiel 34. Well might Gerhardsson
raise the question whether the parable of the good Samaritan is
not derived from, or at least very similar to, Old Testament
passages of this type.[7]

But if the basic motif of the parable is familiar territory, the
advent of the Samaritan after the failure of the Temple functionaries is surprising and distinctive. The image of the shepherd
may be familiar, but he is not presented as a Samaritan shepherd,

[6] B. Gerhardsson, *The Good Samaritan – the Good Shepherd* (Lund: Gleerup;
Copenhagen: Munksgaard, 1958): 3.
[7] Ibid.: 9–22.

any more than the Messiah is represented as a Samaritan, or
enemy of Israel. It is true that one strain of Jesus' teaching—in
true biblical style—evinced concern for the poor, the outcast
and even, on occasion, the Samaritan. And it is equally true
that shepherds were considered to be outside the accepted circles
of Judaistic piety. But the combining or fusing of the shepherd
and the Samaritan motifs, and the manner in which this is
achieved in the parable, are distinctive and arresting. Here, if
anywhere, is the crux of the parable. The Fathers rightly identified the basic motif; they were less successful in appreciating
the sophistication of its expression in the parable.

Luke uses the parable of the good Samaritan as an interpretation of the two great commandments, enlarging upon
the implications of Deuteronomy 6:5 and Leviticus 19:18. The
lawyer in Luke's context 'tests' Jesus (cf. Deut. 6:16). His question
is about the commandments and 'life' (Deut. 5:33, 6:24), and
the parable is often taken to illustrate what it means to love your
neighbour (cf. Lev. 19:9–18). If this is the real purpose of the
parable, it contains a tantalising degree of indirection. One may
readily conclude that this line of interpretation fails to account
for the sophistication of the parable.

Luke's interest in Samaritans is a commonplace of New
Testament studies, but it is much more complex than is often
recognised. He does not always present them in a favourable
light, but appears to keep the Samaritan mission in mind when
ordering his material. Thus, he includes the story of Jesus'
rejection in a Samaritan village as an episode in his journey to
Jerusalem and his *analepsis* (9:51–56). His journey entails
pilgrimage, manifests eschatological concern and recalls the
Elijah motif of Malachi 3:1. It certainly has a much greater
affinity with John 4:4–42 than with Matthew's prohibition
against entering any Samaritan town (Matt. 10:5), and it
suggests that relations with the Samaritans were a lively issue in
Jesus' ministry and in early Christian mission. More particularly,
the story demonstrates that Jesus experienced the same kind of
response in Samaritan as in Judaic towns (cf. Luke 10:10f.).
Implicit in the rejection, however, is the exception the
Samaritans took to Jesus' avowed destination, Jerusalem. The
socio-religious context thus asserts itself as counter-productive
to Jesus' eschatological ministry. Samaritan hostility to Jewish

pilgrims is even documented in Josephus.[8] In spite of Luke 10:1, any suggestion that the disciples were engaged in a mission to Samaria at this point is extremely low key. As John Nolland puts it, 'the event prefigures later mission to the Samaritans (Acts 8:4–25) rather than itself being an instance of mission to them.'[9] Yet Jesus' rebuking of James and John for calling for prophetic judgement in the tradition of Elijah at least suggests that Jesus left the door open for a better understanding of God's ways when his own immediate purpose had been accomplished. When Samaritans would eventually hear this story, they would note that Jesus refused to condemn their village for its original lack of response.

The story of the ten leprous men (Luke 17:11–19), with its overtones of the Naaman story and the other Gospel accounts of cleansing from leprosy, is distinctive because of the return of one of them to give thanks to Jesus. This man was a Samaritan. While it is not stated that the other nine were Jews, the Samaritan's gratitude to Jesus is underlined, possibly for Christological reasons, and the paradox is noted that none came back to praise God in Jesus' presence except one *allogenēs*. The exaggeration makes the point. Luke's story is not anti-Jewish nor pro-Samaritan (if there seems to be such a suggestion, it is countered by 9:51–56), but it suggests that those alienated from Jewry can and will respond in gratitude and faith to God's work in Christ. Nolland notes in parenthesis that, in a secondary way and in the context of Luke–Acts, the story 'secures a foothold for the Samaritan mission,' as 7:9 does for the Gentile mission.[10]

We come now to the parable of the good Samaritan, the legacy of which has been to invest the term 'Samaritan' with powerful overtones of compassion and loving concern for those in dire straits. Although the primary audience of Jesus' parable was Jewish, not Samaritan, we wish to raise here the question of how the parable would be heard in a Samaritan context, or at least with the Samaritan mission in mind, and to question whether Luke has been influenced by this in his presentation of the story Jesus told.

---

[8] Cf. Josephus, *Ant.* 20.118–23; *War* 2.232–33.
[9] J. Nolland, *Luke 9.21–18.34: Word Biblical Commentary*, vol. 35B (Dallas, Texas: Word Books, 1993): 535.
[10] Ibid.: 847.

To begin with, the story told to a Samaritan audience narrates an event from a different culture, involving characters to whom the audience was indifferent, if not antipathetic. The hearers would recognise the world it evoked as dangerous, a world where people were beaten up, where Samaritans trod at their peril, and where priest and Levite were representatives of an alien cult from which one could expect nothing. The arrival of the Samaritan mid-scene is thus no less surprising to this audience than to a Jewish one, but his subsequent actions are received eagerly. He performs the duties of the Law, which the priestly guardians of the Temple so conspicuously failed to do, and does so with style and assurance. He is hero and model. Audience satisfaction is at its height as the lawyer is forced to answer Jesus' question in a way he does not relish. 'Go and do likewise,' for this audience, means 'Go and act as the Samaritan did.' The imperative phrase is a didactic addition to the parable, which transforms the parable into an exemplary story. It is a moral tale with a specific focus, rather than a parable proper. Its wider import for the Samaritan mission is that Samaritans, far from being excluded from the covenant of grace, are as capable of fulfilling the Law of God as their priestly Jewish counterparts—and sometimes do it better! Unlike his co-religionists from the Temple, Jesus did not condemn the Samaritans but had occasion to single some of them out as examples of gratitude or compassion, or faithfulness to Torah.

If the Fathers brought to the text a highly developed allegorical method of interpretation, designed in the end to distil spiritual meaning from the baser elements in the mixture, and if—as we suggest—Samaritan hearers brought their predispositions to the text and marginally influenced its form, modern readers also bring their presuppositions to the text. Prominent among these is the priority of historical perspectives, sometimes understood in fairly crude terms. In order to overcome the alleged excesses of the allegorical method, critical scholarship has appealed to contextual criteria to identify the 'real' setting of the parable in the life of Jesus and perhaps even to hear again the *ipsissima verba* of Jesus. Thus, Jülicher, Jeremias and others have focused on the socio-religious significance of priest, Levite and Samaritan in order to reveal the dynamics of the story and its implicit message, an approach that is too well known to require detailed recapitulation here.[11] It is important to note, however, that the pinpointing of such contextual features involves the selection of a particular perspective on the evidence. The interpreter assumes a relatively single-minded concentration on the Jew/Samaritan divide as the hermeneutical clue to the parable and its setting. The Samaritan emerges as the exemplar of self-sacrificial love for neighbour which refuses to allow religious and racial divisions to inhibit the duty of mercy, unlike the two Temple officials whose response can be explained, but not excused, on contextual grounds also. But matters may not be as simple as that. The context may presuppose other perspectives than those recognised by traditional approaches. For example, a socio-economic reading of the contextual evidence would suggest that Temple officials were popularly regarded as parties to economic oppression, the Temple being much involved in land-owning and taxation, and that the Samaritan was a particularly un-likeable entrepreneur who had taken advantage of the Herodian displacement of Jews in the North to make his fortune. The story remains an illustrative parable, but the terms of reference are subtly different. Economic and political considerations thrust themselves to the fore, and the parable incidentally but fiercely counters stereotypical attitudes based on them. Hence the perspective in which the evidence is viewed is extremely important. But how is one to be guided by perspective?

A helpful approach is to discern the leading perspective presupposed in the telling of the parable in the context of Jesus' ministry conducted mainly in towns and villages of Lower Galilee. The audience is assumed to be Jewish. With whom would such an audience identify? They would identify with the victim, a fellow Jew, the innocent target of violent action all too common in the dislocated society to which they all belonged. He ends up in the ditch, badly bruised and beaten, and the Jewish audience is there with him in spirit and imagination. 'It could have been one of us!' The perspective of the parable is thus, in Funk's

---

[11] It is well surveyed, for example, N. Perrin, *Jesus and the Language of the Kingdom* (London: SCM Press, 1976): 91–107, especially.

memorable phrase, 'the view from the ditch.'[12] What the Jewish audience and the man in the ditch are looking for is a compassionate character, concerned for their plight and so fulfiling the law of God. In theological terms, the audience sees the need for an act of grace. The Jewish listeners expect one of their own to show compassion. But the plot of the parable explodes their conventional image of how grace is enacted. The view from the ditch is that of a hated Samaritan face looming above. What can be expected but a final act of hatred? In the reversal of role from stereotypical opponent to supreme helper, the expectation of the Jewish audience is positively assailed. No figure could be more alien to them than the Samaritan—on religious, racial, economic and even political grounds. No other figure could have acted in such contradiction of stereotype. The parable puts the question, 'Which one of these three acted as neighbour . . . ?' The answer is unavoidable, however articulated. The moral quality of his action cannot be denied.

The parable is far from being merely illustrative (despite Luke's exhortative appendix). It operates as a true parable. That is, it juxtaposes to the known world of the hearers an alternative realm of being which challenges and seeks transformation of their life-world. Charges of lack of realism or credibility are beside the point. The parable inducts the hearers into a narrative world with which they readily identify. It is precisely because they are brought to such a degree of engagement with it that the sudden twist of the plot has such dramatic force. Here is an unveiling of alternative possibility. More than that, here is an undeniably moral and religious scenario which expressly contradicts their expectations and presuppositions and shows them for what they are. And the modern reader readily discerns that these issues have a validity which is not confined to the ancient context. The parable crafts an image of divine reality invading the conventional world of

---

[12] Robert W. Funk, *Parables and Presence: Forms of the New Testament Tradition* (Philadelphia: Fortress Press, 1982): 32; idem., *Language, Hermeneutic, and Word of God* (New York: Harper & Row, 1966): 214; also 'The Good Samaritan as Metaphor', *Semeia*, 2 (1974): 74–81. Elsewhere I have discussed this way of reading the parable. J. I. H. McDonald, 'The View from the Ditch – and Other Angles,' *Scottish Journal of Theology*, 49, 1 (1966): 21–37. Articles in *Semeia*, 2 by D. Patte, G. Crespy, and J. D. Crossan are also relevant to the present discussion.

first-century Palestine. The Fathers were right to look for something beyond the literal or historical dimension.

The parable arguably originated in a Jewish setting and is much more likely to have its source in the ministry of Jesus than in the inventiveness of Luke. It has no explicit christological features of the kind that might give rise to the suspicion of secondary interpretation. And when the Samaritan mission context is itself seen as secondary, the case for a *Sitz im Leben* in Jesus' ministry becomes compelling. Contrary to the way it is often represented, this is a parable *par excellence*. According to Funk 'there is no other parable in the Jesus tradition which carries a comparable punch.'[13] The parable also broadly affirms the patristic perspective, not in terms of highly worked allegory nor Christological development, but in terms of its basic motif or tenor. The audience identifies with the victim. The tenor of the parable is the unexpected manifestation of life-giving compassion. The first Jewish hearers, like the victim, are recipients of the parabolic action. The movement of the action is radically from beyond the ordinary. This super-compassionate movement is identifiably the action of God, yet meted out through a traditional enemy. But to receive compassion, even through an alien agent, moves one to become compassionate. In so far as there is an exemplary aspect, it is that of *imitatio dei*: one must imitate the divine action. This aspect the Fathers tended to overlook.

What does this parable tell us about the moral and religious issues in the ministry of Jesus during Second-Temple Judaism in Palestine? What does it signal about Jesus as teacher?

The parable underlines the fact that Jesus' teaching does not come out of the blue, but is grounded in the religion and morality of Israel. The topics of Law and Temple and Covenant are addressed implicitly. The Lukan setting of the parable is, of course, secondary. In a formal sense, the debate about the great commandment leading into the parable is a separate issue, which is related in all the Synoptic Gospels. That debate has no necessary connection with this parable, although the connection is appropriate enough.[14] Moreover, Luke's use of

[13] Funk, *Parables and Presence*: 65.
[14] Cf. V. P. Furnish, *The Love Command in the New Testament* (London: SCM Press, 1973): 34–38.

'eternal life' may be taken as editorial. In setting the parable as he did, however, Luke has used his material with sensitivity.[15] The parable is about the nature of the life to which God calls his people; and it is also an exploration of the implications of the Torah—summarised in the double commandment—for life in community. Luke's setting gives the parable an intelligent introduction to the issues it raises, rather than an integral piece of received tradition. It is no less valuable for being so.

The religion and morality of Israel were based on Law and Covenant. The parable presupposes acceptance of the Law as the rule of faith and life, but questions sharply the existing Temple cult. It raises starkly the Law's requirement of unconditional love and responsibility for neighbour. The alternative scene the parable presents raises the question of love for God, for the action of the Samaritan does not spring from the ethos of any social group. The parabolic scenario represents God's way—a strange and unconventional way—and is presented as such to the people of the Covenant. The result is an assault on exclusive and self-interested views of 'covenant' (scripted in priest/Levite) a concept that is capable of gross distortion. The Covenant undoubtedly implied gracious election and commission, but did not necessarily set the chosen people on a higher moral and religious plane than others, for God is also in covenant with his whole creation. The Law itself enjoined responsibility for the alien and the needy in Israel.[16] The Temple figures depict its distortion. The Samaritan symbolises the outsider or enemy, not simply as a child of God but—even more powerfully—as the agent of God. The covenantal realm of meaning is thus stretched to the limit, towards a new openness. As V. P. Furnish indicated, citing E. Fuchs:

> While the rabbis emphasised the *periphery* of the circle within which neighbour love should be operative and discussed the problem of a longer and a shorter radius, the

---

[15] See especially Kenneth E. Bailey, *Poet and Peasant* and *Through Peasant Eyes* (Grand Rapids: Eerdmans, 1983): 33–56.

[16] E.g., Exod. 22:21–27; 23:6–12; Lev. 19:9–18; 33–34; 23:22; Deut. 24:11–21; 29:9–15.

parable stresses the *mid-point* of that circle (love) and allows the periphery to extend endlessly outward. Concrete deeds of love, not casuistic definitions of love's limits, should be of concern.[17]

Doubtless this theme was congenial to Luke. That does not mean that it is the product of his activity as redactor. There is a hermeneutical centre to Jesus' ministry. Knowledge of the Law is assumed. His teaching presupposed in turn, that insight into the meaning of Law and Covenant was essential to right action. His role as teacher—whether prophetic or messianic—was to prompt such insight. Parable in the teaching of Jesus interrogates conventional views and practices in the light of the Covenant of God, and calls for a radical transformation through obedience.

Parables are essentially stories.[18] Jesus as narrator uses them to project something of the faith story of Israel to the mind of his contemporary audience. His parables are the ways of God with his people. They appeal to the imagination; in that sense they are metaphoric. They represent perspectives on a given issue, sometimes so surprising that one is arrested mentally by the possibilities they present. Jesus' parables engineer a 'cosmic disclosure'.[19] They engage the audience, then as now. They give reality to an alternative world, juxtaposed to the world of the receptor, and thereby challenge or subvert the 'received world.'[20] Jesus, as the teller of parables, perfected an instrument lying to hand in the tradition of Israel.

The implications of this style of teaching ministry are fascinating. By giving reality to an alternative world, parables not only image divine reality but also actualise it within the narrative structure. The rule of God presses upon the hearers, acquires imminent actuality, and calls for decision. Jesus the parable teller (like Jesus the healer or exorcist) is the agent by which the kingdom of God is actually performed 'in the midst' of his

---

[17] Furnish, *Love Command*: 45; cf. E. Fùchs, 'Was heist "Du sollst deinen Nachsten lieben wie dich selbst"?', in *Gesammelte Aufsatze* II (Tübingen: J. C. B. Mohr, 1960): 5.

[18] Cf. C. Westermann, *The Parables of Jesus in the Light of the Old Testament* (Edinburgh: T&T Clark, 1990): 181–82.

[19] Cf. I. T. Ramsey, *Christian Discourse* (London: SCM Press, 1965).

[20] See Shillington, chapter 1 above, esp. p. 16.

hearers. Hence Jesus the storyteller becomes part of the story of God's working in his creation.[21]

Parables, therefore, are transmitted in the context of the story of Jesus; and since Jesus embodied his own teaching, it is not surprising that they were often heard or read as interpreting his own ministry. Thus, the good Samaritan is heard as the story of the good Shepherd and thus also of Jesus himself. But parables are also received as transparent upon the hearers' own world. The story Jesus told, like the story of Jesus, intersects the story of their lives. It confirms, challenges or transforms the hearers' story. Unfortunately, it is much more comfortable to be confirmed than to be challenged or transformed; hence there is a temptation to make the parable confirm by depriving it of its strangeness or otherness. Something like this may well have happened when the parable of the good Samaritan was told later in a Samaritan context. It allowed Samaritans to identify with the hero as Samaritan and thus be confirmed as true disciples of Jesus, in contrast to the Jewish Temple figures in the parable.

The intersection of the parabolic story and the hearers' life story is therefore critical. It is bound up with the perspective in which the parable is understood, and with the way the two horizons merge. There are certain safeguards against distortion. One is the cohesion of the parabolic story with the story of Jesus himself. If a parable seems at odds with that setting, second thoughts are necessary. Another safeguard is fidelity to the structure of the plot and to the way the story is told and heard. In these respects, the interpretation of the Fathers scores well, although the parable is contextualised not simply in Jesus' ministry but in the entire story of salvation. Such insight is not to be minimised, but in the hands of the Fathers the parable loses its provocative, moral challenge. It becomes instead a confirmation of the faith of the church. When this parable is allowed to speak its 'word' authentically, the result is a challenge to change, rather than a confirmation of the *status quo*.

This parable of Jesus issues in a critique of the Temple system in the negative picture of the priest and Levite.[22] Such a critical stance could not avoid controversy. There is substantial evidence

---

[21] Cf. B. Chilton and J. I. H. McDonald, *Jesus and the Ethics of the Kingdom* (London: SPCK, 1987): 110–31.

[22] Cf. Farris, chapter 2 above, pp. 30–31.

of controversy about Jesus' interpretation of the Law within Second-Temple Judaism; not all of it can be written off as *post eventum*.[23] The controversy, directly or indirectly, hit against some of the most explosive aspects of Judaism: accepted beliefs, the question of authority or authorisation, the Temple, the Sabbath, the question of purity . . . The parable of the good Samaritan appears to censure the elevation of cultic over moral duties, and thus to criticise cultic values. In this respect, this parable might be held to recapitulate prophetic criticism of the separation of Temple worship from social justice. The parable coheres with other actions of Jesus in relation to the Temple, not least the dramatic act of casting out from the Gentile court buyers and sellers and overturning the tables of the money-changers (Mark 11:15–19). Whatever its detailed historical grounding, this act is widely accepted as precipitating Jesus' execution.[24]

The fundamental criterion for Jesus was moral rather than cultic purity. 'Blessed are the pure in heart' (Matt. 5:8).Yet the scope of his teaching shows that he interpreted purity not simply in terms of an inner relation with God but also in terms of the social praxis of God's people. The parable is addressed to a lawyer in Luke 10, and that conjures up for us the whole debate about accommodating the Law to the pragmatics of daily life. Hence the desire to limit the connotation of the term 'neighbour,' not to speak of 'covenant.' This kind of issue underlies much of Jesus' controversy with the Pharisees, yet such debates were also within Israel. What is daring and subversive is the role of the Samaritan, not because he controverts the Torah but because he fulfils its requirements in the letter and the spirit. The circle of God's people is thus dramatically extended; yet the criticism is from within Israel and from shared premises, and looks towards the renewal of God's people. But anyone who shifts the paradigm of Israel's identity in this way can expect the disapproval of the establishment and of much popular sentiment. He is likely to be marginalised or rejected by those who consider it their duty to maintain traditional patterns.

Is there theological significance in the astonishingly daring device of making the Samaritan not only the agent of God

---

[23] See e.g. N. T. Wright, *Jesus and the Victory of God* (Minneapolis: Fortress Press, 1996): 439–42.
[24] Cf. E. P. Sanders, *Jesus and Judaism* (London: SCM Press, 1985).

but also the incarnation of divine grace? Recall the gulf that separates the image of shepherd from that of Samaritan. The image of the shepherd may be that of a humble outsider but is otherwise positive. The image of the Samaritan is not only that of the 'other', the outsider, but also of the renegade, the putative enemy.

Functionally, the 'other' (Samaritan) is essential to the parable. Without him the story would operate entirely within the closed world of Israel as it was. Doubtless, a more domestic cast of characters could have been deployed to make a point, but the parable would not effect transformation. The 'other' subverts the cosy picture. He is the world shatterer. He is the stimulus towards creating a new world. In this respect, he is the instrument of the God who is wholly Other, who cannot be identified with any object of this world, not even the Temple of Jerusalem, although he may be seen to operate through people and through natural forces.

The Other comes in narrative rather than in image. True, the parabolic image is strong and memorable, but it is what the Samaritan *does*—and the fact that it is he who does it and not the Temple clerics—that matters. This action is more than religio-social commentary, for the 'other' is also 'enemy.' In parable, there is no reason why God should not speak through enemy as through friend. In using this device, Jesus presents a picture of moral reality in such a way that the shortcomings and failures of conventional religious practice cannot but be admitted. God is thus the enemy, the judge, the subverter of Israel's entrenched and institutionalised ways of Second-Temple Palestine of Jesus' time.

God as enemy? Is this a valid theological concept, or a Freudian nightmare? It has its dangers, and can be used only in carefully defined ways. The most direct commentary on it is provided by Ahab's reaction to Elijah on the issue of Naboth's vineyard: 'Have you found me, O my enemy?' (1 Kings 21:20). Enemy, because the prophet brought to the surface the king's suppressed awareness of wrongdoing. God is enemy—as grace is inimical—to those who would hide moral reality (the call of goodness and integrity) from themselves. God and grace are inimical because they are transformative: they break down defences and rationalisations and seek change in practice. The parable is a means of entering into a given situation, subverting it and seeking response to a clarified moral vision.[25]

If we dare to apply the term 'theologian' to Jesus—and it may be important to do so—we must recognise the kind of theologian he is. He is a Jewish (not a Christian) theologian in the prophetic tradition, who frequently conveyed his message by the indirect means of parabolic narrative subverting known worlds. Magnificent as they are (and accurate in many respects), the Fathers' interpretations and Luke's Samaritan version blunt the edge of the theology of Jesus through an ecclesiastically domesticated Christology on the one hand and a prejudicial moralism on the other. Jesus' eschatological radicalism stands over against Christian as well as Jewish moral self-justification. The quest of the historical Jesus may be for ever elusive, yet resonating through the mists of tradition and antiquity is a discernible, authentic voice, speaking in parables; and one may endorse the verdict of at least some of his contemporaries: 'Never man spoke like this man.'

[25] See further, McDonald, 'The View from the Ditch.'

Parables of the Land

'Land' continually moves back and forth between literal and symbolic intentions . . . A symbolic sense of the term affirms that land is never simply physical dirt but is always physical dirt freighted with social meanings derived from historical experience. (Walter Brueggemann, *The Land* [1977]: 2)

4

The Foolish Landowner
(Luke 12:16b–20)

The Parable of the Rich Fool

MARY ANN BEAVIS

The Text in Translation

The estate of a certain rich man brought forth abundantly. And he spoke to himself, saying, 'What shall I do, because I don't have a place to store my produce?' And he said, 'I shall do this—I shall pull down my granaries and build greater ones, and gather together my grain and my goods, and I shall say to my self (*psychē*), "Friend (*psychē*), I have many goods stored for many years: Eat, drink, be merry."' But God said to him, 'Fool! This night they shall demand your life (*psychē*) from you; and whose will the things that you have prepared be?'[1]

In a recent commentary on the parables of Jesus, B. B. Scott observes that the parable of the foolish landowner[2] 'has not been of major interest in the history of parable interpretation, nor has it been at the centre of controversy. . . . Its meaning is apparent. And that meaning is the meaning found in Luke's Gospel.'[3] Few recent scholarly articles have been devoted to it,[4] and many contemporary monographs on the parables give it

---

[1] Author's translation. Unless otherwise indicated, translations of biblical passages are from the New Revised Standard Version.

[2] I have chosen to use 'The Foolish Landowner' instead of the familiar title (The Rich Fool) for reasons that will become apparent later in this essay.

[3] B. B. Scott, *Hear Then the Parable: A Commentary on the Parables of Jesus* (Minneapolis: Fortress Press, 1989): 127.

[4] Recent exceptions are J. D. M. Derrett, 'The Rich Fool: A Parable of Jesus Concerning Inheritance,' *Heythrop Journal*, 18 (1977): 131–51; J. Birdsall, 'Luke xɪɪ, 16ff. and the Gospel of Thomas,' *Journal of Theological Studies*,

little or no coverage.[5] The fact that this parable seems so unproblematic is, ironically, somewhat daunting to the interpreter. What can be said about a parable whose interpretation has been so 'stable, predictable, and unafflicted by the obscurities that so torment the other parables?'[6]

The interpretation that follows will attempt to read the parable from a novel perspective. First, in keeping with the purpose of this book to open windows on the historical figure of Jesus,[7] the parable will be situated within the Jewish Wisdom tradition, as an expression of Jesus' mission as prophet and messenger of divine Wisdom (Sophia).[8] Moreover, it will be argued that, far from being a simple warning against selfishness, this parable is 'subversive speech'—in the sense of politically revolutionary speech—using William R. Herzog's model of the parables of Jesus as 'pedagogy of the oppressed.'[9] Finally, I shall show that traditional interpretation of the parable has cast God (v. 20) in a harsh and oppressive role, thus inadvertently and

---

13 (1962): 332–36; G. Gaide, 'Le Riche insense Lc 12, 13–21,' *Assemblés du Seigneur*, n.s. 49 (1971): 82–89; E. W. Seng, 'Der reiche Tor: Eine Untersuchung von Lk. xii 16–21 unter besonderer Berlicksichtigung form- und motivgeschictlicher Aspekte,' *Novum Testamentum*, 20 (1978): 136–55.

5 Derret, ibid.: 131, asserts that the parable 'has not been handled well since Jülicher, and the general ignorance concerning it is astounding.' Among monographs that neglect this parable are J. D. Crossan, *In Parables: The Challenge of the Historical Jesus* (New York: Harper & Row, 1973); M. A. Tolbert, *Perspectives on the Parables: An Approach to Multiple Interpretations* (Philadelphia: Fortress Press, 1979); E. Linnemann, *Parables of Jesus: Introduction and Exposition*, trans. from 3rd German ed. by J. Sturdy (London: SPCK, 1966); Dan Otto Via, *The Parables: Their Literary and Existential Dimension* (Philadelphia: Fortress Press, 1967); F. H. Borsch, *Many Things in Parables: Extravagant Stories of New Community* (Philadelphia: Fortress Press, 1988).

6 Scott, *Hear Then the Parable*: 127.

7 See Shillington, 'Purpose and Method of the Book,' in chapter 1 above, pp. 2–4.

8 M. Hengel, 'Jesus als messianischer Lehrer der Weisheit und die Afange der 'Christologie,' in *Sagesse et Religion, Colloque de Strasbourg, Octobre 1976* eds. Jean Leclant, Jan Bergman, Jean Pépin, et al. (Paris: Presses universitaires de France, 1979): 147–88; E. Schüssler Fiorenza, *Jesus: Miriam's Son, Sophia's Prophet: Critical Issues in Feminist Christology* (New York: Continuum, 1979): 139–41.

9 William R. Herzog II, *Parables as Subversive Speech: Jesus as Pedagogue of the Oppressed* (Louisville: Westminster/John Knox, 1994).

inaccurately contributing to what psychoanalyst Alice Miller calls 'poisonous pedagogy.'[10]

The parable survives in two forms: Luke 12:16b–20 and Gospel of Thomas 63:1.[11] With the significant exception of J. D. Crossan,[12] most interpreters agree that the Lucan version is closer to the parable of Jesus.[13] Although, of course, the original, oral form of the parable can never be retrieved, I shall treat the Lucan version as the more authentic expression of Jesus' teaching.

The parable shows many affinities with Hellenistic-Jewish Wisdom and apocalyptic traditions.[14] The parable is often compared with passages in Sirach and 1 Enoch:

> There is a man who is rich through his diligence and self-denial, and this is the reward allotted to him: when he says, 'I have found rest, and now I shall enjoy my goods!' he does not know how much time will pass until he leaves them to others and dies (Sir. 11:18–19, RSV). Woe unto you who gain silver and gold by unjust means; you will then say, 'We have grown rich and accumulated goods, we have acquired everything that we have desired. So now let us do whatever we like; for we have gathered silver, we have filled our treasuries (with money) like water. And many are the laborers in our houses.' Your lies flow like water. For your wealth shall not endure but it shall take off from you quickly for you have acquired it all unjustly, and you shall be given over to a great curse (1 Enoch 97:8–10).[15]

[10] Alice Miller, *For Your Own Good: Hidden Cruelty in Child-rearing and the Roots of Violence* (New York: The Noonday Press, 1990).

[11] The Gospel of Thomas reads: 'There was a rich person who had a lot of money and said, "I will use my money so that I may sow and reap and plant and fill my storehouses with fruit, so that I won't need anything." This was what the person thought. But that night the person died. Those who have ears, let them hear.' Translation in Burton H. Throckmorton, Jr., *Gospel Parallels: A Comparison of the Synoptic Gospels*, 5th ed. (Nashville: Thomas Nelson, 1992): 124.

[12] J. D. Crossan, 'Parable and Example in the Teaching of Jesus,' *Semeia*, 1 (1974): 63–104.

[13] E.g., Birdsall, 'Luke XII, 16ff.:' 332–36; Seng, 'Der reiche Tor:' 149; Joseph A. Fitzmyer, *The Gospel According to Luke* X–XXIV, The Anchor Bible, 28 (New York: Doubleday, 1985): 971; Scott, *Hear Then the Parable*: 130–31.

[14] Seng, 'Der reiche Tor:' 142–47, gives a lengthy list of the parable's echoes of the Wisdom tradition.

[15] Quotation from James H. Charlesworth, ed., *The Old Testament Pseudepigrapha*, vol. 1 (Garden City, NY: Doubleday, 1983): 78.

The critique of the rich man (*anthrōpou tinos plousiou*) who
behaves foolishly (*aphrōn*) is redolent of the strands in the
sapiential literature that deal with the theme of the disposition
of wealth, including the hedonistic pessimism of Ecclesiastes
[Qoheleth/Preacher] (e.g. Eccl. 2:18–24; 6:1–6; cf. Luke
12:19b) and the exhortations to almsgiving and rebukes to the
unjust rich in Proverbs, Sirach and Wisdom (e.g. Prov. 11:24–
27; Sir. 29:8–13; Wisd. 2:6–11). The attitude of the landowner
expressed in his dialogue with his 'soul' or 'self' (*psychē*)—'eat,
drink, be merry' (v. 19b)—recalls the words of the Preacher:
'There is nothing better for mortals than to eat and drink, and
find enjoyment in their toil' (Eccl. 2:24).[16] The fact that, in the
parable, God calls the man a 'fool'[17] for espousing this philosophy
indicates that the story is unsympathetic to this expression of
worldly wisdom. The parable is more in line with the teachings
of the 'kindly spirit' of divine Sophia (Wisd. 1:6) that condemns this kind of solipsism as foolish and wicked (cf. Wisd.
2:1–11).[18]

A model of the historical Jesus that has gained increasing
acceptance in the past two decades is that of Jesus as prophet
and messenger of divine Wisdom. Scholars have located Wisdom
teaching in virtually every stratum of the gospel tradition,
especially Q, Matthew and John.[19] Several scholars have detected

---

[16] Similar sayings are found in Tobit (7:9–11) and Greek wisdom (cf. J. M. Creed,
The Gospel According to St. Luke [London: Macmillan, 1930]: 173; F. W. Danker,
Jesus and the New Age: A Commentary on St. Luke's Gospel [Philadelphia: Fortress
Press, 1988]: 248).

[17] The term *aphrōn* is a strong expression of foolishness; see Kenneth E. Bailey,
*Through Peasant Eyes: Poet and Peasant and a Literary-Cultural Approach to the
Parables of Jesus.* Combined ed. (Grand Rapids: Eerdmans, 1983): 67.

[18] *Contra* Drury, who sees this parable as a Lucan creation which expresses the
'common sense' wisdom of Qoheleth that 'after the crisis of a man's death
life goes on without him and his goods go to others' (John Drury, *The Parables
in the Gospels* [New York: Crossroad, 1985]: 137). J. D. Crossan, who regards
the version in the Gospel of Thomas as the more original form of the parable,
observes that it 'does not presume that the farmer has done anything wrong.
He is simply rich and has the planning problems of such a status. But riches
do not save you from death's unexpected arrival' (idem, *The Historical Jesus:
The Life of a Mediterranean Jewish Peasant* [HarperSanFrancisco, 1991]: 275).

[19] See, e.g., John S. Kloppenborg, *The Formation of Q: Trajectories in Ancient Wisdom
Collections* (Philadephia: Fortress Press, 1987): 171–245; Ronald A. Piper,
Wisdom in the Q-tradition: The Aphoristic Teaching of Jesus (Cambridge:
Cambridge University Press, 1989); Fred. W. Burnett, *The Testament of Jesus-
Sophia: A Redaction-Critical Study of the Eschatological Discourse in Matthew*

the influence of the Wisdom tradition in the ministry of Jesus. Seán Freyne speaks of Jesus as a Wisdom teacher whose pedagogy was folk wisdom, rooted in human experience and in the Galilean countryside, in contrast to the elite court circles that collected the Old Testament Wisdom traditions.[20] J. D. G. Dunn admits that Jesus seems to have regarded himself as Wisdom's messenger.[21] Similarly, Martin Hengel argues that the image of Jesus as prophet and messenger of divine Sophia goes back to Jesus himself.[22]

The work of feminist biblical interpreters especially has underlined the influence of the Wisdom tradition, and the figure of divine Wisdom, on Jesus and primitive Christianity.[23] The attributes of Sophia, or woman-Wisdom, as personified in Proverbs (1:20–33; 8:1–9:6), Sirach (4:11–19; 6:18–31; 15:1–8; 51:13–22), and Wisdom (6–19) include creativity, generosity, industry, beauty, truthfulness and care for the people of Israel. She teaches wisdom to human beings, loves righteousness and abhors wickedness and foolishness. Those who despise her exhortations to seek knowledge and the fear of the Lord will inevitably come to grief by their own perversity. To those who welcome her instruction, she is a faithful companion. Wise kings and holy prophets are her instruments. Wisdom also denounces those who abuse the poor (Prov. 14:31, 22:22–23; Sir. 4:5–6), and urges the rich to be generous to those in need (Prov. 21:13, 22:9; Sir. 4:1–8, 14:3). The creator will listen to the poor who curse the stinginess of the selfish rich (Sir. 4:4-6). This

---

(Lanham/New York/London: University Press of America, 1981); F. Christ, *Jesus Sophia: Die Sophia-Christologie bei den Synoptikern* (Zurich: Zwingli-Verlag, 1970); Fiorenza, *Jesus*: 141–54. Kloppenborg assigns the story of the foolish landowner to Q (*Formation of Q*: 92, n. 5), as does Burton L. Mack, *The Lost Gospel: The Book of Q* (HarperSanFrancisco, 1993): 77–78.

[20] Seán Freyne, Galilee, *Jesus and the Gospels: Literary Approaches and Historical Investigations* (Philadelphia: Fortress Press, 1988): 259–60.

[21] J. D. G. Dunn, *Unity and Diversity in the New Testament* (London: SCM Press, 1977): 221, 231.

[22] Hengel, 'Jesus'.

[23] E.g., Fiorenza, *Jesus*: 139–41; Elizabeth Johnson, 'Jesus, the Wisdom of God,' *Ephimerides Theologicae Lovanienses*, 61, 4 (1985): 276–89; Susan Cady, Marcia Ronan and Hal Taussig, *Wisdom's Feast: Sophia in Study and Cele-bration* (HarperSanFrancisco, 1990); Virginia Mollenkott, *The Divine Feminine: The Biblical Imagery of God as Female* (New York: Crossroad, 1994): 101–02.

theme is intensified in the apocalyptic development of the
Wisdom tradition typified by 1 Enoch (1 Enoch 97:8–10). The
Wisdom orientation of the parable of the foolish land-owner
supports the contention that this is an authentic parable of Jesus,
who understood himself as a prophet sent by divine Wisdom,
and who was remembered as such by his earliest followers.[24]

As mentioned earlier, a recent book on the parables by Herzog
offers a model of interpretation that may be applied to Luke
12:16b–20.[25] Herzog's starting point is the work of Paolo Freire,
a contemporary Brazilian activist and educator, who has used a
radicalised form of literacy education to bring peasants to an
awareness of their oppression by the dominant class.[26] As well as
learning to read texts, the peasants, in dialogue with teachers
and learners, learn to 'read their culture, including its systems
of domination, exploitation, and marginalization.'[27] Part of this
process includes 'codifications,' which involve the learners'
decoding of visual images (like a photograph or a sketch) that
objectify some aspect of their culture ('moments in the daily life
of the oppressed')[28] in dialogue with a teacher-facilitator. The
next step is the learners' 'problematization' of oppressive social
structures, followed by communal action and social transformation. As Herzog puts it:

> No longer the passive recipients of an imposed world or the
> active analysts of how oppression works, the oppressed become
> subjects capable of making history by remaking their society.
> They accept their vocation as historical subjects, and they
> become agents of humanization in a dehumanizing society.[29]

The entirety of this educational process Freire calls 'con-
scientisation' (conscientizacao),[30] a transformation from the
dominated consciousness of the oppressed to a consciousness
capable of creating opportunities for liberation.[31]

---

[24] Fiorenza, Jesus: 146–47.
[25] Herzog, Parables.
[26] The germinal work by Freire (a prolific author) is The Pedagogy of the Oppressed
(New York: Continuum, 1970). The original Portuguese manuscript was
translated into English in 1968. This chapter can only convey the merest
sketch of Freire's (or Herzog's) thought.
[27] Herzog, Parables: 20.
[28] Ibid.: 21.
[29] Ibid.: 22.
[30] Freire, Pedagogy: 54.
[31] Ibid.: 54–56.

Herzog sees both Freire and Jesus as 'pedagogues of the oppressed,' and likens the parables to the pictorial 'codifications' used by Freire and his colleagues:

> Without invoking the entire program developed by Freire, it is possible to propose that Jesus used parables to present situations familiar to the rural poor, to encode the systems of oppression that controlled their lives and held them in bondage. Living in a visual culture, Freire used pictures as codifications; Jesus, who lived in an oral culture, used story-telling.[32]

He interprets two groups of parables, one group in which the world of oppression is 'problematised' (Matt. 18:23–35, 20:1–16, 25:14–30; Mark 12:1–11; Luke 16:19–31, 19:11–27), and one in which the consciousness of the oppressed is opened up to liberating possibilities (Luke 11:5–8; 16:1–9, 18:1–8; 9–14). Herzog argues that the parables of Jesus (as opposed to the interpretations imposed upon them by the Evangelists) must be read as codifications of the oppressive social systems at work in agrarian Palestine, which at the same time contain the seeds of social transformation. For example, Herzog interprets the parable of the wicked tenants (Mark 12:1–12) as an expression of the exploitive relationship between the landowner and the tenants, which erupts into a self-defeating spiral of violence. Readers/hearers of the parable are left with the question of whether there is an alternative to the futility of violent resistance.[33] The parable of the unjust steward (Luke 16:1–9) shows a situation in which 'the weak' (the steward and the debtors) are able to turn the tables on the powerful (represented by the master of the estate), thus providing a glimpse of a world where emancipation from economic and social oppression is possible.[34] Like Freire, Jesus used such parables, grounded in the harsh realities of everyday life in a stratified agrarian society, to bring his Palestinian peasant audiences to a critical awareness of their social marginalisation and oppression, and to open up new visions of social life.

An initial reading of some of the interpretations of Luke 12:16b–20 that have been offered in the past century offers

[32] Herzog, *Parables*: 27–28.
[33] Ibid.: 98–113.
[34] Ibid.: 233–58.

limited encouragement for a reading of the parable as 'pedagogy of the oppressed.' The story has often been interpreted as a warning to individuals against over-confidence in human resources, and forgetfulness of the fleeting quality of human life and of mortal dependence on God.[35] Several exegetes also emphasise the loneliness of the rich man.[36]

Several recent interpretations that bring us closer to Herzog's approach are less individualistic/existential, emphasising rather the social/communitarian implications of the story. For example, Esler sees the closest parallel to Luke 12:16–21 in 1 Enoch 97:8–10 (quoted above), with its scathing denunciation of the unjust rich.[37] Scott evaluates the rich man's plan to warehouse his bumper harvest against the obligation to use wealth and bounty for the good of the village.[38] Horsely regards the parable as directed not to the rich but to 'ordinary poor people' illustrating the 'futility of building up a surplus that one holds onto for oneself' and the deleterious social effects of the 'self-protective tendency' that results from deprivation.[39] Derrett sees the rich man's foolhardiness in his failure to distribute his surplus to the poor.[40] Similarly, the social-critical interpreters Schottroff and Stegemann see the foolish landowner as a brazen speculator who stores his grain in new silos so that he will be able to sell it at an exorbitant profit in hard times.[41]

Not only do the interpretations which see the landowner's offence in social/communitarian rather than individualistic/existential terms bring us closer to Freire/Herzog's 'problem-

---

[35] E.g., Gaide, 'Le Riche insense:' 88–89; Seng, 'Der reiche Tor:' 152; Drury, *Parables*: 137; Claus Westermann, *The Parables of Jesus in the Light of the Old Testament* (Edinburgh: T&T Clark, 1990): 189; John R. Donahue, *The Gospel in Parable* (Philadelphia: Fortress Press, 1988): 178. Similarly Jeremias, *Parables*: 123; Fitzmyer, *Luke*: 971–72; Danker, *Jesus*: 247–49.

[36] Donahue, *Gospel*: 178; Bailey, *Peasant Eyes*: 64–66.

[37] Philip Francis Esler, *Community and Gospel in Luke-Acts: The Social and Political Motivations of Lucan Theology* (Cambridge: Cambridge University Press, 1987): 189–90.

[38] Scott, *Hear Then the Parable*: 139.

[39] Richard A. Horsley, *Jesus and the Spiral of Violence: Popular Jewish Resistance in Roman Palestine* (Minneapolis: Fortress Press, 1993): 258.

[40] Derrett, 'Rich Fool:' 131–40.

[41] Luise Schottroff and Wolfgang Stegemann, *Jesus and the Hope of the Poor* (Maryknoll: Orbis, 1986): 97. Similarly, Walter E. Pilgrim, *Good News to the Poor: Wealth and Poverty in Luke-Acts* (Minneapolis: Augsburg, 1981): 111. Cf. Freyne, *Galilee*: 247.

posing' hermeneutic but also it is supported by what we know about ancient Mediterranean psychology, which, as Malina and Neyrey point out, was 'dyadic, not individual.'[42] That is, in antiquity, 'the unit of social analysis is not the individual person but the dyad, a person in relation with and connected to at least one other social unit, in particular, the family.'[43] The ancient person experienced him/herself not as a distinct, unique personality but as a member of a group interrelated to others within a horizontally and vertically organised social system.[44] This is apparent in many of the parables of Jesus, which, although they appear simple to modern readers, depict people and situations embedded in complex networks of relationships, obligations and expectations that reflect the class structure and group-awareness of ancient people, e.g. the unjust steward (master, steward, debtors; Luke 16:1–8), the good Samaritan (Samaritan, Jew, priest, Levite, robbers, innkeeper; Luke 10:29–37), the wicked tenants (master, tenants, slaves, heir; Mark 12:1–11), the unmerciful servant (king, slave, wife, children, fellow slaves, torturers; Matt. 18:23–35).

Although the foolish landowner is the only human character mentioned in Luke 12:16b–20, like other parables of Jesus, the story presupposes that the rich man is enmeshed in a web of social and economic relations that ancient audiences would have recognised without effort. The man is *rich* and *owns land* (*chōra*, 'landed property' or 'estate'). Ancient listeners would have assumed that the man did not work his own land, but that he had slaves or (more likely) tenants to do the work for him. Although not explicitly mentioned in the parable, ancient listeners would have assumed that a man of property would have a family and an extensive network of patrons and clients.[45] The question in verse 20b—'and the things you have prepared, whose will they be?'—implies an awareness that the man has heirs.

According to historians of antiquity, in the Roman empire, including Palestine, land was the principal source of wealth, and

[42] Bruce J. Malina and Jerome H. Neyrey, 'First-Century Personality: Dyadic, Not Individual,' in *The Social World of Luke-Acts: Models for Interpretation*, ed. Neyrey (Peabody, MA: Hendrickson, 1991): 67–96.

[43] Ibid.: 73.

[44] Ibid.: 73.

[45] See Scott, *Hear Then the Parable*: 205–08.

the goal of the elite classes, to which the landowner would have belonged, was to amass and consolidate land holding.[46] One of the principal ways in which lands became available for purchase by the rich was the loss of smallholder land through debt, which resulted in the peasant becoming the new landowner's tenant.[47] The listeners would have known that the rich man was likely to be an absentee landlord, residing in the city, who administered his lands through hired agents liable to misuse their power.[48] As MacMullen observes, there is ample evidence that tenant farmers were subjected to both economic exploitation and physical abuse by landowners and their bailiffs.[49] Tenants, already poor, were pressed for rents by their masters' servants, and for taxes by the state.[50] Neither landlords nor state authorities scrupled to collect their dues by violent means.[51]

Within this socio-economic context, the landlord's decision to build new barns to store his produce takes on a sinister quality. As several of the interpreters cited above have suggested (Derrett, Schottroff and Stegemann, Pilgrim), the soliloquy in verses 15–19, in which the man plans to build new barns to store the produce and lay it up for 'many years,' implies his intent to hoard the grain and sell it when a shortage drove up the price.[52] The uncertainties of rural life, combined with the warehousing of crops by urban landowners, could lead to desperate hunger among the peasantry. MacMullen cites examples from the first and second centuries CE in which villagers were reduced to eating vetch and other virtually inedible plant matter such as bulbs and roots.[53] G. E. M. de Ste. Croix observes that absentee landlords were so effective at exploiting the countryside that, during famines, the fruits of peasant labour might all be stored in cities.[54]

---

[46] Ramsay MacMullen, *Roman Social Relations* (New Haven/London: Yale, 1974): 4–6, 48–54; G. E. M. de Ste. Croix, *The Class Struggle in the Ancient World* (London: Duckworth, 1981): 120–33.

[47] Douglas E. Oakman, 'The Countryside in Luke-Acts,' in *Social World*: 157.

[48] MacMullen, *Social Relations*: 5–6.

[49] Ibid.: 5, 13. Cf. Oakman, 'Countryside:' 168.

[50] MacMullen, *Social Relations*: 34–35.

[51] Ibid.: 5–12, 35–37.

[52] MacMullen finds evidence of this practice as early as the first-century CE (37–38). See also de Ste. Croix, *Class*: 219–21.

[53] MacMullen, *Social Relations*: 33.

[54] de Ste. Croix, *Class*: 219.

The portrait that emerges of the landlord is that of a character who would have been familiar to, and despised by, the Galilean peasants to whom Jesus brought the teaching of divine Wisdom. In fact, since Jülicher, the pericope has been classified by most interpreters not as a 'parable proper,' based on metaphor, but as an exemplary story, based on literal events, like the Good Samaritan (Luke 10:29–37), the Rich Man and Lazarus (Luke 16:19–31) and the Pharisee and the Tax Collector (Luke 18:9–14). Jeremias classed it among those parables so vividly told that they probably rose out of recalled incidents.[55] It is not difficult to imagine that Jesus' listeners would, at least initially, have smiled at the prospect of the landowner's sudden demise, and agreed with God's (and presumably Jesus') estimation of him as a fool—as do all of the modern interpreters cited in this chapter. However, the ancient listeners might have disagreed with the vast majority of contemporary interpreters who view God as the direct agent of the rich man's untimely death. The verb *apaitousin* in 12:20a, God's verdict on the fool, usually translated as a passive ('this night your soul **is demanded** of you'), is actually an active verb in the plural with an unidentified subject ('this night they [shall] demand your soul of you'). This plural where one would expect a singular (*apaiteō*, 'I [God] demand your soul' or *apaitetai*, 'your soul **is demanded**') is usually explained as a Semitic theological passive (thus the passive reading in most translations),[56] or, less often, as presupposing 'angels of death' as its subject.[57]

A reading that would more readily have presented itself to an audience of Galilean peasants (and which may have been explicit in Jesus' telling of the story) would involve the killing of the man by human agents. Peasant uprisings, tax revolts and brigandage in the face of the kind of ruthless exploitation represented by the landowner are a well-documented feature of ancient history.[58] If, as suggested above, the rich man was an absentee landowner,

[55] J. Jeremias, *The Parables of Jesus*, 1st ed. (London: SCM Press, 1954): 20.

[56] E.g., Fitzmyer, *Luke*: 974. Of the three other examples of this usage in Luke offered by Fitzmyer (6:38, 16:9, 23:31), only 16:9 seems to be unequivocal; however, the plural *dexōntai* may be a deliberate parallel with the same verb in 16:4.

[57] As suggested by W. Grundmann, *Das Evangelium nach Lukas* (Berlin: Evanglische Verlangsanstalt, 1959): 258.

[58] Oakman, 'Countryside:' 168–69.

he would not have been immune from reprisals. MacMullen vividly depicts a situation that might well apply to the subject of the parable: Someone who hoarded grain in time of shortage or brought defilement in the eyes of the gods or in any way attacked the whole community risked mob violence.

> 'People would pick up anything that lay in the street cobbles, broken tiles, rocks—and let fly. . . . If it availed nothing against a powerful citizen in a strong house, the mob tried arson. . . .'[59]

Of course, listeners might also have pictured the man on a visit to his estate and vulnerable to attack by hostile tenants (cf. Mark 12:1–11) or brigands, although there is evidence to suggest that landowners of the mid-first century were disinclined to spend much time in the country.[60] On this interpretation, God's address to the fool in the night-vision of 12:20 is an announcement of the death by human violence that the man has brought upon himself, not the prelude to a divine execution.

Jesus' audience is left with the question of who will own the man's hoarded wealth (v. 20). A violent death has snatched the landowner's possessions away from him, but the assassins will not benefit from his goods; nor will the poor. Another rich man will inherit, or buy, the estate, and the man's killers, whether they are caught or escape, will be no better off. Like the question that concludes the parable of the Wicked Tenants (Mark 12:9), the conclusion of this story codifies the self-defeating nature of revenge and violence.[61]

This reading of the parable is in line with the Jewish Wisdom traditions in which the wicked and foolish are brought down by their own perversity. Jesus, as the emissary of divine Wisdom, criticises both the rapaciousness of the elite and the violence of rebels and bandits. However, it runs counter to the near consensus of interpreters that the rich man's death is God's direct punishment for his foolishness.

Not surprisingly, this feature of the story is minimised or glossed over by most interpreters.[62] Oesterley noted that the exact

[59] MacMullen, *Social Relations*: 66.
[60] de Ste. Croix, *Class*: 241.
[61] Cf. Herzog, *Parables*: 113.
[62] Including myself, in 'Parable and Fable,' *Catholic Biblical Quarterly*, 52 (1990): 489.

manner in which the death sentence is carried out is not specified: 'it is a dramatic way of expressing the divine will; in modern speech: "Man proposes, God disposes."'[63] Fitzmyer admits that God's taking of the man's soul 'may seem unjust,' but sees the fool's failure to consider God by using wealth on behalf of others as justifying the parable's fatal conclusion.[64] Donahue blames the fool's death on his failure to realise that his life was 'on loan' from God.[65] Richard Wenham holds that the man's sudden death at the hand of God is justified by the 'terribly serious and dangerous' implications of foolishness in the Wisdom literature.[66] Bailey sees the voice of God as breaking through the rich man's self-absorption and confronting him with a 'chilling vision' of himself.[67] Scott places the killing as a remove from God by seeing the agents of destruction as the angels of death: 'The kingdom's coming is not an apocalyptic intervention; God does not seek to right the kingdom's misuse by an apocalyptic destruction of evil. Rather the man will die in his sleep!'[68] Jeremias held that in the original form of the parable, the moment of crisis was not the man's death, but the coming of the kingdom.[69] Gaide reminds his readers that the death of the rich man is a 'parabolic sketch' (*trait parabolique*) whose significance surpasses the literal sense of the story.[70]

Such efforts to exonerate God in the death of the landowner illustrate the biblical-theological—if not the historical-critical—difficulty of a parable of Jesus that ends with God summarily executing a person for greed, selfishness and foolishness.[71] From the perspective of the 'pedagogy of the oppressed,' it is difficult to see how a story with such an ending could open up liberating, non-violent possibilities for its hearers. Rather, the message conveyed by a parable in which God is the agent of the man's demise is reminiscent of the kind of 'poisonous pedagogy' that

[63] W. O. Oesterley, *The Gospel Parables in the Light of Their Jewish Background* (London: SPCK, 1936): 171.
[64] Fitzmyer, *Luke*: 972.
[65] Donahue, *Gospel*: 178.
[66] Richard Wenham, *The Parables of Jesus: Pictures of Revolution* (London: Hodder & Stoughton, 1989): 140.
[67] Bailey, *Peasant Eyes*: 67. Similarly, Pilgrim, *Good News*: 112.
[68] Scott, *Hear Then the Parable*: 139.
[69] Jeremias, *Parables*: 123.
[70] Gaide, '*Le Riche insensé*': 88–89.
[71] Although such an outcome is not unthinkable for Luke (cf. Acts 5:1–11).

psychoanalyst Alice Miller censures in her critique of hidden cruelty in historical and contemporary child-rearing practices.[72] Miller traces the roots of adult violence to the abuse, manipulation and scare tactics used by parents and teachers to control children. One example she offers from a nineteenth-century encyclopaedia of pedagogy is illuminating:

> Finally, it will be useful to call to mind the dubious and transitory nature of merely material things by occasionally pointing out appropriate illustrations of this: the sight of a youthful corpse or the report of the collapse of a commercial house has a more humbling effect than often repeated warnings and censure.[73]

The Lucan Jesus uses the parable in a similarly frightening way, to warn two brothers squabbling over their inheritance rights (Luke 12:13–15) against the dire consequences of greed. Luke's crude portrayal of God as a judgemental and lethal patriarch who kills human beings as a punishment for their deviant conduct (cf. Acts 1:18–19, 5:1–11) is considerably different from that of the parable of Jesus, in which the landowner's death by human hands is the (futile) outcome of his own social violence. The Lucan 'exemplary story' offers an instance of self-satisfied greed harshly addressed by a punitive God reminiscent of Rita Nakashima Brock's description of atonement Christology as teaching divine child abuse.[74] In contrast, the 'problem-posing' parable of Jesus, the prophet of divine Wisdom, raises questions and dilemmas with liberating possibilities for the hearers. Will the man's death truly result in justice for his tenants? Are the man's killers really justified in taking his life? Characterised by divine Wisdom rather than human foolishness, are different relationships between rich and poor, oppressor and oppressed, possible?

---

[72] Miller, *For Your Own Good.*

[73] Ibid.: 23. The quotation is from K. G. Hergang, ed., *Päidagogische Realenzyklopädie* (1851).

[74] Rita Nakashima Brock, 'And a Little Child Will Lead Us: Christology and Child Abuse,' in *Christianity, Patriarchy and Abuse: a Feminist Critique*, eds Joanne Carlson Brown and Carol R. Bohn (New York: Pilgrim Press, 1989): 42–61.

5

Vulnerable Promise from the Land
(Mark 4:3b–8)

The Parable of the Sower/Soils

DONALD PETERS

The Text in Translation

A sower went out to sow. And as he sowed, some seed fell on the path, and the birds came and ate it up. Other seed fell on rocky ground—where it did not have much soil (*gē* i.e. land/soil), and it sprang up quickly, since it had no depth of soil (*gē*). And when the sun rose, it was scorched; and since it had no root, it withered away. Other seed fell among thorns, and the thorns grew up and choked it, and it yielded no grain. Other seed fell into good soil (*gē*) and brought forth grain, growing up and increasing and yielding thirty and sixty and a hundred-fold.[1]

The genius of the parable form is its ability to challenge the readers/listeners wherever and whoever they are, whether on the Jewish holy land of first-century Palestine or peasants on the subsistence farms of North-eastern Brazil where we worked for five years, from 1988 to 1992. On one occasion during those years of volunteer work I observed a peasant farmer perched on a steep, protracted field of pineapple, making his way among the rows. From my Canadian prairie perspective, this was no place to farm. The land was dry, hard and stony, but valued highly by the peasant farmers who lived there. 'Who would ever buy such land?' I asked. The response, 'When the rain comes, the land will produce. It will be green here.' The scene in North-eastern

---

[1] Parallels in Matt. 13:3b–8; Luke 8:5–8a and Gos. Thom. 9.

Brazil reminded me of agricultural practices in biblical times: of the land that promised life to the people, of the rainy season, of sowing, of reaping, of rocks and thorns and hard places. The farmer in the pineapple field, the sower and the soil in the parable, are imprinted in my memory.

The Brazilian experience with peasant farmers furnishes one perspective from which to interpret this parable of Jesus. The same story/parable can be read in different ways to evoke different responses: in the holy land of first-century Palestine responses peculiar to that situation, and in Brazil responses related to that situation. This difference is felt sharply in someone moving from an industrial economy, such as that of Canada, to a more agrarian economy, such as that of the Brazilian peasant farmers. Similarly, within the variety of Synoptic contexts (Matthew, Mark, Luke) different responses to the story of Jesus can readily be observed.

Before turning attention to the distinctive usage of the parable by each of the three evangelists, a note should be made about the existence of a version of the parable in the Gospel of Thomas.[2] The general distinctiveness of the sayings in the Gospel of Thomas suggests that the parable existed in the pre-Synoptic tradition. There is no scholarly consensus on the literary relationship between the Gospel of Thomas and the Synoptic Gospels.[3] The parable in the Gospel of Thomas shares essential elements with the canonical Gospels: road, bird; rock, lack of root; thorns, suffocation; good soil, plentiful production. The

---

[2] 'Jesus said: "Behold, the sower went out, he filled his hand, he sowed (the seed). Some (seeds) fell on the road. The birds came (and) gathered them up. Others fell on the rock and did not send root down into the earth, and did not send an ear up to heaven. And others fell among thorns. They choked the seed, and the worm ate it. And others fell upon the good earth, and it brought forth good fruit up to heaven. It bore sixty-fold and one hundred and twenty-fold."' Gos. Thom. 9, cited in *Synopsis Quattuor Evangeliorum*, ed. Kurt Aland (Stüttgard: Deutche Bibelstifiung, 1976): 518.

[3] For example, Werner Georg Kümmel, *Introduction to the New Testament*: translated by Howard Clark Kee, 17th ed. (Nashville: Abingdon Press, 1977), 75, believes that the Gospel of Thomas is not independent of the Synoptic Tradition but cites the Synoptics according to the oral tradition and freely alters them. Helmut Koester, '*GNOMAI DIAPHOROI*: The Origin and Nature of Diversification in the History of Early Christianity,' in James M. Robinson and Helmut Koester, *Trajectories through Early Christianity* (Philadelphia: Fortress Press, 1971), p. 129, asserts that the Gospel of Thomas is independent of the Synoptic Gospels.

expression 'up to heaven' in Thomas (two occurrences in the parable) perhaps reflects the gnostic conceptual framework for the document. If the Gospel of Thomas is independent of the Synoptics, we have before us four versions of the parable. If the Gospel of Thomas is dependent on the Synoptics we still have three versions of the parable embedded in their respective literary contexts, each version reflecting its place and usage in the particular Gospel.

Further, we assume that the parable *received* by each of the evangelists is not exactly the same as the parable *transmitted* by them. We can detect with reasonable confidence the redactional hand of each evangelist at work. This process, as we shall see, is also based on certain assumptions: (1) that there is a literary relationship among the Synoptic Gospels; (2) that Mark, as a written source, is used independently by Matthew and Luke; and (3) that Matthew and Luke independently shared another source known as Q.[4] Following on these assumptions, the place to begin our investigation of the parable of the sower/soils is the Gospel of Mark, where we will attempt to uncover hints of Mark's redactional hand.

That the parable of the soils belongs to the pre-Markan tradition is based on four observations: Mark 4:3–8 forms a distinct unit within the parable pericope itself (Mark 4:1–9), the parable of the soils is found in the Gospel of Thomas without introductory comment; chapter 4 of Mark is structured around the theme of seed parables, which may well have been connected in an earlier stage of the tradition.[5] These considerations taken together suggest that Mark inherited the tradition of the parable of the soils and used it for his own purposes within the Gospel.

The thread that Mark used to seam his editorial material to the pre-Markan Soils parable tradition is discernible: Mark 4:1–2 suggest a geographical setting beside the sea for the teaching of the chapter. Mark uses the term 'parable' in Mark 4:2 and repeats the term six times in the rest of the chapter. The term 'Listen!' (Mark 4:3a) is not essential to the parable itself, but

---

[4] For a detailed analysis and review of the Synoptic Problem, see Kümmel, *Introduction*: 38–80.

[5] Mark 4:3–8 (parable of the soils), Mark 4:26–29 (seed growing secretly) 4:30–32 (mustard seed); Robert A. Guelich, *Mark: Word Biblical Commentary*, vol. 34a (Dallas: Word Books, 1989): 197.

serves as a second introduction to the parable and as a complement to the conclusion (Mark 4:9), which likewise focuses on hearing.[6]

Moreover, the parable proper is found in verses 3b–8. Since this is a distinct literary unit, and since the *exact* content of the pre-Markan tradition is lost to us, it would be unproductive to speculate on possible Markan modifications to the tradition. There is no distinctively Markan vocabulary in 4:3b-8. His redactional contribution to the parable, if there was any, is difficult to identify.[7] This much can be stated with confidence: the pre-Markan tradition, utilised by Mark and inherited by Matthew and Luke, was very similar to what we have in Mark 3b–8, set out at the head of this chapter.

The parable contrasts the results of sowing two sets of seeds. The first set (4:4–7) becomes subject to three adverse growing environments: the path, the rocky ground and the thorns. The result is agricultural disaster owing to predators, the climate and plant competitors. A second set of seeds encounters rich soil and, in contrast to the first set, yields three degrees of productivity: thirty-fold, sixty-fold and one-hundred-fold.[8]

Four kinds of sowing conditions are described where the type of land (pathway, stony soil, thorns and good soil) is the primary factor. Secondary factors (birds, heat and thorns) add to the destructive effect of the primary factor (the land) for the first set of seeds. The contrast between the three disastrous results with the three productive results of sowing is deliberate. If the parable belonged to the pre-Markan tradition, we should not necessarily assume that the interpretation given in Mark 4:13–20 belonged to that tradition.[9] The precise original context of the parable of Jesus may be lost, except that it was probably told

---

[6] Ibid.: 195ff.

[7] I suspect that the redundancies in verses 5 and 8 indicate that Mark has tampered with his source.

[8] Guelich, *Mark*: 195. See also, Norman Perrin, *Jesus and the Language of the Kingdom* (Philadelphia: Fortress Press, 1976), p. 162.

[9] B. Gerhardsson, 'The Parable of the Sower and Its Interpretation,' *New Testament Studies*, 14 (1967–68): 187 argues that the parable was constructed for the interpretation it received in the Gospels! Most commentators agree with Bultmann that the interpretation is secondary: Rudolf Bultmann, *History of the Synoptic Tradition*, rev. ed., trans. John Marsh (New York: Harper & Row, 1963): 187. See also, Perrin, *Jesus and the Language of the Kingdom*: 8, who argues that the interpretation is secondary.

in Lower Galilee. While the parable explicitly compares two types of land, it offers no explicit explanation of the reality for which it is a mirror.[10]

It may be that agriculture is used in this parable, as it is in the traditions of Judaism, as an eschatological metaphor.[11] Following this line of thought, the parable echoes the eschatological nature of Jesus' ministry and the vulnerability of God's eschatological activity through the work of Jesus.[12] Accordingly, Jesus teaches, performs signs, and seeks response. Some will respond in a life-changing way. Some will not. The ministry of Jesus is not guaranteed a positive effect on all who hear. Yet the message will get through to some who, in turn, will be nurtured, and will be productive.

The wider context of Mark's Gospel, and the fourth chapter in particular, reveal more of Mark's purpose and his application of the parable. We can observe several Markan emphases that have bearing on Mark's application of the parable of the soils. First, 'hearing' is a prominent theme in chapter 4. The parable sequence begins with the command, 'Listen' (4:3a). Mark concludes the parable of the soils with the corollary command, 'He who has ears to hear, let him hear' (4:9). A slight variation of this statement is repeated in verse 23, while in verse 24 Jesus instructs his listeners to 'Take heed what [they] hear.' Beside verse 3a, Greek forms of the verb 'to hear' are used an additional seven times in the chapter (4:9, 12, 15, 16, 18, 20, 33). In the interpretation of the parable (4:13–20), there are four groups of listeners to 'the word.' The first three groups hear but do not understand. Those of the last group hear, understand and accept the consequences of that word for their lives and deeds.[13]

A second theme has to do with the stature of the disciples in the Gospel of Mark. Mark's editorial addition to the parable (v. 9) implies a distinction between those who could and those who could not hear. In the Markan sequence, the following verses

[10] Cf. Shillington, 'The Land,' in chapter 1 above, pp. 9–11.
[11] In reference to Mark 4:3–8, Bultmann, *History of the Synoptic Tradition*: 202, cites 4 Ezra 8:41. 'For just as the husbandman sows much seed upon the ground and plants a multitude of plants, and yet not all which were sown shall be saved in due season, nor shall all that were planted take root; so also they that are sown in the world shall not all be saved.'
[12] Guelich, *Mark*: 197.
[13] Gerhardsson, 'Parable:' 179–82.

(10–12) explain why some can hear and some cannot. Some, namely the disciples, have been given the secret of the kingdom of God. Others have not. Those who have been given the secret ask for (4:10–12) and receive (4:13–20) explanations. And with respect to the completion of the parable sequence in the chapter, we are told that while Jesus spoke to the people in parables (seemingly without their being able to understand), 'privately, to his own disciples, he explained everything' (4:34).

Mark develops this theme consistently throughout the sequence. That which is hidden is made manifest; that which is secret comes to light for those with ears to hear (4:22–23). Those who 'have', like the disciples, will receive more. Those, who do not 'have', like the scribes (2:1–12, 16; 3:22), the Pharisees (2:24, 3:2), and, perhaps, even the well-intentioned who were astonished at Jesus' words and deeds (1:22, 27; 2:12), will lose what they have (4:24–25).[14]

What lies in the background of the parable sequence, and throughout the Gospel of Mark, is the concept of the messianic secret.[15] Jesus commands that his miraculous deeds should not be publicised (1:44), he withdraws from populated areas as his reputation spreads (1:45), and he commands that the unclean spirits, which know his true identity, conceal that fact (1:34, 3:11–12). Boobyer suggests that '[the] prevailing idea is apparent: to the general public the full messianic nature of events is not to be communicated; some are not granted the privilege of such revelations.'[16] However, the idea of the messianic secret is an interpretive theory used to understand the direction of Mark's Gospel. The theory should not be applied more consistently than Mark would have applied it. As it happens in Mark, the secret of Jesus' identity cannot be kept. The word spreads and, despite Jesus' withdrawing in the face of public attention, the crowds persist in finding him.

On the other hand, while some are granted insight into the messianic secret, their vision does not remain unblurred. The disciples have been given to know the secrets of the kingdom of

---

[14] Guelich, *Mark*: 197ff. makes the point about the Markan emphasis in these verses.

[15] Kümmel, *Introduction*: 90–92.

[16] G. H. Boobyer, 'The Redaction of Mark iv. 1–34,' *New Testament Studies*, 8 (1961–62): 68.

God (Mark 4:10–12). But they still need to ask the meaning of the parable of the soils and the seed. Jesus chides them for their ignorance: 'Do you not understand this parable? How then will you understand all the parables?' (Mark 4:13) And the disciples' failure to understand continues throughout the Gospel.[17] The Markan context of the parable of the soils accounts for the fact that there are some who can and some who cannot know. The same context recognises that the disciples know (4:11), and then excuses them, perhaps on the basis of the messianic secret, for not knowing when they should (4:13). Given these considerations, perhaps the parable implicitly recognises that not all seed sown on hostile soil goes to waste, nor does all seed sown on good soil reach fruition.

A third and final observation we will make concerns Mark's use of the material in 4:3b–8. Its function at that point in chapter 4 arises from the thematic direction of the first three chapters. In Mark, Jesus inaugurates the kingdom of God through his words and deeds. The kingdom of God had come, but it is like a vulnerable seed whose success, while guaranteed, is fragile at best. In the introduction to his commentary on Mark, Robert Guelich notes that 'Jesus' message risked a triumphalist misunderstanding by those who saw primarily the glory of the final kingdom in contrast to its vulnerable beginnings.'[18]

The parable of the soils is an apt demonstration of this principle. Boobyer[19] states that the first three chapters of Mark display a number of contrasting themes with respect to response to Jesus and his proclamation: acceptance (1:22, 27; 2:12) versus rejection of the Son of man (2:7; 3:22, 30); popularity (1:33, 37, 45; 2:2; 3:20) versus opposition (2:6, 16, 24; 3:2–6); and some who find forgiveness (3:28) versus some who lose it forever (3:29–30). In this context, even the matter of familial ties is brought under scrutiny (3:31–35). Who belongs to the true family of Jesus? Those who do the will of God are his brother, sister and mother.

There are, therefore, two classes of people: those who are outside and those who are within. The parable of the soils in

---

[17] See as examples: 4:40–41, the stilling of the waves; 6:48–52, Jesus walking on the water; 8:14–21, the question about the loaves.

[18] Guelich, 'Introduction,' *Mark*: xlii–xliii.

[19] Boobyer, 'Redaction:' 68.

Mark continues the theme of rejection and acceptance, of unbelievers and believers, of those outside and those inside. Some soils are unreceptive to seed and are unproductive, but some soil is rich and will yield much fruit.

In studying the Matthean and Lukan texts, we have the advantage of knowing the precise nature of the source material that these later Evangelists possessed. We find that Matthew was very faithful to his source for the parable itself. He omits Mark's 'Listen' (Mark 4:3a), consistently pluralises Mark's 'seed' (Matt.13:4a, 5a, 7a), abbreviates Mark, likely for stylistic purposes (Matt. 13:7–8, cf. Mark 4:7–8), and inverts the order of the plentiful production from good soil (Matt. 13:8: 'some a hundred-fold, some sixty, some thirty'). These alterations of his source are not substantive and leave the essential structure of the parable intact. Accordingly, four types of soil are considered in two sets. The first set of three hostile environments yields unsuccessfully. The second yields at the same production rate as in Mark.

Luke takes greater liberties with his Markan source than does Matthew. While he adds an explanation that the seed that fell along the path 'was trodden under foot' (Luke 8:5), in general, his is a truncated version of Mark. He retains the notion of the three hostile environments for the seed and the one receptive one. But the Markan contrast between the three negative results of the sowing and the three positive yields (30, 60, 100) is lost in Luke: 'And some fell into good soil and grew and yielded a hundred-fold' (Luke 8:8). What is retained, however, is the essential: against the prospect of sowing without success lies the prospect of yielding phenomenal growth.

Both Matthew and Luke reproduce the Markan parable with few, if any, substantive modifications and in accordance with their particular styles. Their ways of using the parable, however, demonstrate some interesting and subtle changes in emphasis.

The first telling remark in the Matthean text which sets a different tone in emphasis comes immediately following the Matthean parable of the soils. In contrast to Mark 4:10, where the disciples ask Jesus concerning the parables, the disciples in Matthew do not ask about the parables, but rather ask why Jesus speaks to the crowd in parables. This is a subtle but significant shift in emphasis and is carried forward consistently throughout the chapter.

The explanation for Jesus' use of parables (Matt. 13:12–15) suggests that Matthew may have had difficulty with the boldness of Mark's explanation (Mark 4:12). In Mark, parables are used almost as a means of having people see without perceiving and hear without understanding. In Matthew, the parables are used because people are already in a state of seeing without perceiving and hearing without understanding. Could it be that parables, much as we understand them today, are used in the Gospel of Matthew to bring unseeing people to sight?

In the Markan text, Jesus' explanation of the parable comes at 4:13–20. The explanation is prefaced by what can only be understood as an insult to the disciples. The disciples, who had been given to understand the secret of the kingdom of God, were still in need of an explanation. 'How then will you understand all of the parables?' Jesus asks (4:13). Matthew not only omits this question and the insult that it implies but replaces the unit with a treatise on the blessedness of the disciples which he borrows from Q (Matt. 13:16–17; cf. Luke 10:23–24). Kümmel observes that 'the disciples [in Matthew] are strongly idealised, so that blame or evidence of failure is eliminated.'[20]

Matthew's parable of the soils is placed within his discourse on parables (chapter 13),[21] in which Matthew takes over the structure of Mark 4:1–34, uses almost all of the Markan material,[22] and weaves in material from Q[23] as well as special Matthean source material.[24] The chapter includes seven parables that

---

[20] Kümmel, *Introduction*: 108. Compare also Mark 6:52 with Matt. 14:33. See also, Gerhard Barth, 'Matthew's Understanding of the Law,' in Günther Bornkamm, Gerhard Barth and Heinz Joachim Held, *Tradition and Interpretation in Matthew*, trans. Percy Scott (London: SCM Press, 1963): 107ff.

[21] On the organisational structure of Matthew's Gospel into five discourses, the parable discourse being the third, see, Howard Clark Kee, *Jesus in History*, 2nd ed. (New York: Harcourt Brace Jovanovich, 1977): 170; and Donald A. Hagner, *Matthew 1–13, Word Biblical Commentary*, vol. 33a (Dallas: Word Books, 1993): 365ff.

[22] The parable of the seed growing secretly (Mark 4:26–29) is the only exception.

[23] The following texts are from Q: the blessedness of the disciples, Matt.13:16–17; the parable of the leaven, Matt. 13:33.

[24] Material unique to Matthew includes: the parable of the weeds, Matt. 13:24–30; the interpretation of the parable of the weeds, Matt. 13:36–43; the parables of the hidden treasure and the pearl, Matt. 13:44–46; the parable of the net, Matt. 13:47–50; and the parable of the Householder, Matt. 13:51–52.

display ecclesiastical and eschatological motifs.[25] The role of the disciples is prominent throughout. Gerhardsson points out that in this chapter, Jesus' instruction includes the crowd as audience up until Matthew 13:36. After that, Jesus is in retreat with his disciples.[26] The contrast between the spiritually inert crowds who do not 'have' and the inquiring disciples who 'have' is accentuated in Matthew. This contrast reaches its climax at the end of the Matthean parable sequence in Matthew 13:51–52. The disciples, having understood all of the parables, are 'scribes trained for the kingdom of heaven' (13:52). In Matthew, the point is clear: The people of the rich soil are the disciples who have been given the secrets of the kingdom of heaven (13:11) and have understood them (13:51).

In contrast to Matthew, Luke does not augment the content he inherited from Mark 4, nor does he strengthen the role of the disciples. Luke uses only seventeen of the verses Mark 4:1–34, and two of these verses are used in another context.[27] Unlike Matthew, Luke adds no new tradition. If it is clear in Matthew that the people of the good soil are the disciples, that conclusion is left much more open in Luke. Luke retains the Markan contrast between the disciples and the crowd. The disciples know the secrets of the kingdom of God while the crowd may only hear those secrets in parable form (Luke 8:10). At the same time, Luke does not draw the same inference as Matthew regarding the exclusive status of the disciples.

It so happens that the introduction (Luke 8:1–3) and conclusion (Luke 8:19–21) to the Lukan sequence suggest another direction. The section is introduced with a note on Jesus' itinerant ministry throughout cities and villages during which Jesus was accompanied by the twelve as well as some women, three of whom are named. At the conclusion of the sequence (8:19–21), Jesus' mother and brothers come to meet him. Jesus responds by stating that his true family is comprised of those

---

[25] Günter Bornkamm, 'End-expectation and Church in Matthew,' in Bornkamm, et. al., *Tradition and Interpretation in Matthew.* 19.

[26] Jesus is in retreat with his disciples for the interpretation of the parable of the weeds (13:36–43), the parables of the hidden treasure and the pearl (13:44–46), the parable of the net (13:47–50), and the parable of the householder (13:51–52). See Gerhardsson, 'Parable:' 173.

[27] The parable of the mustard seed (Mark 4:30–32) is taken up in Luke 13:18–19.

who hear and do the will of God. By using Mark 3:31–35 here, Luke has illustrated his interpretation of the parable of the soils: those who are of good soil hear the word and bring forth fruit (Luke 8:15).[28] By implication, they are the same ones who are of Jesus' true family and, by implication, that group goes beyond the circle of the twelve (cf. Lk. 8:1–3).

One final consideration suggests that Luke expands the circle of the people of the good soil. Mark 4:20 uses the vocabulary of 'hearing', 'acceptance' and 'bearing fruit' to interpret the parable of the soils. The Lukan emphasis on the people of the good soil is decidedly different: 'they are those who, hearing the word, *hold it fast* in an honest and good heart, and bring forth fruit with *patience*' (Luke 8:15, emphasis mine). The Greek terms for 'persistence' (8:15), 'endurance' (8:15), 'temptation' (8:13), and 'faith' (8:12, 13), each unique to the Lukan interpretation, suggest a context of early Christian mission. These subtle changes to the Markan source suggest that Luke's focal point is on the young missionary church.[29] Accordingly, the parable of the soils is an encouragement for adherents to 'hold fast in an honest and good heart' and 'to bring forth fruit with patience' (Luke 8:15).

Mark inherits the tradition of Jesus containing the parable of the soils. Mark's editorial activity in the parable sequence suggests a development of a theme of contrasts between those who are inside and those who are outside. He places the disciples squarely within the circle of those who 'have' and relegates them to good soil. Matthew, who defends Christianity in the eyes of his Jewish readership,[30] perhaps for this reason, eliminates any Markan inference to obduracy on the disciples' part. Luke takes over the Markan tradition and blends in his focus on a young missionary church in its fight for the faith.

Gospel traditions about Jesus are alive. The Evangelists are not merely scribes. They are creative preachers who, while remaining faithful to traditions they received, are able to blend those traditions with their own particular foci. A parable about the land that had poignant significance in its first telling on Palestinian Holy Land took on new significance in the new situations of the Synoptic Evangelists.

[28] Gerhardsson, 'Parable:' 183.
[29] Ibid.: 183–85.
[30] Kümmel, *Introduction*: 141.

The modern interpreter of the parable of the four soils must do no less. The hermeneutical challenge, of course, is to remain faithful to the essence of the parable while allowing the parable as metaphor to affect imagination born from experience. Joachim Jeremias maintains that a parable makes one central point, which can be uncovered through a thorough study of the parable's historical context.[31] For Jeremias, the central point of this parable of Jesus is eschatological. In a context that depicts the hopelessness of the sower's labour, a miracle happens: 'The abnormal tripling, presented in true oriental fashion, of the harvest's yield (thirty, sixty, a hundred-fold) symbolises the eschatological overflowing of the divine fullness, surpassing all human measure.'[32] Despite the appearances and the difficulties, God will bring a triumphant conclusion to the work.

Recent work on the parables frees the approach of Jeremias from the quest of a single salient point from a reconstruction of Jesus' historical context. The recent studies accept the value of Jeremias' contribution to the study of parables but they also recognise the creative power of metaphor that opens onto the interpretation of the parable. Amos Wilder is representative of this school of thought:[33]

> In the parables we have action-images . . . Jesus' com-
> munication, just because it is fresh and dynamic, is necessarily
> plastic. Now we know that a true metaphor or symbol is more
> than a sign, it is a bearer of the reality to which it refers. The
> hearer not only learns about the reality, he participates in it.
> He is invaded by it. Here lies the power and fatefulness of
> art. Jesus' speech had the character not of instruction and
> ideas but of compelling imagination, of spell, of mythical
> shock and transformation.

This approach acknowledges the hearer as participant. What, then, are the compelling images that the parable of the soils brought to the audience of Jesus and to the Evangelists? Two observations come to mind.

---

[31] Joachim Jeremias, *The Parables of Jesus*, 2nd rev. ed. (New York: Scribner's, 1972), pp. 1–22.

[32] Ibid.: 150.

[33] Amos Wilder, *Early Christian Rhetoric: The Language of the Gospel* (New York: Harper & Row, 1964): 84, as cited in Perrin, *Jesus and the Language of the Kingdom*: 130. See Perrin for a good study of the modern interpretation of the parables.

First, as we have seen in our study of the Synoptic Gospels, the parable focuses on exclusiveness versus inclusiveness. Some will hear the word, some will not. Some are entitled to the secrets of the kingdom of God, some are not. Some will bear fruit, some will not. Each of the three Evangelists develops this image of the parable. The Markan literary context, which contrasts those who accept with those who reject the teaching of Jesus, implies that Jesus' disciples are persons of rich soil. For Matthew, this point is made explicitly. The disciples in Matthew are scribes trained for the kingdom of heaven (Matt. 13:52). For Luke the focus is still intact, but the emphasis has shifted from the disciples to the new Christian community. The true family of Jesus are those who hear the will of God and do it (Luke 8:21). These are the people of rich soil.

A second image the parable evokes is eschatological. Jeremias observes that correct interpretation of the parable must consider two periods of time: the period for sowing and the period for reaping. While the image of harvest is eschatological, the focus of the image is not so much on judgement as it is on triumph.[34] Nolland comments that this sower is no typical farmer. He does not care that the seed is wasted: 'In relaxed confidence, Jesus sows generously, assured of an extravagant fruitfulness, no matter how much of the field receives the sowing in vain.'[35] Despite the obstacles, some will hear, and, when they hear, the growth will be outstanding!

These several images the parable would have evoked in the minds of Jesus' audiences, as in the minds of the Evangelists. Contemporary audiences of the biblical tradition are far removed from the setting in which the parable was first heard or read. What salient images does the parable of the four soils evoke for a present-day audience? In his recent commentary on Matthew, Donald Hagner observes that a new hermeneutic, in addition to accounting for the historical context, recognises the 'multivalence of meaning and indeed the free construction of meaning of the parable in relation to the personal situation of the reader.'[36] As active participants in the

[34] Jeremias, *Parables*: 150.

[35] John Nolland, *Luke, Word Biblical Commentary*, vol. 35a (Dallas: Word Books, 1989): 376.

[36] Hagner, *Matthew 1–13*: 364.

audience, what do we bring to our listening to the parable of the soils?

The early Christian tradition focused its attention on exclusiveness versus inclusiveness, and the potential for astronomical growth at the harvest. Today's audience might direct some of its attention to the idea of different kinds of land. It might read the metaphors of the parable against the background of common contemporary experience. Following this line of interpretation, we observe that in our actual experience, we play the roles of soil, sower and seed.

As a metaphor, the soil/land is a measure of our receptivity to the message. Every contemporary reader can readily identify with each of the four types of soil. On the one hand, we recognise the hard places, the stones and the thorns present in ourselves. Our lack of receptivity to the secrets of the kingdom results in failure. On the other hand, we recognise the rich soil in ourselves. Our willingness and ability to hear produces fruit. The metaphor of the sower measures our diligence in performing the tasks of the kingdom of God. The sower is faithful to the task, knowing that most of what is sown will not yield positive results. But the sower spreads all of the seed in confidence that some will reproduce abundantly. The parable's eschatological image of bounty teaches faithfulness in the act of kingdom work.

The metaphor of the seed calls to mind our vulnerability and the ever-fledgling status of the kingdom of God. As heirs of the Christ-message, we will find that our words and deeds are either accepted or rejected. Some seed flourishes. Some seed does not. Even with this attempt to translate the parabolic metaphor into contemporary categories, our cultural and historical context forces us to stretch the point in interpreting the parable. Pineapples in well-stocked supermarkets serve as ample testimony that we are far removed from the terrain of the sower. Norman Perrin observes that 'for the man of the technological West, for whom agriculture is agribusiness carried on both scientifically and on an enormous scale, The Sower and The Lost Sheep would really seem to have died as metaphors.'[37]

---

[37] Perrin, *Language*. 203.

The task of the modern interpreter is to reclaim the insight of the metaphor. This chapter represents one more attempt to do so. Perrin's observation about the death of the metaphor of the sower in the technological West, does not apply to North-eastern Brazil where the peasant sower plies his agrarian trade. We return there to conclude our study of the parable of the soils.

In the faith communities of peasant farmers, the focal points of this parable are undoubtedly the varied soil and the harvest. The peasant people of Brazil understand soil, its pathways, stones and thorns, as did the peasant population of Lower Galilee.The Brazilian peasants understand crop predators and scorching sun. They know crop failure. They also know success. They see themselves and others in the four soils. Many earn just enough from their labour to stay alive, but not enough to live fully. They live with violence in their communities and within their families. Their dwellings are many kilometres on foot from health care and schools. They understand the reasons why positive change does not come to their lives. Their situation seems hopeless. Yet they do hope and work for better tomorrows for themselves and for their children. Despite the odds, they sow and put faith in the harvest.

In soil like this, most seeds do not grow. But in the parable, for every four lots of seeds thrown, one lot of seeds grows. The Brazilian poor would understand this image because of their vulnerable attachment to the land. They would make immediate application to their social context, recognise their vulnerability within that context, and place faith in their potential to transcend it. Brazilian peasants understand the harvest. They experience dismal failure and, when the conditions are right, astounding success. A Brazilian peasant's exegesis of the parable of the soils would comment on the success rate. When the seeds grow they will produce a great harvest. Some of the work will bear fruit. Some of the effort will not be wasted. For the Brazilian peasant, the parable communicates hope.

The parable of Jesus told first on the Holy Land of Palestine, and recaptured by the Evangelists, remains alive. While the tradition of Jesus remains, the meaning adjusts with every new situation and experience of the community in which the parable is heard again. Each audience in its turn receives the tradition of the parable of the soils and allows it to intersect with experience. In the process, the biblical tradition demonstrates its vibrancy, relevancy and life.

Parables of the Economy

Money should circulate; we should circulate; . . . Let us risk being used, and we will be increased, and the end will be glory, because we made things better for all the others we lived and died with. (Joseph G. Donders, *Jesus, The Stranger* [1978]: 104–105)

6

Saving Life and Keeping Sabbath
(Matthew 20:1b–15)

The Parable of the Labourers in the Vineyard

V. GEORGE SHILLINGTON

The Text in Translation

A landowner went out early in the morning to hire labourers
for his vineyard. After agreeing with the labourers for the day's
wage (*denarius*), he sent them into his vineyard. When he went
out three hours later he saw other people standing idle in the
marketplace, and said to them, 'You also go into the vineyard,
and I will pay you whatever is right.' So they went. When he
went out three hours later, and then three hours after that,
he did the same. At about the eleventh hour [of a twelve hour
day] he went out and found others standing around, and said
to them, 'Why are you standing here idle all day?' They said to
him, 'Because no one has hired us.' He said to them, 'You
also go into the vineyard.' When evening came, the owner of
the vineyard said to his manager, 'Call the labourers and give
them their pay, beginning with the last and then going to the
first. When those hired at the eleventh hour came, each of
them received a day's wage (*denarius*). Now when the first
came, they thought they would receive more; but each of them
also received the denarius. And when they received it, they
grumbled against the landowner, saying, 'These last worked
only one hour, and you have made them equal to us who have
borne the burden of the day and the scorching heat.' But he
replied to one of them, 'My dear man, I am doing you no
wrong. Did you not agree with me for a denarius? Take what
belongs to you and go. I choose to give to this last the same as
I give to you. Am I not allowed to do what I choose with what
belongs to me? Or is your eye evil *(ponēros)* because I am good
(agathos)? (Adapted from the NRSV)

To anyone who thinks of Jesus as a model of fair dealings, the parable of the labourers in the vineyard must come as something of a shock. One group of workers receives an agreed wage for twelve hours of work, while another group receives the same amount for only one hour of work. To make matters worse, the one-hour workers are paid first. 'Here is a story of barefaced injustice'[1] that cannot be resolved by reducing the 'meaning' of the parable to a single, universal point, or by classifying it under any label in particular. 'Hardly any parable in the Gospels seems to upset the basic structure of an orderly society as does this one.'[2] The inherent tension in the structured world (or frame)[3] of the parable is part of its appeal. The paradoxical form draws the reader back to participate imaginatively[4] again in further resolution.

This appeal of the parable is perhaps reason enough to abandon instant resolution provided by an allegorical inter-pretation, to which this parable has been subjected through the centuries, epitomised especially in the interpretation of Irenaeus in the second century.[5] Alas—or perhaps Hurrah!—when one returns to the narrative plot, the scandal of injustice in the reckoning at the end of the parabolic working day still stands beckoning the reader inside the narrative world to feel the tug-o-war once more.

---

[1] J. Jeremias, *The Parables of Jesus*, 2nd rev. ed. (New York: Scribner's, 1972): 37. From the 8th edition of *Die Gleichnisse Jesu* (Göttingen: Vandenhoeck & Ruprecht, 1970).

[2] John R. Donahue, *The Gospel in Parable* (Philadelphia: Fortress Press, 1988): 81.

[3] The term reflects the psychological 'frame analysis' of Erwin Goffman represented by James R. King in an article on this parable, 'The Parables of Jesus: A Social Psychological Approach,' in *Journal of Psychology and Theology*, 19, 3 (1991): 257–67. The frame is 'the structure or organisation that individuals impose upon the chaos served up by the world and from which they derive their sense of reality. A frame is a strip of "experienced activity":' 258.

[4] For further discussion of the role of *imaginative participation* in the inter-pretation of narrative parables see V. G. Shillington, 'Imaginative Participa-tion in Parable Interpretation,' in *The Bible and the Church: Essays in Honour of Dr. David Ewert*, ed. A. J. Dueck, H. J. Giesbrecht and V. G. Shillington (Winnipeg: Kindred Press, 1988): 45–61; and Sallie McFague, *Speaking in Parables: A Study in Metaphor and Theology* (Philadelphia: Fortress Press, 1975): 43–89.

[5] Irenaeus read the different times of hiring as stages in the history of salvation, the denarius as immortal life from the Son of God, *Against Heresies* IV.xxxvi.7.

It is in the nature of parable (whether a modern one of Kafka or an ancient one of Jesus)[6] not to let its reader/participant walk away blithely nodding to the moral of the story. If the parable is metaphor, as I believe it is, then its form and figures and plot are certain to leave 'the mind in sufficient doubt about its precise application to tease it into active thought,'[7] as Dodd first proposed some sixty years ago. What I propose to do here, after a brief review of principal readings of this parable in this century, is to treat the parable as an extended metaphor that points paradoxically to a way of life beyond the received world in which the metaphor itself is rooted. The world beyond, I believe, is not an abstract theological construct unrelated to the cultural, social vicissitudes of the people with whom Jesus associated, who heard this parable about workers in a vineyard in its first telling, but a world of concrete possibility for the same people who lived where Jesus lived. They knew the value of a denarius, and knew also what happened to people who were not so fortunate as to have the denarius in their possession on any given day, especially Sabbath day. The denarius, so I will argue, plays a vital role in the plot of the story as a metaphoric unit of value that equalises the workers, and in some measure also the householder with them.

Of course, any reconstruction of the world of the first audience is tentative, yet necessary for a responsible decoding of the elements of the narrative. Recent social-scientific studies of the Mediterranean world of the New Testament are shedding new light on puzzling texts such as this one about labourers and landowners on Jewish soil in the Mediterranean world.[8]

---

[6] See J. D. Crossan's discussion of the relationship between ancient parables and modern ones in 'Parable, Allegory, and Paradox,' *Semiology and Parables: Exploration of the Possibilities Offered by Structuralism for Exegesis* ed. Daniel Patte (Pittsburgh: The Pickwick Press, 1976): 248–78.

[7] C. H. Dodd, *The Parables of the Kingdom*, rev. ed. (New York: Scribner's, 1961): 5. Cf. J. D. Crossan, *Cliffs of Fall: Paradox and Polyvalence in the Parables of Jesus* (New York: Seabury/Crossroad, 1980): 5, where he defines parable, with reference to Paul Ricoeur's work, as 'narrativity, metaphoricity, paradoxicality.'

[8] E.g. John Dominic Crossan, *The Historical Jesus: The Life of a Mediterranean Jewish Peasant* (HarperSanFrancisco, 1992); Kenneth E. Bailey, *Poet and Peasant and Through Peasant Eyes: A Literary-Cultural Approach to the Parables in Luke* Combined ed. (Grand Rapids: Eerdmans, 1983). (Even though Bailey applies his findings to parables in Luke, the results of his investigation of the cultural,

Until the appearance of Herzog's incisive and provocative social-scientific study of the parables in 1994, interpretations of the parable of the vineyard workers moved minimally beyond those of Dodd and Jeremias, who interpreted it as a parable of the grace of God toward sinners. Dodd, following the lead of Jülicher at the turn of the century,[9] ostensibly denied the validity of an allegorical interpretation of the parable. Instead, he applied principles of Form Criticism to the text to remove the parable 'from its setting in the life and thought of the Church, as represented in the Gospels, and make an attempt to reconstruct its original setting in the life of Jesus.'[10] That 'original setting,' according to Dodd, was the opposition of the Scribes and Pharisees to the unceremonial way Jesus consorted with tax collectors and sinners. The point of the story itself is that 'the employer, out of sheer generosity and compassion for the unemployed, pays as large a wage to those who have worked for one hour as to those who have worked all day.'[11] But for Dodd the meaning of the story is not found within the parameters of the narrative, but outside in 'the facts of the ministry of Jesus.'[12] Dodd's interpretation reveals at once which 'facts' he has in view:

> The divine generosity was specifically exhibited in the calling of publicans and sinners, who had no merit before God. The Kingdom of God is like that. Such is Jesus' retort to the complaints of the legally minded who cavilled at Him as the friend of publicans and sinners.[13]

Ironically, while Dodd decried the allegorical method of interpreting parables, his own interpretation of this parable exhibits

---

social and political world of Jesus applies also to such parables as the labourers in the vineyard in Matt. 20); Seán Freyne, *Galilee, Jesus and the Gospels: Literary Approaches and Historical Investigations* (Philadelphia: Fortress Press, 1988); B. B. Scott, *Hear Then the Parable: A Commentary on the Parables of Jesus* (Minneapolis: Fortress Press, 1989); William R. Herzog II, *Parables as Subversive Speech: Jesus as Pedagogue of the Oppressed* (Louisville: Westminster/John Knox, 1994).

[9] Adolf Jülicher, *Die Gleichnisreden Jesu*, 2 vols (Tübingen: J. C. B. Mohr [Paul Siebeck], 1910). Volume 1 appeared in 1888, was revised in 1899 with the publication of a second volume in the same year. The second volume was revised in 1910.

[10] Dodd, *Kingdom*: 85.

[11] Ibid.: 94.

[12] Ibid.: 95.

[13] Ibid.

the marks of an allegorical approach: the gracious vineyard owner is 'God;' the one-hour workers are 'publicans and sinners;' the twelve-hour workers who complained are the 'legally minded' Scribes and Pharisees. None of this is conveyed in the frame of the parable proper (nor in its immediate context in Matthew for that part). Had the Scribes been in the audience they might have reached Dodd's conclusion, although not directly from the terms of reference in the parable. On the other hand, landless day-workers and householders in Jesus' audience would have found themselves figured in the story explicitly without allegorical ado. Even so, as extended metaphor, this parable admits polyvalent interpretation[14] such as that of C. H. Dodd.

Jeremias worked out his own version of Dodd's form-critical analysis. He calls the story the 'Parable of the Good Employer,'[15] told by Jesus 'for the vindication of the gospel against its critics.'[16] Jeremias rightly sees the emphasis, not on the call to the vineyard, but on the reckoning at the end of the day (20:8–15). The employer is generous. He will not allow the last workers to go home with a pittance for one hour of work. But Jesus did not tell the parable to extol God's mercy to the poor, according to Jeremias. The parable is not about vineyard workers at all.

> 'The parable is clearly addressed to those who resembled the murmurers, those who criticised and opposed the good news, Pharisees for example. Jesus was minded to show them how unjustified, hateful, loveless and unmerciful was their criticism.'[17]

Yet one page earlier Jeremias dared to call the story one of bare-faced injustice. Perhaps this apparent contradiction in Jeremias bears testimony to the paradoxical complexity of the form of this parable. This is not simply a parable about the grace of God for late-comers. There is a perceived injustice in the story that continues to stimulate imagination and beg for interpretation.

---

[14] On the polyvalence of parable interpretation see Mary Ann Tolbert, *Perspectives on the Parables: An Approach to Multiple Interpretations* (Philadelphia: Fortress Press, 1979): 15–66, and Crossan, *Cliffs of Fall*: 65–104.

[15] Jeremias, *Parables*: 136.

[16] Ibid.

[17] Ibid.: 38.

Using various literary and social-scientific approaches, scholars have nuanced the interpretations of Dodd and Jeremias with illuminating results, but ending up with essentially the same general conclusion: this is a parable of grace, the surprising grace that signals the in-breaking of the kingdom of God. Dan Via combined a structuralist approach with an existential interpretation. The parable has the potential of an ironic comedy, but the tragic characters who complain tip the balance of the parable to become an ironic tragedy. The flaw is not in the work of the complainers, but in their *self-understanding*. 'Their desire to have their security within their own grasp caused them to see the incalculable, not as graciousness, but as injustice.'[18] In this interpretation, the parable emphasises grace rejected by the grumbling workers who insist on merit. What Via seems to ignore, however, is that the complainers who worked all day for their denarius were not the recipients of grace at the end of the day. Instead, they were deliberately made to witness others receive the same reward for one-twelfth of the work performed in the cool of the day. The tragedy for the complainers, as Via understands it, is their exclusion from the source of grace ('take what belongs to you and go,' v. 14) by their own 'legalistic understanding of existence, grounded in the effort to effect their own security.'[19]

Robert Funk's analysis[20] likewise stressed the tragic/comic curves in the structure of the story. The householder determines the terms of the narrative within which there are essentially two responses, one that turns tragically downward at the time of reckoning (the all-day workers), and one that turns comically upwards (the one-hour workers). By the canons of ordinariness the response of the first is justified, but the kingdom of God in Jesus shatters everyday justice. 'The mercy of God does not wait upon some future—near or remote—but is already "there" for those who care to quit the immense solidity of the mundane world and step through the looking glass of the parable.'[21] In a

---

[18] Dan O. Via, *The Parables: Their Literary and Existential Dimension* (Philadelphia: Fortress Press, 1967): 152.

[19] Ibid.: 154.

[20] Robert W. Funk, *Parables and Presence: Forms of the New Testament Tradition* (Philadelphia: Fortress Press, 1982): 35–54.

[21] Ibid.: 74. Robert Funk is presently writing a new book on the parables in which he may have revised some of his earlier conclusions.

SAVING LIFE AND KEEPING SABBATH   93

similar vein, Crossan has pointed to the reversal of expectations
which shatters normalcy. 'The owner is *not* one who is especially
generous but one who violates expectations . . . God also shatters
our understanding of graciousness and that is the most difficult
of all to accept.'[22] Granskou, viewing the parable against the
backdrop of the prophetic tradition of Israel, sees ironic humour
in the parable in which divine justice is no respector of special
status. The complaint of the all-day workers was not about social
justice, but about the kind of justice meted out to them in
particular. 'The humor is that their selfishness is so transparent
as to void their case for more pay.' The parable chastises the
first disciples 'who want to have a special place when everyone
else is considered equal.'[23] Achtemeier relates the meaning of
the parable directly to contemporary readers. 'Stripped of the
cloak of our piety, we all stand with those indignant laborers
who were paid last and no more than those who had worked
only one hour . . . How we dislike it when the breaks go the other
way!'[24] Scott observes a 'hierarchical pattern of a patron-client
society' in the parable, but hesitates to exploit the interpretive
possibilities of his observation in his final statement of the
meaning of the parable. He agrees with 'those commentators
who see grace as the major theme of the parable . . . The denarius,
however, is not the metaphor of grace; rather, the need for
workers, the call, is the metaphor.' Scott then tips his hat to
'Paul's argument that with God there is no distinction, that
justification (making right) is through gift (Rom. 3:22–24).'[25]

In 1994, Herzog's work called into question all interpretations
since Dodd that tended to vilify the complainers and applaud
the householder for his God-like generosity. Using his paradigm,
'Jesus as pedagogue of the oppressed,' Herzog divested the
characters of any theological significance, and transferred the

---

[22] J. D. Crossan, *In Parables: The Challenge of the Historical Jesus* (New York: Harper
& Row, 1973): 114–15.

[23] David M. Granskou, *Preaching on the Parables* (Philadelphia: Fortress Press,
1972): 107–108.

[24] Paul J. Achtemeier, 'The Ministry of Jesus in the Synoptic Gospels,'
Interpretation, 35 (1981): 162.

[25] B. B. Scott, *Hear Then the Parable*: 297–98. At the beginning of his discussion
of this parable, Scott agreed with Manson that 'the parables cannot be made
to support the thoroughgoing Pauline and Lutheran doctrine of salvation
by grace alone:' 283. Yet at the conclusion of his discussion Scott ties the
Pauline/Lutheran theme to the strategy of the parable.

vilification from the all-day workers to the householder. Herzog contends that the characters in the parable 'belong to identifiable social classes or groups in advanced agrarian societies. To understand the parable it is necessary to know who appears in its social script.'[26] The vineyard owner is an elite class, because the crop 'can be converted into a luxury item (wine), monetised, and exported.'[27] This elite vineyard owner has unilateral power. The agreement was not a negotiated one. Furthermore, 'the fact that the agora is filled with day laborers at all hours of the day indicated a situation of high unemployment.'[28] Moreover, the householder is far from being generous. He takes advantage of an unemployed work force to harvest his crops without a wage agreement. The way the payment is structured is humiliating and degrading to the ones who worked all day. Stripped of their last vestige of dignity, their physical work, they rise up to challenge the householder's treatment of them. They must defend their honour or die! 'The landowner is shrewd. Having shamed the day laborers, the owner denies their charge; he then picks out their leader and makes an example out of him' in a condescending way.[29] Herzog attempts to read the parable from the place of the peasant farmer[30] who has lost his land to someone like the elite householder who turned the peasant vegetable plot into a vineyard. His interpretation merits a somewhat lengthy quote.

> If the owner is speaking to former free peasants who have been forced into working as day laborers, his claim to the land is akin to rubbing salt in their wounds. How has he gained what belongs to him? . . . Their relationship is not as brothers but as exploiter and exploited. The day laborers have no ground on which to stand. . . . Any vestige of the debt code has been obliterated by his covetous greed. . . . As pedagogue of the oppressed, Jesus would have facilitated

---

[26] Herzog, *Subversive Speech*: 84.

[27] Ibid.: 85.

[28] Ibid.: 86.

[29] Ibid.: 92.

[30] On the hermeneutical possibilities of reading from the social location of someone else, see Fernando F. Segovia, 'Cultural Studies and Contemporary Biblical Criticism: Ideological Criticism as Mode of Discourse,' in *Reading From this Place*, vol. 2, ed. Fernando F. Segovia and Mary Ann Tolbert (Minneapolis: Fortress Press, 1995): 1–17.

their interaction with his codification, posing problem after problem to break their adhesion to the oppressor, to constantly unveil reality.[31]

Herzog's incisive analysis of the social location of this parable has opened new possibilities for its interpretation. By exposing the householder as an elitist oppressor of landless, and therefore powerless, day labourers he has persuasively shifted attention away from a generous God-like householder, like the merciful God of the Jewish Scriptures.[32]

Laudable as Herzog's work is, his analysis uncovers some puzzling pieces not altogether resolved by his interpretation. Among them these: What is the metaphoric significance of the denarius that all alike receive? Why bring the owner, not his steward, face to face with the unemployed in the marketplace? Is there a Jewish understanding of human work-and-rest playing into the parable, especially work-and-rest related to the land? What would have been the reaction of a mixed audience of peasant farmers, gainfully employed landless day labourers, destitute unemployed day labourers, elitist land owners and religious leaders?[33]

At the risk of robbing the parable of its metaphoric power, I shall lay out what I perceive to be the structure of the narrative for purposes of interpretation, omitting the closing line at verse 16, which doubtless belongs to Matthew's redaction. The introductory phrase ('the kingdom of heaven is like,' v. 1) may also have been incorporated by Matthew, as Herzog suggests.[34] Between these two brackets lies the parable proper (20:1b–15).

---

[31] Ibid.: 95.

[32] So Claus Westermann, *The Parables of Jesus in the Light of the Old Testament*, trans. and ed. F. W. Golka (Minneapolis: Fortress Press, 1990): 185, who sees in the story that 'mercy is incalculable,' even though the denarius is the designated sum that everyone in the story, and doubtless in the audience, is quite able to calculate.

[33] Audience criticism is still in its infancy, compared to other exegetical tools, but its role in the interpretation of parables such as this one is strategically significant. The work of J. D. M. Derrett opened the way to the development of this instrument (Herzog's critique of Derrett's reconstructions notwithstanding, *Subversive Speech*: 93), *Jesus's Audience: The Social and Psychological Environment in which He Worked* (London: Darton, Longman & Todd, 1973): 31–159. Cf. J. A. Baird, *Audience Criticism and the Historical Jesus* (Philadelphia: Westminster Press, 1969): 15–173.

[34] Herzog, *Subversive Speech*: 97

The two-phase movement of the narrative reveals a certain chiastic structure, the second phase moving in reverse order to the first.

Phase I: The Received World of Labourers and Landowners (20:1–7)

- first agreement on a denarius for a normal day's work (20:2)
  - later agreements for 'what is right' (20:3–5)
    - last non-agreement for one hour of work (20:6–7)

Phase II: An Alternate Vision for Labourers and Landowners (20:8–15)

- last one-hour workers receive the denarius first (20:9)
- full-day workers receive the denarius as agreed (20:10)
- the case against equality of living dishonourably denied (20:11–15)

The effect of the reversal signals something wrong with the received world of labourers and landowners in Palestinian Jewish life. The steps of Phase I would correspond more or less to the experience of the groups represented in the characters, except perhaps for the appearance of the householder himself in the village marketplace (v. 3, *agora*), instead of his employment manager, otherwise called a 'retainer' in Lenski's analysis of such servants in an agrarian society.[35] The narrative world of Phase I was essentially the real world the people knew and had come to accept: some are fortunate enough to be householders (*oikodespotēs*, v. 1), others get a subsistence wage (*dēnarios* as agreed, v. 2), others receive less than subsistence (*ho ean hē(i) dikaion*, v. 4), while others are without livelihood at the end of the day (v. 7). By the end of Phase II, however, two figures, representing two groups, stand out by their attitude and action: the all-day workers and the householder. If these two types are in the audience both of them are scandalised, the all-day workers, happy not to be empty-handed like their fellow labourers, but also householders who blissfully stockpile profits from the land and the marketplace where Jewish compatriots live and die in destitution. The fact that the householder in the parable comes

---

[35] G. E. Lenski, *Power and Privilege: A Theory of Social Stratification* (New York: McGraw-Hill, 1966): 243–48.' Their basic function was always the same— service to the political elite:' 243.

across as a protagonist in the plot does not mean that such householders in the audience approve of his action. They would protest, perhaps even on religious grounds. Prosperity and property are signs of blessing within the tradition of Israel, and thence also in Jewish tradition. To distribute accrued blessing (profits) to down-and-outs, making them equal with their fellows, could be viewed as folly at best and sacrilege at worst. Similarly, persons able to sustain life from their labour would consider themselves blessed in comparison to those in destitution. Phase II of the parable calls into question this accepted rule of life and world.

The denarius symbolises the necessary means of daily living from working on the land. The opening agreement in Phase I assumes this to be so. By the end of the day, however, people are standing in the marketplace without the necessary denarius as a means of living. The elite householder in the audience is made to see the situation through the eyes of the narrative householder, and is shamed by the narrative householder's response.

The parable does not suggest that the denarius as such was a super-generous wage. The generous act of the householder in the parable is not that he pays a large wage, but that he sees to it that everyone in the marketplace has an equal living share of the land that he owns and operates. To propose, as Herzog does, that the narrative householder, far from being a good man, takes oppressive advantage of poor labourers thwarts the formal force of the parable. This householder does not let the destitute die, whereas the all-day workers were concerned only for themselves, not for their Jewish comrades who were not so fortunate. Herzog pays too little attention to the subjects in the narrative who did not have a full day's wage. Should the householder have paid the one-hour workers one-twelfth of a denarius, which apparently did exist?[36] Would that amount have been 'right' (dikaios, v. 5)? Could they live on such deficient justice? Surely this is the challenge of the parable.

The narrative householder equalises the means of living from the land. He is 'good' (agathos, v. 15), as he claims, not because he is a shrewd business man blest of God, but because he has

---

[36] The coin was called a pondion, so T. W. Manson, The Sayings of Jesus (London: SCM Press, 1949): 220.

learned from his trip to the marketplace at the end of the day
that gross inequality of life exists between worker and worker,
and between the workers and himself. Every Israelite has a right
to life from the land. Herein lies the weakness of Herzog's
argument. He argues for the rights of the fully employed, but
fails to address the destitution of the non-workers in the land of
promise. The parable addresses *that* problem above all. How can
a destitute Israelite honour his religious heritage in the Holy
Land given to sustain life? How can he observe the law of Sabbath
if he has neither work nor livelihood to celebrate on the seventh
day of the week? These are the kinds of teasing questions the
parable of the Jewish Jesus poses.

The meaning of the Jewish Sabbath, while not explicit in the
texture of the parable of the workers and non-workers, hovers
in the background.[37] Since the Maccabean opposition to the
foreign invasion of Jewish life and thought and identity in the
second century BCE, Sabbath keeping became one of the
hallmarks of Jewish self-definition.[38] Jesus is reported in the
Synoptic Gospels as having had some controversy with the Jewish
leaders about the particulars of Sabbath observance.[39] Whatever
one makes of the accuracy of the reported Sabbath controversies
in the Synoptics, the issue of proper Sabbath keeping in
Palestinian Jewish life was clearly alive during Jesus' ministry.
Nor should the conflict between Jesus and the Pharisees over
Sabbath observance be taken to mean that Jesus abandoned the

[37] Parables allude to Scripture and tradition in their own elusive way, as
Seán Freyne has pointed out: 'the artistry with which scriptural allusions or
images and realistic situations have been interwoven into stories which
challenge, provoke and call for a deeper appropriation of the biblical
understanding of God and his ways' calls for more attention, *Galilee, Jesus
and the Gospels*: 256. In this case, the parable of the labourers in the vineyard
alludes to the cycle of 'work-rest-work' of the fourth commandment of the
Decalogue, now broken in the situation of labourers without work at the end
of the day.

[38] J. D. G. Dunn, *The Partings of the Ways: Between Christianity and Judaism and
Their Significance for the Character of Christianity* (London: SCM Press, 1991):
29. 'The *Sabbath* was also maintained and recognized as a distinctively Jewish
institution . . . and rooted in creation itself (Gen. 2:2–3; Ex. 20:8–11).'

[39] Although E. P. Sanders discounts the point as unrealistic in the Palestinian
Jewish setting in which Jesus moved. According to Sanders, 'further consideration of the evidence . . . will lead to the conclusion that there was no
substantial conflict between Jesus and the Pharisees with regard to Sabbath,'
In *Jesus and Judaism* (Philadelphia: Fortress Press, 1985): 265.

notion of rest from work on the seventh day. On the contrary, as Zeitlin has noted, 'neither Jesus, nor his disciples and followers, took the sabbath laws lightly . . . In none of the sabbath controversies is Jesus revealed as denying the validity of the sabbath observance.'[40] What does the Sabbath law, so prominent in the code of the Decalogue (Exod. 20:8–11; Deut. 5:12–15), mean apart from work? How can one observe the Sabbath rest of God apart from the product of work that sustains life? From what does a destitute non-worker rest if not from the labour of his hands?

Sabbath keeping in the command of Exodus 20 is motivated by the celebration of the Creator God who gave the earth to humans who reflect the divine image, who sustain their lives from the gift of the land. As the Creator rested from work on the seventh day, so also should those who bear God's image. 'The seventh day is a day to celebrate completion, achievement, as God does after his six days of creating, about which Genesis 1:31 says, "and behold, it was very good."'[41] The Sabbath command of Deuteronomy 5 is motivated by the deliverance from the slavery of hard taskmasters in Egypt. In both commands to keep the Sabbath, the assumption is that the meaning of Sabbath is found in working gainfully from the gift of the land that the Lord God gave to Israel. On the seventh day, work stops so that God can be honoured. When some have no work to do during the six days, and therefore are without sustenance from the land, God is dishonoured on the sacred seventh day of rest, and the human family is divided.

The Sabbath equalises the participants in Israelite society. Citing H. W. Wolff, Janzen underscores this point. The man-servant and maidservant become one with the master on the seventh day of rest.

> In their activities human beings are separated as masters and servants, strong and weak, gifted and less gifted; but in resting they become equal. Thus the sabbath not only grants a day of rest to all on a regular basis . . . but establishes human

[40] Irving M. Zeitlin, *Jesus and the Judaism of His Time* (Oxford: Polity Press, 1988): 77.
[41] Waldemar Janzen, 'The Theology of Work from an Old Testament Perspective,' *Conrad Grebel Review: A Journal of Christian Inquiry,* Spring (1992): 124.

equality at least once a week. In this way it anticipates the kingdom of God.[42]

The equalising effect of the Sabbath is reflected also in the parable of the *one denarius for all*, as it may be called. The privileged all-day workers and the unfortunate one-hour workers end up with the same means of sustaining their equally human lives. On two counts, therefore, the parable carries an implicit critique of Sabbath observance in Jewish Palestine. First, some cannot truly observe Sabbath as they ought because they have little or no product of work to celebrate come Friday at sundown. Second, the intent of the Sabbath command to equalise the human family is violated by gross inequality of human life in the stratified social situation in agrarian Palestine.[43]

Jewish religious leaders within earshot of Jesus' parable, with a sense of the equalising intent of the Sabbath law they enforce, could hardly miss the cutting edge in Phase II of the parable. Who is truly able to keep God's Sabbath? To celebrate creation and deliverance? Only the fortunate all-day workers and the elite householders with the staff of life from the land could rest from their work on the Sabbath. The unemployed and under-nourished of God's human household could scarcely enter God's rest one day in seven, and be at one with their fellows. The parable implicitly puts a provocative question to the Sabbath regulators: What are you doing to provide work-and-life for the community you call to rest on the Sabbath of the Lord your God?

By the same token, the householders in the audience in the stratified agrarian society of Jewish Palestine are likewise provoked ironically to question the *status quo*.[44] By an accepted standard, a well-to-do householder is 'good' because he is well-to-do, blest of God. The householder in Phase II of the parable

---

[42] Ibid.: 131.
[43] On the inequity between the classes of people in agrarian societies see Lenski, *Power and Privilege*: 295–96.
[44] 'Examples persuade but parables provoke,' J. D. Crossan, 'Parable, Allegory, and Paradox:' 260.
[45] Ibid. Crossan's analysis of the parable of the Good Samaritan as paradoxical reversal also fits this one. The parable 'presents the audience with a paradox involving a double reversal of expectations.' The day labourers, who are expected to empathise kindly with their fellow labourers, do the opposite. The powerful vineyard owner, who is expected to use his position to take advantage of a large, unemployed work force, does the opposite.

is 'good' because he inverts the *status quo*, reverses the expected order of things, reduces his profits, distributes the means of livelihood, equalises life in the Jewish marketplace.[45] Householders in the audience are just as scandalised by the strange twist in the story. They are just as likely to protest as the all-day labourers in the story. Imagine a scene where the parable is first told. In one section of the audience sit fortunate workers, glad to be able to maintain their lives from their labour. In another section a smaller group of self-sufficient householders, happy with their sumptuous lot in Palestinian life. And in another, a larger group of unfortunate, marginalised, destitute expendables.[46] The only group laughing at the end of the story, however, are these last who have no other reason to laugh. 'Blessed are you destitute (*hoi ptōchoi*), because the kingdom of God belongs to you' (Luke 6:20).

---

[46] Expendables end up 'at the bottom of the class system in every agrarian society,' and are those 'for whom the other members of society had little or no need,' Lenski, *Power and Privilege*: 28.

7

Entrusted Money
(Matthew 25:14–28)

The Parable of the Talents/Pounds

JOEL R. WOHLGEMUT

The Text in Translation

For it is as if a man, going on a journey, summoned his slaves
and entrusted his property to them; to one he gave five
talents, to another two, to another one, to each according to
his ability. Then he went away. The one who had received
the five talents went off at once and traded with them, and
made five more talents. In the same way, the one who had
the two talents made two more talents. But the one who had
received the one talent went off and dug a hole in the ground
and hid his master's money. After a long time the master of
those slaves came and settled accounts with them. Then the
one who had received the five talents came forward, bringing
five more talents, saying, 'Master, you handed over to me five
talents; see, I have made five more talents.' His master said
to him, 'Well done, good and trustworthy slave; you have been
trustworthy in a few things, I will put you in charge of many
things; enter into the joy of your master.' And the one with
the two talents also came forward, saying, 'Master, you
handed over to me two talents; see, I have made two more
talents.' His master said to him, 'Well done, good and
trustworthy slave; you have been trustworthy in a few things,
I will put you in charge of many things; enter into the joy of
your master.' Then the one who had received the one talent
also came forward, saying, 'Master, I knew that you were an
harsh man, reaping where you did not scatter seed; so I was
afraid, and I went and hid your talent in the ground. Here
you have what is yours.' But his master replied, 'You wicked

and lazy slave! You knew, did you, that I reap where I did not sow, and gather where I did not scatter? Then you ought to have invested my money with the bankers, and on my return I would have received what was my own with interest. So take the talent from him, and give it to the one with the ten talents.'[1]

For Matthew, the parable of the talents warns of a coming judgement day and the urgency of being prepared. For Luke, the parable of the pounds informs its readers that patience and diligence are needed during the interim before the coming of God's kingdom. Yet might the parable that potentially underlies these extant versions have a different impact when contextualised in the ministry of the historical Jesus? Until quite recently, interpretations of Jesus' parable of the man who entrusted money to his servants (Matt. 25:14–30; Luke 19:12–27) could be depended upon to fall within certain parameters: somehow the story stresses the third servant's failure to take appropriate action, in which case his censure is well deserved. However, several scholars have recently offered radical re-readings of the text, which glorify the recalcitrant third servant and make a monster of the master. Such studies purport to hear the parable from a peasant point of view, a stance which undermines centuries of Western, elitist accounts. The rise of these new perspectives calls for a 'reckoning scene' of our own, in which novel insights are evaluated alongside more conventional ones. Accordingly, this essay traces traditional speculation about an 'original' parable which may be attributed to the historical Jesus,[2] critiques recent efforts to cast the third servant in a different light, and produces an interpretation which ultimately reaffirms older formulations, but nuances them with respect to newer observations about the parable's social world.

When sifting through the available textual evidence, the first problem is the existence of two very similar, yet significantly different, stories. The basic congruency is apparent: a master

---

[1] Luke's parallel parable (Luke 19:12–24) has the monetary unit *mina* ('pound') instead of *talanton*, as in Matthew. Both Evangelists apply a moralistic conclusion to the parable proper (Luke 19:25–27 and Matt. 25:29–30).

[2] Admittedly, such an attribution is tentative, and the issues surrounding it are complex. Here I rely on a general scholarly consensus with respect to the authenticity of the basic parable material in the Gospels.

entrusts money to servants before going on a journey, returns to demand a reckoning, rewards two profit-generating servants, and rebukes a third who hid the trust and thus produced no increase. Simply on the grounds of this outline, it would be plausible to suggest that the parable came down to Matthew and Luke through a common source. However, the variety of detail is sufficient to cast this hypothesis into question. Matthew has three initial servants who are given talents in graded amounts (5, 2, and 1); Luke has ten servants given one *mina* each. Matthew's profitable servants are told they will be put over 'many things;' Luke's are given command of cities. Such discrepancies prompt several scholars to suggest that the story came to the Evangelists via independent Matthean and Lukan traditions.[3] If this is the case, the parable's presence in multiple strands of tradition is an initial indication of a relatively early origin.

Still, there must be an attempt to determine what form of the text is likely 'original.' B. B. Scott is right to observe that the lack of verbal identity between the Matthean and Lukan accounts 'makes impossible a detailed reconstruction of *ipsissima verba Jesu* (the very words of Jesus),' given the highly hypothetical character of such an enterprise.[4] Despite this, Scott maintains that 'an originating structure or pattern that gave birth to the extant versions' is recoverable,[5] and it is to this task that we now turn.

When comparing the Matthean and Lukan versions, the most blatant discrepancy concerns the Lukan description of a well-born man who goes to receive a kingdom, has his leadership contested by his subjects, and proceeds to slaughter his opponents (see Luke 19:12, 14, 27). Given that these details form a discrete story,[6] Lukan conflation (rather than Matthean excision) seems likely. Thus, whether we attribute these additions

---

[3] For example, Jan Lambrecht, *Once More Astonished: The Parables of Jesus* (New York: Crossroad, 1981): 167; C. H. Dodd, *The Parables of the Kingdom*, rev. ed. (New York: Scribner's, 1961): 114; John Dominic Crossan, *In Parables: The Challenge of the Historical Jesus* (New York: Harper & Row, 1973): 100–101.

[4] Bernard Brandon Scott, *Hear Then the Parable: A Commentary on the Parables of Jesus* (Minneapolis: Fortress Press, 1989): 218.

[5] Ibid.: 225.

[6] See Joachim Jeremias, *The Parables of Jesus*, 8th ed., trans. S. H. Hooke (London: SCM Press, 1972): 59, on the possible historical referents for these details. On the other hand, Scott, *Hear*, 223, argues that the theme of a throne claimant is common enough to render historical connections unnecessary.

to Luke himself or to his source, we are justified in preferring Matthew's simpler story-line as the more original.[7] Nevertheless, specific components within that Matthean account must be evaluated independently.

This brings us to the question of where the parable proper ends and where Matthew's application takes over. Beginning at the end, it is a much-repeated observation that the references in Matthew 25:30 to the 'outer darkness' and 'weeping and gnashing of teeth,' which also appear in 8:12 and 22:13, are unique to this Gospel.[8] Consequently, this combination of phrases is likely redactional, and may be excluded from present consideration.

Retreating one step further, we land on Matthew 25:29/Luke 19:26: 'For to the one who has, much will be given, and he will have an abundance, but from the one who does not have, even what he has will be taken.' Once again, this statement recurs elsewhere in the Gospels, this time in Mark 4:25/Matthew 13:12/Luke 8:18. As a result, it has been characterised as a 'free-floating logion,' which, given its presence in both Matthew and Luke, was already attached to the parable at some stage of oral transmission.[9] Of course, by pushing the provenance of the expanded parable back into an earlier oral phase, one must entertain the possibility that Mark abstracted the saying from its parabolic context in the tradition.[10] In response, an appeal is generally made to the fact that the concluding logion does not appear to fit snugly with the story: ostensibly, the third servant's allotment is not taken from him because it is 'only a little,' but because he acted inappropriately with it.[11] Thus, this statement appears not to summarise the story, but rather to deal with discomfort over the fact that, in the end, the richest servant gets even richer.[12] The invocation of such a proverb may have been an attempt to mitigate the sense of injustice. In the light of such

[7] So also Jeremias, *Parables*: 60; Scott, *Hear.* 223; Brad H. Young, *Jesus and His Jewish Parables: Rediscovering the Roots of Jesus' Teaching* (New York: Paulist, 1989): 168.

[8] For example, see Dan O. Via, *The Parables: Their Literary and Existential Dimension* (Philadelphia: Fortress Press, 1967): 114.

[9] See Scott, *Hear.* 224, and his note on a history of similar interpretation.

[10] Lambrecht, *Once More*: 181–182, outlines this argument before refuting it.

[11] Ibid.: 182.

[12] The crowd's protestation in Luke 19:25 ('Lord, he has ten minas!') is an intriguing window onto audience response.

argument, we may also exclude Matthew 25:29/Luke 19:26 from our originating structure, limiting our basic textual examination to Matthew 25:14–28 (roughly Luke 19:12–24).

Having addressed questions of delimiting the parable, several particular queries remain. First of all, how many servants were there—three (Matthew) or ten (Luke)? Joachim Jeremias notes that the reference to the third servant as 'the other' *(ho heteros)* in Luke 19:20 betrays that there were originally three servants.[13] Why the number might have been altered in Luke's version is unclear. Scott suggests that it may be related to the story of the throne-claimant:[14] an expanded coterie of servants is in line with the nobility and kingly aspirations of the master.

A second sticking point concerns the monetary unit involved. Were the servants given talents (Matthew) or minas (Luke)? Many scholars follow Jeremias' position on this issue, which claims that the lesser valued mina (i.e. 100 *dēnarii*) must be original, since the awarding of talents (i.e. 6000 *dēnarii*) would be grossly inconsistent with the master's commendation for faithfulness over 'a few things' (Matt. 25:21, 23; cf. Luke 19:17, 'a very small thing').[15] In the light of Luke's regal expansions (especially the provision of 'cities,' Luke 19:17, 19), the fact that the seemingly insignificant mina is used is an indicator that Luke has not altered it. However, if we posit the mina as the original unit, there is no compelling explanation for Matthew's upward adaptation of the amount. As Scott notes, we are in the awkward position of observing that 'the minas would fit better in Matthew's story and the talents in Luke's story!'[16] Thus, there is no sure basis for deciding on an 'original' amount. John Dominic Crossan may very well be right that the minas are much more 'realistic,'[17] but hyperbole with respect to the amounts and understatement with respect to the master's commendation ('a few things') are certainly within the realm of possibility. In staying, by and large, with the Matthean account, I will use talents as the parable's monetary unit, acknowledging that not much weight can be put on the reading at this point.

[13] Jeremias, *Parables*: 61.
[14] Scott, *Hear*: 222.
[15] Jeremias, *Parables*: 28; see also Via, *Parables*: 114; Lambrecht, *Once More*: 176; Crossan, *In Parables*: 101.
[16] Scott, *Hear*: 225.
[17] Crossan, *In Parables*: 101.

Related to this question of the monetary unit is the issue of the gradation of the amounts: in Matthew, the servants are given sums of five, two and one talent respectively, while in Luke each receives one mina. Interestingly, in the Lukan account it is the investment returns (and the concomitant rewards) that are graded, while Matthew's first two servants both double their capital and receive equivalent commendation. Once again, a firm foundation from which to evaluate originality is absent. On the one hand, the Matthean gradation may be an allegorical expansion connected to the various 'abilities' (Matt. 25:15) employed by believers awaiting the parousia. On the other hand, it may simply be the result of a story-teller's desire for variety.[18] I will again rely on Matthew's account, though maintaining with Scott that 'in the long run it makes little difference to the story's development how much each servant received.'[19]

Having given consideration to the disparities in the opening scene, we now focus our attention on the accounts of the reckoning. Here, the master returns from his journey[20] and settles accounts with his servants. The master's praise of the first servants likely lies somewhere between the two canonical versions. Matthew's 'enter into the joy [or "banquet," *charan*] of your master' is probably a later Christological redaction, reflecting the expectation of an eschatological feast.[21] Luke's cities, on the other hand, may be an embellishment connected to the 'kingdom' theme. Thus, we can offer a tentative reconstruction: 'Well done, good servant! You have been faithful over a little; I will set you over much.'

The atmosphere of geniality dissipates quickly as the third servant makes his appearance. The closing of the Matthean and Lukan renditions are remarkably similar, leaving little doubt about the story's end. The only discrepancy left to sort out is the nature of the third servant's activity: does he bury the money (Matthew) or place it in a cloth (Luke)? Jeremias notes that

[18] So Lambrecht, *Once More*. 176, but his preference for this position based on the claim that the first servant in Luke actually has eleven minas, not ten (cf. Luke 19:16, 25), and thus that Luke has adapted the amounts found in Matthew, is insupportable: the calculations need not be read so literally.
[19] Scott, *Hear*. 226.
[20] 'After a long time' in Matthew is probably an addition related to the view that the parable allegorically describes a coming judgement day.
[21] So Jeremias, *Parables*: 60; Scott, *Hear*. 220.

burying money, according to rabbinic law, was considered an adequate precaution against theft, while the guardian was required to make good any loss in the case of cloth-storage.[22] Although this alone does not give us reason to choose one option over the other, later argument will demonstrate that the third servant is not criticised for irresponsibility in selecting a storage method; thus, in order to avoid suggesting inappropriate causal links, the proposed 'originating structure' will present him burying the money.[23] But is such action to be commended or condemned? Having dealt with the textual problems in the two parable accounts, we now consider alternative views of the third servant's activity.

As indicated in the introduction, most previous interpretations of this parable agree in one major aspect: the third servant is viewed negatively, his rebuke by the master justified. C. H. Dodd concludes that he is 'an unprofitable servant, a barren rascal.'[24] Jeremias alludes to his 'unconvincing excuse.'[25] Dan O. Via discusses the servant's 'breach of trust,' and his 'existential flaw.'[26] However, two recent contributions to parable scholarship have challenged this fundamental consensus, arguing on the contrary that the third servant is the true hero of the tale. At this point, I will summarise the positions of Richard L. Rohrbaugh and William R. Herzog II, before offering an evaluation of their perspectives.[27]

Rohrbaugh acknowledges the situation described above, noting that the third servant 'is universally condemned by Western interpreters as a failure.'[28] It is precisely this viewpoint which Rohrbaugh rejects, arguing instead that 'Jesus' peasant hearers would almost certainly have assumed [the parable] was a warning to the rich about their exploitation of

---

[22] Jeremias, *Parables*: 61 n 51.

[23] Still, before too readily attributing irresponsibility to Luke's servant, we should consider Scott's comment (*Hear.* 225) that the degree of precaution may understandably be contingent on the value of the trust.

[24] Dodd, *Parables*: 118.

[25] Jeremias, *Parables*: 61.

[26] Via, *Parables*: 119.

[27] The similar counter-reading in Megan McKenna's more popular work *Parables: The Arrows of God* (Maryknoll, NY: Orbis, 1994) is further evidence of the proliferation of this perspective.

[28] Richard L. Rohrbaugh, 'A Peasant Reading of the Parable of the Talents/ Pounds: A Text of Terror?' *Biblical Theology Bulletin,* 23:1 (Spring 1993): 35.

the weak.'[29] The emphasis on peasant hearers here is important, for it is a peasant reading which Rohrbaugh attempts, based on the insights of cultural anthropology. At heart, Rohrbaugh wishes to demonstrate that the master's desire to increase his wealth, and the compliance of the first two servants in this endeavour, would have been abhorrent in the peasant milieu of first-century Palestine.

Central to his reasoning is the concept of 'limited good,' which implies that a 'larger share for one automatically means a smaller share for someone else . . . There simply is not enough of anything to go around or any way to increase the size of the pie.'[30] Thus, the significant increases reported in the parable (whether 100 percent in Matthew or up to 1000 percent in Luke) would have been translated by peasant audiences into corresponding losses for their hypothetical compatriots. More generally, Rohrbaugh claims that a distaste for money as a means of exchange (i.e. gaining money as an end in itself, rather than using it to satisfy needs) characterised agrarian workers in Mediterranean cultures. To support this view, he cites from several ancient works which unequivocally describe the rich as evil.[31] Accordingly, he maintains that

> this master can be seen as honourable and such a story seen as good news only if the story is told from the vantage point and value system of the rich—i.e. those who have and use power to extract the shares of others for themselves.[32]

Conversely, from his peasant standpoint, Rohrbaugh sees the third servant's attempt merely to preserve the master's share as an honourable activity: rather than participating in exploitive activity, he defies his master's greed.

One of the major props to Rohrbaugh's argument is a re-interpretation of the version of the parable cited by Eusebius, thought to be from the so-called Gospel of the Nazoreans.[33] In

[29] Ibid.: 38.
[30] Ibid.: 33; see also Bruce J. Malina, *The New Testament World: Insights from Cultural Anthropology*, rev. ed. (Louisville:Westminster/John Knox, 1993): 90–116.
[31] Rohrbaugh, 'Peasant,' 34–35.
[32] Ibid.: 35.
[33] Eusebius, *De Theophania* IV. 22; see Wilhelm Schneemelcher, ed., *New Testament Apocrypha*, vol. 1, *Gospels and Related Writings*, rev. ed. (Louisville: Westminster/John Knox Press, 1991): 162–63.

that variant, one servant squanders the money on prostitutes and flute-girls, one increases the amount, and one hides the talent in the ground. According to Eusebius, three different outcomes result: one is accepted, one is rebuked, and the third is cast into prison. Generally, scholars view this account as a later distortion of Matthew. Jeremias terms it 'a moralistic perversion which the parable has undergone in the Jewish-Christian church.'[34] However, in the literary structure of this version Rohrbaugh finds support for his position. He maintains that the parable is organised chiastically:

   A. squandering servant
      B. multiplying servant
         C. hiding servant
         C'. acceptance
      B'. rebuke
   A'. imprisonment[35]

Consequently, Rohrbaugh insists: (a) that Eusebius could not fathom how the first Matthean servant could possibly have been approved, and thus attempted to show how the most severe punishment was intended for him; (b) that the servant who increased the money was, in fact, rebuked; and (c) that the servant who hid the talent was commended. Rohrbaugh goes on to criticise scholars such as Jeremias and Scott for 'rearranging' the sequence of the servants to suit their own interpretations.[36] To the contrary, he insists, it is the chiastic structure of the story which demonstrates that 'the approval of the behaviour of the third servant . . . is the centrepiece of this Nazorean version of the story.'[37] Rohrbaugh is tentative about his claim that the Nazorean account may be the more original, but definitely regards it as evidence for the honourable nature of the third servant's activity in the eyes of some.[38]

    Building on Rohrbaugh's revolutionary view of the parable, Herzog makes some similar observations, but expands the

---

[34] Jeremias, *Parables*: 58; see also Dodd, *Parables*: 120.
[35] Rohrbaugh, 'Peasant:' 36.
[36] Ibid.: 37.
[37] Ibid.
[38] Ibid.: 37, 38.

perspective in significant respects. He notes that scholars have had a difficult time reconciling the image of a greedy, absentee landlord with the divine figure required by their interpretations, and uses this stumbling block as a springboard to his own re-reading of the story.[39] He outlines the social structure of ancient elite households, in which retainers (themselves relatively advanced in the social hierarchy) would carry out the exploitive activities of wealthy patrons and 'feather their own nests' in the process. Extending Rohrbaugh's insight, Herzog characterises the third servant as a 'whistle-blower:' he 'cuts through the mystifying rhetoric that has dominated the exchange between the elite and his first two retainers, and he identifies the aristocrat for what he is, strict, cruel, harsh, and merciless.'[40] In order to safeguard his power and control, the master cannot allow such an exposure to remain unchallenged; rather, 'the servant must be vilified, shamed, and humiliated so that his words will carry no weight.'[41] Thus the fate of the 'whistle-blower' is the focus of the parable. Herzog suggests that even when he has abandoned his manipulative career, his status among the populace would remain ambiguous: would the people acknowledge and respect his honesty, or would former hostilities vitiate such relationships? As a result, peasant listeners would be forced to consider whose interests would be served if they, mimicking the master, rejected the third servant.

These two radical re-readings of the parable deserve serious consideration. Given the recent impetus in biblical scholarship toward an increased awareness of the social, political and economic implications of our work, interpretations that champion the plight of the poor have immediate appeal. Still, the strength of the arguments goes beyond the present condition of the Western social conscience. Rohrbaugh and Herzog strike a chord by noting that a first-century Mediterranean peasant audience would likely be much more aware of the costs involved in a capitalistic investment scheme than twentieth-century first-world readers. The cross-disciplinary homework has been done: anthropological and sociological examinations of

[39] William R. Herzog II, *Parables as Subversive Speech: Jesus as Pedagogue of the Oppressed* (Louisville: Westminster/John Knox, 1994): 154–55.
[40] Ibid.: 164.
[41] Ibid.: 165.

the stratification of agrarian societies demonstrate the concentration of wealth in a tiny segment of the population.[42] Consequently, it is initially plausible that a story which describes the aggravation of an already inequitable financial distribution would have sent negative shock-waves through an underclass audience.

Nevertheless, before we concur that the more traditional interpretations 'are rendered instantly obsolete,'[43] we must carefully consider whether these explanations offer the best account of the available evidence. My own analysis suggests that these presentations require questioning at a number of places. First of all, Rohrbaugh's use of the material from the Gospel of the Nazoreans must be challenged: quite frankly, he has misread Eusebius. Chiasmus is a powerful interpretive weapon within the academy of biblical studies, but in this case a much more cogent explanation exists for the structure of the parable. We must remember that Eusebius is trying to reconcile two differing versions of the story. Recall Rohrbaugh's proposed literary structure for the text:

    A. squandering servant

        B. multiplying servant

            C. hiding servant

            C'. acceptance

        B'. rebuke

    A'. imprisonment

The key lies in Eusebius' words, which follow his summary of the parable:

> I wonder whether in Matthew the threat which is uttered after the word against the man who did nothing may not refer to him, but by epanalepsis to the first who had feasted and drunk with the drunken.[44]

Rohrbaugh takes this to mean that Eusebius is trying to figure out 'how the rebuke of the third servant in Matthew could really

---

[42] See Herzog, *Subversive*: 56–66; also Douglas E. Oakman, *Jesus and the Economic Questions of His Day* (Lewiston, NY: Edwin Mellen, 1986), 37–80, on economic distribution in first-century Palestine.

[43] Walter Wink, on the back cover of Herzog, *Subversive*.

[44] Eusebius, *Theophania* IV. 22, in Schneemelcher, *New Testament Apocrypha*: 163.

have been meant of the first.'[45] However, Rohrbaugh has hereby
lumped together under the rubric 'rebuke' two things which
Eusebius clearly separates: the 'threat' and the 'word against the
man who did nothing.'[46] The 'threat' here likely refers to the
casting into the 'outer darkness' of Matthew 25:30, which is
strongly reminiscent of the imprisonment described in the
Nazorean text. Thus Eusebius' comment in no way suggests that
he found the 'rebuke' (i.e. the 'word against') the servant who
hid the talent inappropriate.

Following this direction, a more adequate reading of the
parable's structure becomes apparent. The order of the servants
(squanderer, multiplier, hider) is likely taken from the Nazorean
account, and laid as a template over Matthew's version: thus the
first servant becomes the wastrel. At this point, Eusebius must
account for the three Nazorean consequences (acceptance,
rebuke, imprisonment). When he attempts to make a match with
Matthew, he ignores the acceptance of the first servant (since he
has found a closer match at the end), continues with the commendation of the second and the rebuke of the third, and hints that
the final condemnation applies to the first. This order he has
already anticipated in his outline of the parable. This, I maintain,
is a much more probable interpretation of Eusebius, which
supports previous scholarly readings of the evidence and under-
cuts all of the implications which Rohrbaugh attributes to the text.

Despite this serious flaw in Rohrbaugh's argument,[47] it is
apparent that the challenge does not hinge on this point. We
must still come to terms with the general picture presented by
an analysis of the first-century social world. Against this point, I
raise two considerations. Although arguments calling for an 'ideal
structure' can never be decisive, I raise the question: if the third
servant is intended to be the hero, why would the parable not
conclude with his declaration, rather than with the master's
retort?[48] As the parable stands, it is only with great difficulty that

---

[45] Rohrbaugh, 'Peasant:' 36.

[46] For Greek text, see J.- P. Migne, ed., *Patrologiae Graecae*, vol. 24, *Eusebii Pamphili*
(Petit Montrouge, 1857): 688.

[47] Which Herzog, *Subversive*: 152, uncritically accepts.

[48] See Eta Linnemann, *Parables of Jesus: Introduction and Exposition*, trans. from
3rd German ed. by J. Sturdy (London: SPCK, 1966): 15, who raises Bultmann's
'law of End-stress, i.e. the most important thing is described last' (from *History
of the Synoptic Tradition*: 182–88).

we side with the servant in the face of the master's criticism. Rohrbaugh acknowledges this difficulty, but attributes it to an 'elitist point of view,' suggesting that we are 'expected to figure out Jesus' condemnation of the master's attitude.'[49] Unfortunately, no longer being able to adduce Eusebius as proof of such 'figuring out,' Rohrbaugh is left with a problematic lack of evidence. Herzog may be on better ground, arguing that the master's words seal the fate of the 'whistle-blower,' but they are still anti-climactic in the light of the servant's bold statement.

In addition to these minor queries, a more serious difficulty is the explanation for the third servant's 'fear' which apparently motivates him to hide the money he is given (Matt. 25:25; Luke 19:21). If he indeed caches the money out of 'fear,' this would suggest that his action is something other than a heroic defiance of an oppressive system. Conspicuously, Herzog completely avoids any discussion of this component of the parable. Rohrbaugh, on the other hand, recognises the problem, but his treatment is unpersuasive. He attributes this 'fear' to the hardness of the master, claiming that '[n]o doubt the servant was afraid—especially since he had tried to act in an honourable fashion even though, knowing the greedy master as he did, he had reason to fear reprisal.'[50] In other words, Rohrbaugh attempts to deal with the 'fear' in two ways. First, he projects it into the present tense of the reckoning scene: the servant's present fear before the master is due to the risky character of his past action. Second, Rohrbaugh portrays the third servant as having buried the money in spite of his fear. Thus, I now ask: are these observations borne out by the text? Given my previous reluctance to posit specific vocabulary items which go back to the originating parable, a lexical argument at this point may be suspicious. Nonetheless, the presence of certain grammatical features in both Matthew and Luke demands investigation.

Both canonical versions of the parable describe the third servant's fear as a past action: Luke uses the imperfect 'I was afraid' (*ephoboumēn*), while Matthew employs the aorist participle, 'having been afraid' (*phobētheis*). Thus, while it seems probable that the servant in the reckoning scene is fearful, the fear of

---

[49] Rohrbaugh, 'Peasant:' 38.
[50] Ibid.: 36.

which he speaks describes a past condition. The more serious alternative proposed by Rohrbaugh is that the third servant acted as he did despite his fear. Unfortunately, Luke's account strains against such a reading. There, the servant's statement of fear is linked to his concealment of the money by an explanatory 'for' (*gar*, Luke 19:20–21); i.e. he hid the money in the cloth, for he was afraid of the master. Such a construction hardly suggests resolute defiance. Matthew's variation (25:25) is no more conducive in this respect. Literally, it reads, 'And having been afraid, having gone out, I hid your talent in the ground.' It is possible that the first participle might be read concessively, i.e. 'even though having been afraid . . .' but such instances are rare, and generally demand stronger contextual evidence.[51] Thus, the more likely reading indicates that the servant's fear motivated his subsequent concealment of the money.[52] The fact that both the Matthean and Lukan accounts lean in this direction offers little foundation for arguments that suggest that the servant realised his peril, but nevertheless acted nobly.

Having summarised the views of Rohrbaugh and Herzog, and having raised some basic objections to their positions, the question remains: is there something here which can augment, enrich, or correct more traditional formulations? Can we accept and use their portrait of oppressive elites using the retainer class to exploit the peasants? I indeed suggest that we can use their description, without necessarily capitulating to their conclusions. Rohrbaugh posits that audience sympathies would have aligned strongly with the third servant; Herzog proposes that they should have. In the previous scholarly literature, Scott comes closest to their position. Like Rohrbaugh, he concludes that hearers identify with the final servant, but insists that the parable's power lies in the inappropriateness of such sympathy: adopting the servant's depiction of the master is inconsistent with the master's magnanimous treatment of the first two servants.[53] Milder forms of sympathy can be found in writers such as Dodd, who maintains

---

[51] See BDF §§417–18. The one example given in §418(1) for the concessive use of the conjunctive participle is hardly parallel to our text: in Matt. 7:11/ Luke 11:13 the 'how much more' construction offers strong contextual evidence for that particular reading.

[52] See Jacques Dupont, 'La Parabole des Talents ou des Mines,' *Revue de Théologie et de Philosophie*, 19 (1969): 388.

[53] Scott, *Hear.* 232, 234.

that the third servant is convinced of his own prudence and honesty until the end.[54] Even such a view, I argue, is still too generous toward the third servant.

To the contrary, Herzog's identification of the servants with the 'retainer class' lends credence to a sustained audience opposition to the third servant. Herzog classifies the retainer-servants as 'powerful figures' which comprised from about 5 to about 7 percent of agrarian populations.[55] Such figures would not have been exempt from peasant hostility. In fact, 'one of their roles was to shield elites from popular violence and resentment directed against the exploitive and oppressive policies of the elites.'[56] It is on the basis of this social configuration, that Herzog articulates the liminal position of the 'whistle-blower': turned out by the master, suspect in the eyes of the masses. Herzog hints that such suspicion is unjustified in light of the retainer's action. However, if one holds that the servant is indeed culpable, then the social realities of peasant-retainer relationships would serve to reinforce an audience's antipathy toward him.

This leads us to an attempt to explain the narrative dynamics of the parable. The master gives an amount of money to his servants, and leaves on a journey (Matt. 25:14–15). Thus, the parable creates a 'crisis-moment' immediately: each servant must decide what he will now do. Matthew and Luke wish to prolong the length of the master's journey, since his return represents the anticipated parousia. In reality, however, the time between the master's departure and arrival is incidental. The important action occurs instantaneously: the first two servants go 'at once' (Matt. 25:15–16; Gk. *eutheōs*, 'immediately') and trade, while the third digs in the ground and hides the money. Luke makes it clear that the servants are to trade with the capital (Luke 19:13), but the language in Matthew is initially ambiguous. The master 'hands over' (*paradidōmi*) his wealth, but specific terminology which refers to 'entrusting' money (i.e. for safeguarding) is not used here.[57] However, the following verses quickly dispel much

---

[54] Dodd, *Parables*: 117.

[55] Herzog, *Subversive*: 61, 157; so also J. Duncan, M. Derrett, 'Law in the New Testament: The Parable of the Talents and Two Logia,' *Zeitschrift für die neutestamentliche Wissenschaft* 56 (1965): 185.

[56] Herzog, *Subversive*: 61.

[57] See Josephus: *katatithēmi* in *Ag. Ap.* ii. 208; *parakatathēkē, hoi pepisteumenoi* in *Ant.* iv. 285–88.

of the ambiguity. By comparison to the profitability of the first two servants, the third servant is shown to have misread the master's intentions, and questions about the outcome arise.[58] Herzog claims that peasant anger would immediately be directed toward the 'successful' retainers, since listeners would 'fill in the details' about how their increases were obtained.[59] However, given popular opposition to the retainer class, audiences may very well have relished the prospect of the third servant 'taking a fall.'

When the master returns and settles accounts, the servants are divided into two mutually exclusive categories: those who actively traded with the money (designated *agathos*, 'good', Matt. 25:21, 23), and those who did not (designated *poneros*, 'evil', Matt. 25:26). Here we see that the amount earned is not important—the master implies that even banking the money and collecting the interest would have been acceptable (Matt. 25:27). Also, the scenario does not include a servant who traded with the money and lost it. Appropriate action is implicitly connected with gain and reward. Since, in the world of the parable, the servants' achievements inevitably result from their decision, it is that initial decision which is held up as commendable.

The parable builds to a climax at the end, and the emphasis falls on the fate of the third servant. He admits to hiding his capital out of fear of his master, whom he describes as being 'a hard man' (Matt. 25:24). Apparently, the servant believed that losing the money through trading would infuriate his master, and perhaps incur a harsh penalty, and accordingly he refused to risk such a venture.[60] In anger, the master responds to the third servant's portrait of him by claiming that such a perception should have driven the servant to secure at least a minimal increase (leaving the money with bankers); consequently, the third servant's money is taken from him and given to the first.

The third servant's position is reinforced through the irony of the agricultural images present in the parable. The master is

---

[58] Crossan, *In Parables*: 101; also Bernard Brandon Scott, *Jesus, Symbol-Maker for the Kingdom* (Philadelphia: Fortress Press, 1981): 43; 'the audience is now forewarned that by comparison the fate of the third servant does not bode well.'

[59] Herzog, *Subversive*: 162.

[60] So Dodd, *Parables*: 117.

accused of 'reaping' where he has not 'sown,' and 'gathering in' where he has not 'scattered seed' (Matt. 25:24; Luke 19:22 contains only the first image). However, that which the servant has 'planted' (i.e. 'hidden in the ground') has produced no yield; in barren fashion, it returns only itself. To be sure, Rohrbaugh and Herzog argue that this is precisely the point. For peasant listeners, increasing one's share would have been an abhorrent action. To this point, I insist that the amazing gains reported on the entrusted sums in the parable are exactly that, amazing. The brevity with which their acquisition is described is not designed to provoke investigation, but rather amazement. Against Herzog, I do not believe that listeners would have been enraged through reflection on the hypothetical sources of such revenue, but rather would have laughed at the third servant for missing out on such an apparently glorious opportunity.

If, as I maintain, the parable of entrusted money as spoken by Jesus was not about vilifying elitist oppression, or about responses to a 'whistle-blower,' to what then does it point? Numerous interpretations identify the money allotted in the parable with the Jewish law, and thus find in the story a polemic against the scribes and/or Pharisees as over-zealous and exclusionary protectors of that law.[61] Without dismissing this perspective, it is also possible to see here a more general call to appropriate responses in light of God's in-breaking kingdom.[62] In scorning the third servant for his misguided action, audiences themselves are implicated for their failure to take steps which would lead them to share in the kingdom's 'wealth.' What those 'steps' are, the parable does not specify. It does not seek to be overly didactic, but rather to generate a situation in which the plight of a despised 'other' becomes one's own. In this way, we need not ignore or refute observations about the social inequities of the first-century Mediterranean world. Instead, such insights suggest that lower-class listeners, drawn in by the opportunity to scorn a representative of their oppression, would be left wondering whether such sport was all that Jesus intended.

The parable of the talents/pounds has not always fared well by comparison with Jesus' other sayings. Robert Funk claims that

---

[61] For example, Jeremias, *Parables*: 61–62; Dodd, *Parables*: 119; Scott, *Hear*. 234; Lambrecht, *Once More*. 186.

[62] See Crossan, *In Parables*: 119; Lambrecht, *Once More*. 184, 186–87.

it lacks 'provocative power,' and insists that 'the hearer is not caught in a parabolic snare because there is no snare.'[63] Recent interpretations of the story have sought to attribute to it an incisive critique of ancient exploitation. Although I maintain that the third servant is clearly no heroic rebel, considerations of the parable's social world do help to explain how it might have drawn in and challenged Jesus' listeners.

---

[63] Robert W. Funk, *Parables and Presence: Forms of the New Testament Tradition* (Philadelphia: Fortress Press, 1982): 58.

8

Exposing the Depth of Oppression
(Luke 16:1b–8a)

The Parable of the Unjust Steward

PAUL TRUDINGER

The Text in Translation

There was a rich man who had a manager, and charges were brought to him that this man was squandering his property. So he summoned him and said to him, 'What is this that I hear about you? Give me an accounting of your management, because you cannot be my manager any longer.' Then the manager said to himself, 'What will I do, now that my master is taking the position away from me? I am not strong enough to dig, and I am ashamed to beg. I have decided what to do so that, when I am dismissed as manager, people may welcome me into their homes.' So, summoning his master's debtors one by one, he asked the first, 'How much do you owe my master?' He answered, 'A hundred jugs of olive oil.' He said to him, 'Take your bill, sit down quickly, and make it fifty.' Then he asked another, 'And how much do you owe?' 'He replied, 'A hundred containers of wheat.' He said to him, 'Take your bill and make it eighty.' And his master commended the dishonest manager because he had acted shrewdly.

This parable of the unjust steward is recognised as one of the most difficult to interpret of all Jesus' parables. In the present time, we have come to expect a surprising reversal of accepted norms and cultural practices from these remarkable stories. But the shock effect of this tale, in which the manifest meaning implicitly approves outright fraudulent behaviour, goes considerably beyond the shock effect of a hated Samaritan coming to the aid of a waylaid Jew, or the wastrel son getting the barbecue party, almost to the point of embarrassment. Why would Jesus have told such a tale?

The authentic parables are disturbing, teasing tales that arouse the interest of the hearers. In their first telling in Palestine they were bound to evoke discussion on profound issues relating to the human condition and to everyday living, as they continue to do still. By all accounts, this is one of those authentic parables that Jesus told. Its strangeness made it easy to remember for transmission through the tradition into the Gospel of Luke. It is one of three parables[1] with a reasonably extensive narrative form, each one of them having only a single source, but all three being coded red in publications of the somewhat controversial Jesus Seminar.[2] Scholars of the Seminar consider the narrative part of the parable of Luke 16:1–8a to be the authentic words of Jesus. Despite the fact that the three single-source parables do not meet the criterion of multiple attestation, there is something compelling about this parable in Luke 16, as also the parable of the good Samaritan and the labourers in the vineyard, that led the Seminar members to say, 'That's Jesus.' The majority judgement of the Seminar members on the parable of the unjust steward was that it concluded with verse 8a. I am treating this as a correct judgement for the interpretation that follows.

The question of the original story's ending is one of long standing in the plethora of commentaries and studies on Luke. Both Jeremias[3] and Crossan[4] consider verse 8a as interpretative commentary either by Jesus himself, or by transmitters of the story in the primitive Christian communities. Either way, the 'master' (kyrios) in verse 8a refers to Jesus and not to the steward's master. Jeremias believed that it was virtually unbelievable that

---

[1] The other two being the labourers in the vineyard (Matt. 20:1–15) and the good Samaritan (Luke 10:29–36).

[2] The red code represents the authentic words of Jesus as judged by the Jesus Seminar. The Seminar gave the red code to Luke 13:1–8a. Verses 8b–9 are in black, which means that these words are not in 'the primary data base for determining who Jesus was;' Robert W. Funk, B. B. Scott and James R. Butts, *The Parables of Jesus: Red Letter Edition, The Jesus Seminar* (Sonoma: Polebridge Press, 1988): 21.

[3] Joachim Jeremias, *The Parables of Jesus*, 6th ed., trans. S. H. Hooke (New York: Scribner's, 1963): 46.

[4] John Dominic Crossan, *In Parables: The Challenge of the Historical Jesus* (New York: Harper & Row, 1973): 109–110.

the steward's master would, under any circumstances, commend such dishonest behaviour on the part of the steward. But the steward's behaviour may not necessarily be fraudulent despite the evidence on the surface. The apparent fraud is part of the 'teasing' quality we have come to expect of such parables of Jesus. But the master's commendation, likewise on the surface structure, appears in conflict with the fraud. Crossan believes the closing commendation somewhat weakens the enigmatic quality of the story, a quality he regards as a hallmark of a genuine story of Jesus. Crossan therefore treats 8a as commentary and not part of the parable proper.

Crossan's position notwithstanding, the story gives a feeling of incompleteness without verse 8a as part of it. Furthermore, the enigmatic quality tends to be heightened even more by the concluding commendation of apparent fraud. The master's commendation taken as part of the parable proper, hard questions about the parable's possible meanings arise, the kinds of questions the parables of Jesus tend to raise. Moreover, for the purpose of this chapter, I am treating Luke 16:1b–8a as the original parable of Jesus.

The parable (1b–8a) is set within a larger context that concludes with verse 13. The additional verses (8b–13) serve as windows through which we can view the work of early interpreters of Jesus' story. Verses 8b–13 may reflect, in some parts, the original redactional activity of Luke himself, but not necessarily. They may well be interpretations drawn from other early church communities whose conclusions Luke simply reports. With that assumption in place, the insights in 8b–13 may shed some light on the parable's original setting and the possible meaning(s) an audience might have picked up from Jesus' telling.

Whether Jesus always had a specific meaning in mind in telling a story or whether he intended, rather, to engage his listeners in serious discussion about the human condition—to have them go away unravelling the arresting oddities, and grappling with dichotomous situations in these stories about everyday life—are open to questions. Jülicher[5] insisted that a parable was *never* an allegory: that it had one essential point to make, often found in

---

[5] Adolf Jülicher, *Die Gleichnisreden Jesu*, 2 vols (Tübingen: J. C. B. Mohr [Paul Siebeck], 1910).

the punchline, and that no great significance should be drawn from the details of the story. Until recently, these assertions have had a most salutary effect on parable interpretation. In present scholarly discussion, however, the notion of there being only one central point in a parable is no longer considered axiomatic. We cannot even say with certainty that Jesus *never* told an allegorical tale. He almost certainly would have been familiar with the story Nathan told David (2 Sam.12:1–4), and similarly may have made some of his indictments against injustice in such a form. The Hebrew *mashal*, presumed to be the Semitic counterpart to *parabolē*, can refer to several kinds of utterances: riddles, to which the teller knows the answer, conundrums whose solutions are often in the form of word-plays, allegories, proverbial aphorisms, and also stories of the genre of Jesus' parables. Generally, Jülicher's warning against allegorical interpretations of these stories is well founded. The Synoptic writers/editors did choose the Greek term, *parabolē*, to describe these tales, not *allēgora*.[6] A *parabolē* is a trajectory of co-ordinate points, like the flight-path of a ball tossed in the air. A basketball player or an Australian Rules footballer may size up its trajectory and catch it ten feet in the air. Others may catch it at waist level, or on the first bounce. Others may wait until it comes to a stop on the ground before they 'get it.' The point is, stories like these may be understood at various levels of insight, or more accurately, from various perspectives. Dan Otto Via[7] sees parables as 'art objects' with an inner dynamic, or explosive power, which may fire off in different situations in which the stories are heard.

Expanding briefly on two issues raised above about this parable of the dishonest steward, first, the parable is *not* an allegory. Whatever its meanings are, they must be found within the narrative structure of the story itself (1b–8a). That is to say, we should read the parable *synchronically,* not allegorically or diachronically.[8] Interesting as these kinds of inter-

---

[6] Cf. Paul in Gal. 4:21–31.

[7] Dan Otto Via, *The Parables: Their Literary and Existential Dimension* (Philadelphia: Fortress Press, 1967).

[8] E.g. R. L. Collins, 'Is the Parable of the Unjust Steward Pure Sarcasm?' *Expository Times*, 22 (1910/11): 525–26; Fred Lenwood, 'An Alternative Interpretation of the Parable of the Unjust Steward,' *Congregational Quarterly*, 6 (1928): 366–73.

pretations are, they scarcely represent legitimately the story Jesus told.[9]

Second, interpretations that point to the parable's original meaning in the light of the moralistic pronouncements in verses 8b–13 are dubious. While not strictly allegorical, many of these readings of the parable are *diachronic*; that is, they derive the significance of the story by reference to situations and issues outside of the parameters of the tale itself. These moralistic readings would hardly have occurred to an audience of Jesus in Palestine. These pronouncement sayings have been placed in the context of the parable by Luke, and must reflect in some way his redactional activity. Dodd states bluntly that the evangelist has appended to the parable 'a whole series of morals' which probably represent 'the current exegesis in that part of the church to which he belonged.'[10] Whether they accurately tell us what Luke himself thought the parable meant cannot be said with any certainty. As much as anything, they reflect Luke's (and/or the primitive communities') attempt to resolve the *bafflement* presented by the parable proper. They do indeed give us perspectives from which to assess very early attempts to make Jesus' message relevant to situations in which the followers of Jesus found themselves. Nor is it inconceivable that some of these statements are essentially remembered sayings of the historical Jesus. He may have said such in some contexts: 'Those who are faithful in small matters may be trusted to be faithful in larger issues,' or, 'You cannot serve God and mammon.' Whether any of these utterances were made in the context of this particular parable is hard to say. The first (16:10) would more properly relate to the parable of the talents (Matt. 25:14–30), and the second saying (16:13) supports Jesus' words about where to 'lay up our treasure:' in heaven and not on earth 'where moth and rust corrupt' (Matt. 6:24ff.). The saying in 16:8b, comparing the shrewdness of the 'sons of this world' with an apparent lack of street-wise savvy on the part of the 'sons of light,' is assumed (in many commentaries) to be the 'common interpretation' of the parable.

[9] Cf. A. T. Cadoux, *The Parables of Jesus: Their Art and Their Use* (New York: Macmillan, 1931): 135ff.

[10] C. H. Dodd, *The Parables of the Kingdom*, revised ed. (London: Nisbet, 1961): 29.

If we were to accept Jülicher's injunction that we should not make much of the details of the story but look for the one plain meaning, often found at the close of the parable, then verse 8a provides a strong commendation of shrewd resourcefulness. The possibility exists that ingenious strategy was one of the issues raised in audience-discussion, which undoubtedly followed Jesus' telling of this tale. Former editor of *The Expository Times*, A. W. Hastings, assumed so: '*Presumably* Jesus *meant* to say, "if only you would put as much thought into your religion as a business man puts into his business, even a bad business man into a bad business, you would make a greater success of it."'[11] This, in my view, is a somewhat presumptuous assertion supporting a somewhat simplistic view of the parable's significance. As stated previously, however, a good tale will usually occasion lively discussion: How decisive and resourceful can one be? What is the right use of wealth? How is justice faithfully meted out between employer and employee?

Among the most puzzling of all the sayings ever recorded as coming from the lips of Jesus is the one in 16:9: 'And I tell you, make friends for yourselves by means of unrighteous mammon so that when it fails they may receive you into the eternal habitations.' I take this to be an authentic word of Jesus, probably uttered in the context of the discussion that followed Jesus' telling of this parable. Because of its puzzling nature, and on account of its wide use by other interpreters as a clue to the original meaning of this parable, this saying will be accorded greater space in this chapter[12] than other interpretative sayings in verses 8b–13.

Almost all these interpretations, however, are diachronic readings of the parable and do not elucidate the original thrust of the story. Such diachronic readings present several difficulties.

First, some diachronic interpretations claim that, *in contrast* to the way in which the steward sought to manipulate material goods in order to have his master's debtors receive him into their homes, the followers of Jesus should use money to give alms to the needy. The needy, it was believed, would 'put in a good word'

[11] A. W. Hastings, 'Entre Nous,' *Expository Times*, 39 (1928): 582, italics mine.
[12] The saying figures into my final conclusions about the significance of this parable.

for their benefactors at the time of their death and guarantee them a place in heaven. Or, perhaps more simply, that the giving of alms would be rewarded by God, in the spirit of Matthew 25:34ff. 'Come, blessed of my Father, inherit the kingdom . . . for I was hungry and you fed me . . .'[13] This line of interpretation is not persuasive. Crossan makes the point in several places[14] that Jesus' mission and his understanding of the kingdom of God as a radically egalitarian society in which the 'open table' and 'open healing' obtained is to be strongly *contrasted* with the practice of *almsgiving*. This practice in a subtle way often lets people off the hook from a genuine engagement in working for justice in society. By analogy, it is much easier for me to write a cheque payable to the Salvation Army than to give up my Saturday mornings helping in one of their half-way houses. Crossan puts it pertinently: 'Generous almsgiving may be conscience's last refuge against the terror of open commensality.'[15] I once heard Crossan say in discussion that if a pious person had made the claim in speaking with Jesus that he had been very generous in alms-giving, Jesus would probably have responded by asking, 'But why are people so reduced to poverty that they have been forced to the embarrassment of having to beg for alms?' Crossan's point is well taken, and throws into serious question any interpretation of the parable that proposes almsgiving as reflecting the mind of Jesus in the telling of the parable.

Second, attempts have been made to interpret the parable by *contrasting* the steward's dishonest use of 'dirty money' to win friends with the exhortation to the followers of Jesus in verse 9 to make friends for themselves *without* the use of 'unrighteous mammon.' This interpretation takes the common translation of the Greek text ('by means of unrighteous mammon,' *ek tou mamōna tēs adikias*) to be a mistranslation of the original Aramaic form of the saying. The original Aramaic form is said to have used the Semitic preposition *min* (apart from), which was rendered in Greek as *ek* and then translated 'by means

---

[13] Francis Williams, 'Is Almsgiving the Point of the "Unjust Steward"?' *Journal of Biblical Literature*, 83 (1964): 293–97.

[14] E.g., John Dominic Crossan, *The Historical Jesus: The Life of a Mediterranean Jewish Peasant* (HarperSanFrancisco, 1991): 341.

[15] Ibid.

of.'[16] Wansey speculated that the adverbial *ektos* (without, outside of) was in the original Greek version and by a haplological error in transmission the *-tos* ending of *ektos* was omitted.[17] He draws from this the conclusion that the parable was really about friendship that cannot be bought.

Third, A. Jannaris, a post-classical Greek scholar, believed it unthinkable that verse 9 as it stands in the *textus receptus* should have come from the lips of Jesus. That would have Jesus approving of the unethical Machiavellian doctrine of the end justifying the means. Jannaris therefore suggested changes in punctuation, construing *dexōntai hymas* ('they may receive you') as the end of a sentence in question form: 'Shall I tell you to make friends by means of unrighteous mammon so that when it fails they may receive you.' He then translated the next sentence (beginning with *eis tas aiōpnious skēna . . .*) thus: 'In the everlasting habitations he that is faithful in the least thing is also faithful in much . . .'[18] The point again is to *contrast* the behaviour of the steward with that required of those who hope to attain 'everlasting habitations.' He conveniently omits the next words, 'and he that is dishonest in small matters is dishonest in great ones,' which presumably are also governed by 'in the everlasting habitations.' One would think that the dishonest would not be functioning at all in the eternal habitations! Furthermore, I doubt whether *eis* ('in/into') with the accusative can be rendered in a locative sense as '*in* [rather than "into"] the eternal habitations.' I rather think not.

Fourth, another interpretation *contrasts* the steward's behaviour with that expected of a follower of Jesus in the form of *a fortiori* argument. The steward took care of his material, worldly future by his decisiveness and ingenuity. *How much more* should the 'children of light' act decisively and earnestly in the light of the coming *eschaton* and their

[16] H. F. B. Compston, 'Friendship Without Mammon,' *Expository Times*, 31 (1919/20): 282; R. B. Y. Scott, 'The Parable of the Unjust Steward,' *Expository Times*, 49 (1937/38): 235. The preposition *ek* could be rendered 'from, apart from, out of, by, by means of,' depending on the syntax.

[17] J. C. Wansey, 'The Parable of the Unjust Steward: An Interpretation,' *Expository Times*, 47 (1935/36): 39–40.

[18] A. N. Jannaris, 'The Unrighteous Steward and Machiavellianism,' *Expository Times*, 13 (1901/2): 129–30.

future in it. Such eschatological interpretations[19] clearly reflect the later preaching of the primitive church and are not properly the stuff of the story itself on the occasion of its first telling. Pointing to the bottom line of the parable in which the master shows extraordinary forbearance, Bailey relates this diachronically to the kingdom of God critically presented to the sinner. God's mercy and forgiveness are the sinner's only hope of salvation. This comes close to making the parable into an allegory.

Fifth, some see this significance of this parable as a harbinger of a later event. Karl Barth preached a sermon on the parable along this line. The sermon was published in a pre-Second World War volume of his sermons entitled *Suchet Gott, so werdet ihr leben*.[20] Barth assumes that 'the master' (*ho kyrios*) of verse 8a refers to Jesus who commended the steward in the story for his actions: in total disregard for the master's claim on the debts owed, and eliminating the distinction between 'mine and thine,' the steward cancelled the debtors' obligations, thus 'relieving them of their burdens.' Fraudulent though these actions were, as Barth admitted, the final outcome nevertheless provided a foretaste of the coming age of the Spirit when the members of the early church fellowship held all goods in common. Jesus' words in verse 9 are then a directive to the children of light not to let money be their master. They should rather use their money to relieve the burdens of others. This is undoubtedly a good evangelical preaching point and certainly an imaginative suggestion. Yet Barth has given a thoroughly diachronic reading of the text, and not a very accurate one analogically. The steward did not relieve the debtors of their entire burdens, but only of a fraction of them. Barth's reading does support Crossan's insistence on Jesus' vision of an egalitarian society. Yet it seems to me very doubtful that such a meaning would have been in the mind of Jesus as he told the story.

All of these five diachronic readings have the parable directing the attention of the hearers to the issue of their salvation in the

[19] Jeremias, *Parables*: 181–82; Norman Perrin, *Rediscovering the Teaching of Jesus* (New York: Harper & Row, 1967): 109ff.; Kenneth E. Bailey, *Poet and Peasant and Through Peasant Eyes: A Literary-Cultural Approach to the Parables in Luke* Combined ed. (Grand Rapids: Eerdmans, 1983): 86f.
[20] Summed up in William F. Boyd, 'The Parable of the Unjust Steward,' *Expository Times*, 50 (1938/39): 46.

light of a coming eschatological crisis, the means of attaining it through their charity, their rejection of material concerns, their decisiveness and resourcefulness, and their reliance on the mercy and grace of God. I can well imagine all these issues being prominent in primitive Christian preaching, but they do not stem intrinsically from the inner dynamic of the story itself.

On the one hand, the parable as *parabolē*, a trajectory, will not bear Jülicher's insistence on one plain meaning usually found in the story's punch line at the end. On the other hand, allegorical and diachronic readings do not belong to the thrust of the story in its original setting. Polyvalent meanings should not be confused with allegorical and diachronic readings. Parables lend themselves to polyvalence.[21] Hence, details of a parable should play a significant role in seeking the purport of its message. The details are not simply like the filigree work on a candle-holder, not essential to our seeing the candle's flame, the central point of the story. Dodd was quite right in averring that a parable is 'a metaphor . . . drawn from nature or common life,' which, 'by its vividness and strangeness' leaves the hearers 'in sufficient doubt about its precise meaning to tease (them) into active thought.'[22] Now, the significance of most everyday events is intimately bound up with the details of the situations people experience. To appreciate fully that significance requires attention to the cultural, political, economic, ethical, and religious values at play in those situations. Linnemann's assertion is noteworthy in this regard, that 'a firmly established result of recent parable interpretation is that the parables of Jesus refer to the historical situation in which they were told.'[23]

The details of a parable proper encode elements from everyday life in Jesus' audience in Lower Galilee. The persons in the story are no strangers to the hearers. Two distinct scenarios (with variations) are viable for reading this parable in its original setting, and to each of which the saying in verse 9 can form a synchronic interpretative application.

[21] John Dominic Crossan, *Cliffs of Fall: Paradox and Polyvalence in the Parables of Jesus* (New York: Seabury/Crossroad, 1980): 65ff.

[22] Dodd, *Parables*: 16.

[23] Eta Linnemann, *Parables of Jesus: Introduction and Exposition*, trans. from 3rd German ed. by J. Sturdy (London: SPCK, 1966): 22.

Recent publications about the socio-politico-economic problems experienced in the agrarian setting of rural Galilee, and of the influence of the burgeoning urban growth on rural village life,[24] enhance our understanding of the parables. Small landholders were having their farms expropriated by wealthy creditors, usually as a result of poor seasons. These creditors, most of whom were absentee landlords, rented the land to tenant farmers. The tenants often failed to produce enough to sustain their lives and pay their debts, so they lost their tenancy. Again, exorbitant rental rates demanded by the landlords were assessed in terms of the goods produced. The result in many cases was that tenant farmers were unable to pay their rent, lost their tenancy, and were forced into the class of labourers, hired haphazardly on a daily basis. They became pickers and diggers—strenuous work for little pay. These were the 'expendables' with little hope of economic security. They frequently were reduced to the lowest of the low by being forced to become beggars. The landlord would hire agents or stewards to run this whole enterprise, collect the rents and make sure that the land was properly worked, the crops advantageously harvested. These agents were members of the retainer class. Though not rich, the retainers were not reduced to poverty, as long as they held their position in the service of the landlord.

Many of these absentee landlords and their retainers in this area were Jewish. Although the Torah forbade usury, elitist landlords charged exorbitant amounts to tenants and to members of the merchant class who were under contract to the landlord. The amounts charged could be paid in produce from the land or in the equivalent in monetary value. The amount (produce in the case of this parable) would include hefty interest rates not overtly cited as such in the narrative. Included in these debt amounts would also be the agent's own profit cut. The landlord left all these arrangements in the hands of his stewards

---

[24] William R. Herzog II, *Parables as Subversive Speech: Jesus as Pedagogue of the Oppressed* (Louisville: Westminster/John Knox, 1994): 53–73; see also Crossan, *Historical Jesus*; and Richard L. Rohrbaugh, *The Biblical Interpreter: An Agrarian Bible in an Industrial Age* (Philadelphia: Fortress Press, 1978); idem, 'The Pre-Industrial City in Luke-Acts: Urban Social Relations,' in *The Social World of Luke-Acts: Models for Interpretation*, ed. Jerome H. Neyrey (Peabody, MA: Hendrickson, 1991): 67–96.

whom he trusted, and with whom he had no argument regarding their ways of extorting interest as profit for themselves, provided that *he* got a large return. By locating the parable within such a setting, some of the story's details become pertinent to its interpretation.

The steward's self-assessment, 'I cannot dig and I'm ashamed to beg,' is more than a mere indication of his lazy nature, as Crossan avers.[25] Herzog's suggestion carries more weight. The steward, faced with the prospect of becoming an expendable with a hopeless future greatly heightens the nature of the potential calamity in which he finds himself.[26] Herzog contends that the debtors are more likely to be merchants than tenant farmers, on the evidence of the size of the debts as calculated by Jeremias[27] and Breech.[28] Such yields of grain and oil indicate very large land holdings and a very rich landlord, not the yields from a small tenant farmer's plot. The yields indicate produce handed over to a merchant on contract to sell the goods in a town or city market. The workers farming these crops and harvesting these orchards would have been mere pawns in the game and would have seen very little of the monetary profits stemming from their labour. They were expendables who would have felt keenly the injustice arising from the landlord's unconscionable greed and the steward's handling of the estate.

Many commentators commonly hold two assumptions about this parable. One is that the steward's actions were of a thoroughly fraudulent, cheating nature. Although the steward is party to a totally unjust system, his actions in this case may not have been dishonest. Nearly a century ago, Margaret Gibson suggested (admitting that she did not have much evidence about how stewardship functioned at that time) that the steward may simply have been renouncing his own exorbitant profits without 'defrauding his master.'[29] Much more recently Duncan Derrett has made the case from Mishnaic law, especially as it related to agency and usury, that the steward in the parable forgives the

[25] Crossan, *Parables*: 109–110
[26] Herzog, *Subversive*: 242.
[27] Jeremias, *Parables*: 181; T. W. Manson, *The Sayings of Jesus* (London: SCM Press, 1949): 292.
[28] James Breech, *The Silence of Jesus* (Philadelphia: Fortress Press, 1983): 108.
[29] Margaret D. Gibson, 'On the Parable of the Unjust Steward,' *Expository Times*, 14 (1902/3): 334.

debtors that portion of the debt attributable to the interest, possibly also the insurance, and also part of his own profit. The latter seems less likely. In this case, again, the agent is not acting dishonestly. If both landlord and agent are Jews, as may be assumed, the agent is acting in accordance with the Torah's demands, which forbid the practice of usury. One consequence of this would be that the master 'would get an undeserved reputation for piety.'[30] This conclusion fits well within the parameters of the parable, and will receive further consideration in due course.

The other assumption normally held is that the steward ended up losing his job. The story doesn't say that. It indicates that his tenure was threatened on account of rumours of mishandling of funds, but the final outcome was to depend on the account that the agent would give of his stewardship. The 'bottom line' of the parable in which the master commends his agent for his shrewdness may well indicate (and I am taking it so) that when the steward did put his case, the master found himself put 'over a barrel' on the usury issue. To save face the landlord had to accept the fact that the agent's action in waiving the amount attributable to interest was honest, albeit in a scheming, roguish way. Neither the steward nor the master underwent any genuine conversion to the Torah's demands: they are made to appear Torah-observant. They cover their hypocrisy and greed with a thin patina of piety. What has happened in the end is that the steward has beaten the landlord at his own game.

This account leads into my first interpretative scenario. The story may well be a parabolic version of an actual situation that Jesus heard about from local villagers. In any case, it is not an inconceivable occurrence in the daily life of those times as described above. Jesus tells the story to an audience familiar with the characters and situations in the parable: peasant folk, poor tenant farmers, and probably some diggers and beggars. 'The common folk heard [Jesus] gladly,' says Mark (12:37). One can imagine Jesus telling the story with a wry smile on his lips, one eyebrow raised, and perhaps a twinkle in his eye. His hearers, mainly victims of injustices perpetrated in the agrarian economy

---

[30] J. D. M. Derrett, 'Fresh Light on St. Luke XVI: 1: The Parable of the Unjust Steward,' *New Testament Studies*, 7 (1961): 216ff.

of the villages of Lower Galilee, would see the irony. They may even see the funny side of the tale in which the elitist landlord was forced to forego a sizeable gain in income through the shrewd actions of his agent. There would not be much love lost between those in Jesus' audience and the landlords, nor yet between the audience and the agents. But that would not stop the audience from seeing the humour of the situation.

Russell Baker, in his introduction to the final episode of Dickens' *Martin Chuzzlewit* presented by Masterpiece Theatre, remarked that there is always something comic in the downfall of a very greedy person. And that view is perhaps seen in this parable. Jesus in Luke adds biting sarcasm to the irony of the story understood in this way when he speaks (16:9) of those who try to 'buy' friendship with their wealth. Let them enjoy their welcome into the 'eternal tents,' he says. The oxymoronic nature of that phrase, setting 'eternal' (*aiōnious*) as a qualifier to a dwelling as transitory as a tent (*skēnē/skēnas*), surely comes across as utter sarcasm. Friendships and relationships attained through material wealth can bring no lasting bliss.

Dan Otto Via's interpretation treats this parable as an example of an existentialist picaresque tale: the person falls in the slime and comes up smelling like roses. This view is somewhat similar in mood to the scenario proposed here, though Via draws different conclusions about Jesus' intent in telling the story. The narrative depicts a disastrous situation, followed by a decisive action and a happy ending. For Via, this means that the threatening future is ameliorated by this comic, existentialist story and the hearers are reminded that 'our well-being does not rest ultimately on our dead seriousness.'[31] The ironically comic feature is only one aspect to this parable, and one that was probably incidental to Jesus' intention. To suggest that the parable is comic irony amounts to not much more than an exhortation to retain a good sense of humour, and experience the relief that it brings.

The second scenario I propose as a viable way of interpreting the parable follows more closely the interpretative methods of William Herzog. He asks a very different set of questions from those normally addressed to narrative parables like this one:

[31] Via, *Parables*: 159–62.

'What if the concern of the parables was not the reign of God, but the reigning systems of oppression which dominated Palestine in the time of Jesus? . . . What if the parables are exposing exploitation rather than revealing justification?'[32] Herzog then sees this parable arising out of a situation of peasant resistance, not in terms of physical revolt but by 'subtle sabotage.'[33] Rumours are already in circulation among the peasants that discredit oppressors, such as the steward within their reach. Merchants would likewise do anything they could to bring the agent down.[34] This would place the peasant folk and/or the merchants in a stronger bargaining position. This setting in life would likely have given rise to the tale of the unjust steward. The villagers and/or the merchants would praise the master for the reduced burden placed on them occasioned by the steward's actions. This would probably induce the master to accept the reduction of the debts in order to save face and make him look like a generous man. But the peasants and tenant farmers and merchants would also be putting themselves under a new obligation to the landlord on account of his generosity.

Being in debt to the estate, however, they would hardly be in a position to sustain the steward were he to lose his position. Were that to happen they would surely not be displeased. The steward's actions, therefore, were not really directed to relieving the lot of the debtors, but were, according to Herzog, a desperate attempt to retain his position. The steward's approach would be two-fold: (a) expose those who had accused him, inasmuch as they had accepted the reduced obligation and were themselves, therefore, guilty of cashing in on the master's resources; and (b) emphasise to the master that since he, the steward, had been trusted to write the contracts—hidden interest and all—he knew he would have to take the blame should the contracts appear to be usurious.[35] In being willing to shoulder such blame in the course of his duty to see that the master received huge gains from the enterprise, he would prove his faithfulness and worth as a steward. The master sees the point and commends the steward (16:8a). Herzog concludes that in using the only weapon

[32] Herzog, *Subversive*: 7.
[33] Ibid.: 252.
[34] Ibid.: 253.
[35] Ibid.: 256.

at hand, namely the spreading of the rumour of the agent's fraudulency, this action of the weak and oppressed resulted in the master 'eating crow,' so to speak. The steward brought a limited respite to the debtors, but had his own weaknesses exposed at the same time. Still, he kept his job. Herzog's argument here is not very compelling, as I understand it.

Some basic elements of this account, however, are worthy, and form a basis for my own much less complicated (though not simplistic) reading of the parable. Jesus is telling a story of a typical confrontation between landlords and tenants/merchants, with the steward as a go-between. The situation is one in which the weak and oppressed are royally shafted in a system that is maintained by greed and exploitation through and through. The indebtedness of the tenants/peasants, workers/merchants is exorbitantly high even after the steward's cunning has somewhat reduced their burden. The master and the steward are made to look generous and Torah-keeping, but this hypocrisy only adds insult to injury. It effects a band-aid amelioration in the face of a totally unjust system, and Jesus and his 'expendable' hearers can see through it. Jesus tells the story *in anger* to expose the depth of oppression inflicted on the poor. The steward's plan to make friends by his manipulation of the material assets at his disposal again only underscores the depth of the injustice: it cannot bring any real, lasting hope to those oppressed. His welcome into the houses of those he helped by his machinations brings no lasting benefit, even though the steward thought it would guarantee him a brighter future. It is an illusory benefit, an 'eternal *tent*,' to use the concluding sarcastic utterance of the Lukan Jesus in verse 9. Jesus, instead, is working for a fully egalitarian society as Crossan rightly insists, a society where expendables and acts of oppression and injustice no longer exist. This is Jesus' vision of the kingdom of God. In this realm all can find acceptance. Here all can experience that integrated, full-orbed quality of life in just and compassionate human relationships. In stark contrast to the 'eternal tents,' this kind of life is the eternal life that God wills for all humankind.

In summary, these two scenarios do not pretend to expound a single meaning of this parable. The authentic parable of Jesus, as asserted earlier, will evoke a wide variety of issues for lively imaginative discussion. This story raises questions of faithfulness, of forgiveness, of the responsible use of wealth, of the need for decisiveness in crisis, and of the value of resourcefulness. None of these areas of human concern need be ruled out as inauthentically arising from the telling of this story. Indeed, a major feature of a parable is its power to tease the minds of its hearers into active thought.[36] This, in turn, may seem to imply that Jesus did not intend some parables, such as this one, to have any precise application. Having said that, though, Jesus was not simply throwing out to his hearers an arresting, puzzling story in which he himself took no particular position. I have proposed two lines of interpretation which stem from the teasing elements within the story itself, and not from the implied influence of later accepted doctrinal, liturgical, or pastoral norms of the primitive church or the Lukan evangelist. The scenarios I have set forth make sense as viable reflections of the position Jesus took in relationship to the situation of which he spoke in parable.

[36] Dodd, *Parables*: 5.

Parables of the People

As an architect, before erecting a large edifice, examines and tests the soil in order to see whether it can support the weight, so a wise lawgiver does not begin by drawing up laws that are good in themselves, but considers first whether the people for whom he designs them are fit to endure them. (Jean-Jacques Rosseau, *The Social Contract and Discourse on the Origin of Inequality* [1967]:46)

9

A Dysfunctional Family and Its Neighbours
(Luke 15:11b–32)

The Parable of the Prodigal Son

RICHARD L. ROHRBAUGH

The Text in Translation

There was a man who had two sons. The younger of them
said to his father, 'Father, give me the share of the property
that will belong to me.' So he divided his property between
them. A few days later the younger son gathered all he had
and travelled to a distant country, and there he squandered
his property in dissolute living. When he had spent everything, a severe famine took place throughout that country
and he began to be in need. So he went and hired himself
out to one of the citizens of that country, who sent him to
his fields to feed pigs. He would gladly have filled himself
with the pods that the pigs were eating; and no one gave him
anything. But when he came to himself he said, 'How many
of my father's hired hands have bread enough and to spare,
but here I am dying of hunger! I will get up and go to my
father, and will say to him, "Father, I have sinned against
heaven and before you; I am no longer worthy to be called
your son; treat me like one of your hired hands."' So he set
off and went to his father. But while he was still far off, his
father saw him and was filled with compassion; he ran and
put his arms around him and kissed him. The son said to
him, 'Father, I have sinned against heaven and before you; I
am no longer worthy to be called your son.' But the father
said to his slaves, 'Quickly, bring out a robe—the best one—
and put it on him; put a ring on his finger and sandals on his
feet. And get the fatted calf and kill it, and let us eat and

celebrate; for this son of mine was dead and is alive again; he was lost and is found!' And they began to celebrate.

Now his elder son was in the field; and when he came and approached the house, he heard music and dancing. He called one of the slaves and asked what was going on. He replied, 'Your brother has come, and your father has killed the fatted calf because he has got him back safe and sound.' Then he became angry and refused to go in. His father came out and began to plead with him. But he answered his father, 'Listen! For all these years I have been working like a slave for you, I have never disobeyed your command; yet you have never given me even a young goat so that I might celebrate with my friends. But when this son of yours came back, who has devoured your property with prostitutes, you killed the fatted calf for him!' Then the father said to him, 'Son, you are always with me, and all that is mine is yours. But we had to celebrate and rejoice, because this brother of yours was dead and has come to life; he was lost and has been found.'

In traditional exegesis, the parable of the prodigal son has been understood as a story about repentance, forgiveness and a churlish older brother.[1] Perhaps it is. However, a number of

---

[1] The list of commentators on this story is truly formidable. Thus there have been literary studies (Sellew, Kozar, Ramsay, Tannehill, Talbert, Crossan), legal studies (Derrett, Pöhlmann), structuralist studies (Patte, Scott, Grelot, Giblin), psychological studies (Tolbert, Via, Hein, King), studies of ancient parallels (Fisher, Foster, Aus, Ernst) and Old Testament motifs (Hofius), studies of patristic use of the parable (Thieme, Frot, Derrett, Barnard), along with a host of theological and homiletical treatments. In fact, articles, commentaries and studies of it abound in such numbers that a comprehensive bibliography is neither possible nor useful.

It may be helpful to note for the interested reader where good overview treatments can be found. In addition to the standard commentaries, we strongly recommend two important contributions which cover much of the available work on the parable: Bernard B. Scott, *Hear Then the Parable: A Commentary on the Parables of Jesus* (Minneapolis: Fortress Press, 1989): 99–125; and Kenneth E. Bailey, *Poet and Peasant and Through Peasant Eyes: A Literary-Cultural Approach to the Parables in Luke.* Combined ed.(Grand Rapids, MI: Eerdmans, 1983): 158–206. Both studies reflect on the literary, legal and cultural issues, and both take into account earlier discussions of the parable's authenticity. The latter is now not widely questioned, though for an exception see Heiki Räisänen, 'The Prodigal Gentile and his Jewish Christian Brother (Luke 15:11–32),' in *The Four Gospels 1992: Festschrift Frans Neirynck.* vol. 2, eds F. Van Segroeck, et al. (Leuven: University Press, 1992): 1617–1636. Räisänen's unconvincing case is heavily dependent on (1) a soteriological reading of the story and (2) heavy speculation about allegorical equivalents (see below) for the story's characters. He is led to the latter because he cannot

commentators have pointed out that the term 'repentance' is in fact never mentioned, that the younger son's return seems motivated primarily by his stomach, and that initially he is more inclined to *work* his way back into the family circle rather than depend on divine grace or family generosity.[2] Moreover, when one steps back from the traditional title of the parable it is not difficult to see that it is not really about a prodigal son at all (who does not appear after v. 24). Rather, it is about the troubles of a generous, if somewhat erratic, father with his *two* rather difficult sons. It is really a kinship story. In fact, as we shall argue below, the story could quite plausibly be titled, 'A Dysfunctional Family and its Neighbours.'

Instead of coming at this story with the usual pre-understandings of Western soteriology, therefore, we propose a new approach, which attempts to set it as closely as possible in the socio-cultural milieu out of which it came. Above all, this means recognising what Western exegesis frequently overlooks: it was originally a Mediterranean story, told by a Mediterranean storyteller, for a Mediterranean audience.[3] Our intent is thus to ask what this type of Mediterranean kinship story might have evoked in the minds of ancient Palestinian peasants when they first heard it from one of their own kind.

To some, of course, concentrating on this original audience of Jesus might seem a risky option since it is unlikely that Luke's setting/audience corresponds to that of Jesus, and Luke

---

imagine a 'representative equivalent' for the older brother in the *Sitz im Leben Jesu*. The latter would not be necessary, of course, if the former were not a presupposition.

With the best recent studies, we also recognise that the story is not an allegory, or as Kenneth Bailey (*Poet and Peasant*: 159) puts it, 'the father is not God *incognito*.' Of course this is not to say that the actions of the father cannot be symbolic of the actions of God; that theological possibility remains. So J. Jeremias, *Rediscovering the Parables* (New York: Scribner's, 1966): 101.

[2] E.g., Bailey, *Poet and Peasant*: 173–80.

[3] For an introduction to the use of cultural anthropology in the study of the New Testament see John H. Elliott, *What is Social Scientific Criticism?* (Minneapolis: Fortress Press, 1993) and Bruce J. Malina, *The New Testament World: Insights from Cultural Anthropology*, rev. ed. (Louisville, KY: Westminster/John Knox, 1993). We must also acknowledge our indebtedness to the ground-breaking work of this type done on the story by Kenneth E. Bailey. While Bailey does not come at it from the point of view of anthropology as a discipline, his vast experience living in the Middle East has spawned the most provocative cultural work on the parable to date.

is nearly all we have to go on.[4] It is plausible, however, to presume a rather general audience that could well have included Pharisees, scribes, tax collectors and sinners, as Luke suggests, but likely included others as well.[5] In fact, since 90 percent of agrarian populations were typically rural farmers, and since the story itself is about just such a village setting, perhaps we can assume that Galilean peasants were also among the original hearers.[6] The value of this strategy is that it allows us to ask about the impact of the story without treating it as a *theologoumenon*[7] or allegorically pigeonholing each of the characters ahead of time.[8] We can simply ask what a story about settling a family quarrel might have suggested to the kind of rural audience Jesus typically addressed.

It is difficult for modern North Americans and Europeans reading the New Testament to set aside the individualism with which we view the world. But ancient Mediterranean peasants were not individualistic. Instead they were what anthropologists call 'dyadic' persons. They 'internalise and make their own what others say, think and do about them because they believe it is necessary, for being human, to live out the expectations of

---

[4] B. B. Scott, *Hear then the Parable*: 103, has correctly pointed out there are three audiences in view here: the historical audience of Jesus, the audience in the story-world of Luke and Luke's own audience (his implied readers).

[5] Some literary critics would object to looking past the Lukan performance of the parable to something hypothetically behind it. But our interest is not in the *ipsissima verba Jesu* or some pre-Lukan form of the parable. We offer no comment on *Traditionsgeschichte* in either the wide or narrow sense. We are simply trying to ask how this story might have hit someone who came at it without the pre-conditioning of the Lukan setting.

[6] As Halvor Moxnes points out, the special parables in Luke tend to focus on full members (as opposed to either *marginales* or administrator bureaucrats) of the typical village. Since the parable presumes slave ownership (15:22), the picture is of a substantial village landowner. By contrast, he notes that the parables in Mark focus on nature. *The Economy of the Kingdom* (Philadelphia: Fortress Press, 1988): 55–56.

[7] Scott (*contra* Jeremias), *Hear then the Parable*: 118.

[8] The typical allegory imagines the father as God incognito, the older son as a Jew (or a Jewish Christian: Räisänen) and the younger son as a Gentile Christian. The subtle anti-Semitism of such interpretations is to be deplored. Whatever claim to sense such a reading makes in patristic exegesis (Ambrose, Augustine, et al.) and elsewhere, it makes no sense whatever at the level of Jesus. As noted above, the recent study of Räisänen in which such allegorical speculation is rife is the result of pre-deciding that this is a traditional soteriological tale.

others.'[9] For them, the psychological center is not the isolated ego, the individual. It is the family.

In peasant societies identity is thus family identity, not individual identity. A moniker like 'James the son of Alphaeus' speaks volumes: a son's identity is derived from his father. Family members are deeply embedded in each other socially, economically and psychologically, hence the loyalty they owe each other is simply categorical.[10] They watch each other constantly for hints that kin-group loyalty is weak and any member acting outside the pattern of the family is deeply resented. When describing a family celebration, for example, the first-century Roman poet Ovid puts it bluntly, 'Let the innocent appear; let a disloyal brother stay far, far away.' Interestingly, Ovid counts among the 'disloyal' any brother with an excessive interest in inheriting the property, that is, 'anyone who thinks his father is still too much alive.'[11]

If family solidarity was of first importance, solidarity with the village was second. In a world characterised by social and geographical immobility, the ancient Mediterranean family and village formed what anthropologists call a 'closed' social network.[12] Tightly knit circles of family and friends lived in close proximity over long periods of time and developed deeply felt community attachments. Even though peasant families were normally quite self-sufficient, very few of them, even larger three-generational ones, could manage without calling on neighbours for economic and social support.[13] For an isolated individual it was almost impossible—as the prodigal soon found out.

Equally important to village solidarity was social conformity. Everyone was always subject to the constraints of the village. As May Diaz explains:

> Characteristically, in the peasant community, where the nonconformity of one frequently is seen as a threat to the

[9] Ibid.: 67.
[10] Juliet du Boulay, 'Lies, Mockery and Family Integrity,' in *Mediterranean Family Structures*, ed. J. G. Peristiany (Cambridge: Cambridge University Press, 1976): 393.
[11] *Fasti* 2, 617.
[12] Eric R. Wolf, *Peasants* (Englewood Cliffs, NJ: Prentice-Hall, 1966): 84–90.
[13] May N. Diaz and Jack M. Potter, 'Introduction: The Social Life of Peasants,' in *Peasant Society: A Reader*, eds Jack M. Potter, May N. Diaz and George M. Foster (Boston: Little, Brown & Company, 1967): 156.

cohesion of the whole, the limits are very narrow. The individual wishing to maintain viable face-to-face relations with his fellow villagers finds that he must play the economic game according to local rules. He dares not risk ostracism by becoming a free agent, for he depends on those around him for extra hands in building a house and for harvest, for spouses for his children and for assistance at birth, death and famine.[14]

In short, social conformity was a matter of survival. It meant that peasant groups had to maintain sharp boundaries between insiders and outsiders, between themselves and all others. 'Who belongs and who does not is clearly demarcated; "we" and "they" are unmistakable.'[15] Obviously going to a 'far country' where one was a stranger was not really a very good idea.

Such social solidarity has typically been the strongest in what anthropologists call 'closed' villages, that is, those in which land is not considered by the locals to be alienable.[16] It is stronger still in societies where the population is largely non-literate. In such settings, land claims are not written public records but a matter of collective memory. They depend on and are reinforced by open participation in non-kinship-based associations. Thus breaking solidarity with the village could literally result in land claims being 'forgotten.'

Obviously then a family's honour is dependent upon constant public re-affirmation of loyalty to the village.[17] A good illustration can be seen in the way those acquiring excess wealth were expected to give back to the community.[18] By spending lavishly on rituals or feasts of various kinds, a family both acquired prestige and demonstrated solidarity with neighbours. Similarly, when dyadic contracts resulted in labour exchanges among neighbours, they were then 'validated and celebrated by ritual

---

[14] May N. Diaz, 'Introduction: Economic Relations in Peasant Society,' in *Peasant Society*: 50–51.

[15] Ibid.: 52.

[16] Lev. 25:23. Elites, of course, had no such view. For a full discussion of the fact that Israelite peasants in the first century retained the old notion of the unalienability of land, see David A. Fiensy, *The Social History of Palestine in the Herodian Period: The Land is Mine* (Lewiston, NY: Mellen, 1991).

[17] On the concept of 'honour' and its role in family well-being, see Malina, *New Testament World*: 28–62. For the economic consequences thereof, see pp. 90–116.

[18] Diaz, *Economic Relations*: 54.

and ceremony, by drinking, feasting and dancing, so that participants feel they have gained in enjoyment for what they have contributed in work.'[19] In this way wealth enhanced rather than weakened community solidarity.

That family solidarity is a peasant ideal, however, does not mean it is always a reality. Family conflict is a fact of peasant life. Conflict between father and sons is often intense and usually revolves around inheritance rights, marriage (and the establishment of an independent family), and, in early youth, a son's demand for his own way in matters of work and entertainment. When generational conflict of this sort threatens family stability, mothers are often pushed into the role of buffer or family reconciler.[20]

Fraternal rivalries can also cause serious conflict in peasant families.[21] Sons commonly live in a father's house even after marriage, but on a father's death a major restraint on fraternal tension disappears. At this point, rivalries frequently result in brothers establishing separate nuclear families. If uncontrolled, of course, such rivalries threatened the kind of instability that destroys everyone in the group.[22]

Yet another kind of conflict frequently interrupts family-village solidarity. Inter-family rivalry and competition can be intense. 'Eavesdropping, gossiping about neighbours, inventing scurrilous explanations of events, lying to destroy another's reputation' are all common events in village life.[23] If such conflict was the result of friendly rivalry, of course, it could often be construed as 'fun.'[24] But if over serious matters, corrective

---

[19] Ibid.: 53.

[20] Perhaps the best known case is the quarrels in the family of Herod the Great. Josephus recounts the beginnings of the troubles. They were spectacular indeed, including murder, intrigue, multiple divorces, land and inheritance disputes, etc. For a fine kinship study of the Herodian family and refs to Josephus, see K. C. Hanson, 'The Herodians and Mediterranean Kinship,' *Biblical Theology Bulletin*, 19/3, 19/4 (1989), 20/1 (1990).

[21] J. G. Peristiany, 'Introduction,' in *Mediterranean Family Structures*: 8.

[22] The story of sibling rivalry is especially strong in the tradition of Israel. As Scott points out, the 'younger brother' motif is prevalent in the Old Testament despite Deut. 21:15–17 (*Hear Then the Parable*: 112. See there the Midrash on Psalms 9, which Scott cites to indicate that the tradition continued long past New Testament times.)

[23] Du Boulay, 'Lies, Mockery and Family Integrity:' 392.

[24] Ibid.: 395.

measures had to be taken quickly to prevent disaster. Villagers especially fear the mockery of others.

> On discovery of some offence, the discoverer immediately relates it to his or her friends and relations, and in no time the story is all round the village and everyone is, as they say, 'laughing.' The more serious or ludicrous the offence is, the more people mock the principals of it. The more they laugh, the more the victims of the laughter are humiliated, because the chief ingredient of laughter is lack of respect, and it is this above all that is the enemy of reputation and self-esteem.[25]

As we shall see below, conflict of this sort is a serious risk to the family of the prodigal.

A final matter we must address before turning to a reading of the parable itself, is the unalienability of land. This simply means that land-rights are not exclusively individual, hence land cannot be sold in perpetuity. In many peasant societies this militated against the use of wills. Land was considered to belong to past and future generations, not merely to present occupants, and thus the current owner was not free to dispose of property according to personal whim.[26] That view began to modify in the late Roman republic, however, as the use of wills became widespread.

Yet as David Fiensy's recent study has shown, the old idea that God owned the land was very much alive among Israelite peasants (though certainly not among elite groups) in the Herodian period.[27] A peasant would even buy the land of a kinsman in economic trouble rather than let it slip from family control (Lev. 25:25). Endogamous or defensive marriage strategies had the same intent.[28]

One result was that a peasant's emotional attachment to the land remained significant. As Robert Redfield put it in his classic study of peasant cultures, 'The land and he [the peasant] are parts of one thing, one old-established body of relationships.'[29]

---

[25] Ibid.: 394.

[26] Jane F. Gardner and Thomas Wiedemann, *The Roman Household: A Sourcebook* (London: Routledge, 1991): 117.

[27] Fiensy, *Social History*: 1–20. As Lev. 25:23 puts it: 'The land shall not be sold in perpetuity, for the land is mine, for you are strangers and sojourners with me.'

[28] Malina, *New Testament World*: 129–42.

Thus expulsion from the land was not only an economic disaster, it was a social one. It meant loss of honour, broken survival networks, and disintegration of the family unit. The bitterness of Psalm 137 and the rejoicing of Psalm 126 are witness to this emotional investment in land lost and regained.

Because land is life to a peasant, every effort is made to keep it together and in the family—though not all peasant societies use the same strategies for doing so. Primogeniture is one such strategy and usually means that younger sons are given moveable wealth or forced to move elsewhere and find other means of support. Villages practising primogeniture are usually typified by 'alliances based on marriage and fictive kinship between multi-generational groups' with common interests.[30] By contrast, where land is split up among heirs the resultant community is more likely to be an 'intertwined network of nuclear families.'[31] Since the land was indeed split in Israel (Deut. 21:17), networked nuclear families are thus to be expected—exactly the pattern we see in the parable of the prodigal son.[32]

In sum, we can now say that much more is at stake here than losing and gaining an errant son, traumatic as that event would be. The wellbeing and future of an entire extended family is at stake. Its honour and place in the village, its social and economic networks, even its ability to call on neighbours in times of need are all at issue. If the family were to lose its 'place,' no one would marry its sons or daughters, patrons would disappear, and the family would be excluded from the necessary economic and social relations. Families that do not maintain solidarity with neighbours are quickly in trouble.

With this bit of socio-cultural background, it is time to turn to the parable story itself. If we can presume the attitudes described above for at least some of Jesus' hearers, and at the same time if we can resist traditional soteriological readings, perhaps we can see the story in a new light. It is not that the

---

[29] Robert Redfield, *Peasant Society and Culture* (Chicago: University of Chicago Press, 1956): 28.

[30] Diaz, 'Economic Relations': 51.

[31] Ibid.

[32] This is what Emmanuel Todd calls the 'endogamous community family,' typical of some portions of the Mediterranean world. It is one of the seven family types he analyses in *The Explanation of Ideology: Family Structures and Social Systems* (Blackwell, 1985): 133–54.

many traditional readings are necessarily wrong, it is simply that we wish to bracket the received wisdom for the moment in order to concentrate on new possibilities.

'There was a man who had two sons; and the younger of them said to his father, "Father, give me the share of property that falls to me." And he divided his living between them' (15:11–12). A family with two sons is blessed. Male children were an economic asset and thus considered a gift from God.[33] Keeping sons together, especially in the face of the usual tensions over marriage and inheritance, was difficult but desirable. As J. D. M. Derrett points out, attempts to avoid squabbles after his death might be the one circumstance that would lead a father to divide an estate ahead of time.[34] Many commentators have noted, however, that it is highly unusual for a son to press a father for his share of the inheritance while the father is still alive. Bailey argues that this means the son wishes his father dead,[35] an attitude reflected in the quote from Ovid above. Scott agrees, though he thinks it a possible occurrence even if not the norm.[36] As Sirach 33:19–23 puts it:

> To a son or wife, to a brother or friend, do not give power over yourself, as long as you live; and do not give your property to another, lest you change your mind and must ask for it. While you are still alive and have breath in you, do not let anyone take your place. For it is better that your children should ask from you than that you should look to the hands of your sons. Excel in all that you do; bring no stain on your honour. At the time when you end the days of your life, in the hour of death, distribute your inheritance.

Or as the Babylonian Talmud comments: 'Our Rabbis taught: three cry out and are not answered: he who has money and lends it without witnesses; he who acquires a master; he who transfers his property to his children in his lifetime.'[37] In other words, the father who does not wait is a fool. He has given his place as head

---

[33] Malina, *New Testament World*: 108.
[34] J. D. M. Derrett, 'Law in the New Testament: The Parable of the Prodigal Son,' *New Testament Studies*, 14 (1967): 59.
[35] *Poet and Peasant*: 161–69.
[36] *Hear Then the Parable*: 109–11.
[37] *Baba Mezia*, 75b. Cited by Bailey, *Poet and Peasant*: 110.

of the family to a son and thereby destroyed his own honour and authority.

This is obviously a family in trouble. The younger son has no (sense of) shame or family loyalty. Moreover, careful reading of this opening line indicates that the older son is no better. Only Bailey, coming as he does from a lifetime of living in Middle-Eastern villages, notes that on hearing that the elder was to get his share as well ('he divided his living between them') the reader would expect a loud and immediate outcry of refusal.[38] That this brother is silent indicates he too is shameless and disloyal. Yet even Bailey has not taken seriously enough the fact that the father too is suspect because he gives in without protest or apparent necessity. Villagers (or readers) hearing this would have been dumbfounded. None of the characters in the story has acted properly to this point; all apparently lack a sense of propriety and shame. What kind of family is this? Villagers would be wondering if the family could even continue to function.

In the light of earlier comments about the solidarity of family and village, however, it is necessary to see that more than internal family relations are at stake here. Even if this shameful episode took place in private, it would only be a short time before the whole village knew what happened. Since nonconformity is seen as a threat, village gossip networks are very effective in spreading stories about those who break the rules. What the shameful behaviour of the father and his two sons would signal to other villagers, therefore, is the need to close ranks against this family quickly lest the contagion spread. Thus it is not only internally that the family is crumbling, so also are its relations with village neighbours.

'Not many days later, the younger son gathered all he had and took his journey into a far country, and there he squandered his property in loose living; and when he had spent everything, a great famine arose in that country, and he began to be in want' (15:13–14). Given the normal peasant attachment to land and family, this is a shocking notice indeed. The son is expected to stay at home, and it is especially in the interests of his mother that he do so. Obviously he should maintain his father in his old

[38] Bailey, *Poet and Peasant*: 168.

age,[39] but his presence means far more than that to his mother. He is the surety of her place in the family. J. G. Peristiany describes her position:

> If bearing a son is likened to the growing of roots in one's own home, his departure, especially his premature departure after a quarrel with his father, is responsible for the sentiment of intense insecurity. A mother is thus prepared to make any sacrifice in order not to lose him.[40]

A peasant hearing of the younger son's scandalous departure, then, would recognise that *both* parents had been damaged. We usually forget about the mother, but peasants would not.

The story notes that, in taking off, the younger son 'gathered all he had'—presumably meaning that he sold off his portion of the land.[41] That of course violates the peasant norm of unalienability. It is not as if the younger son got nothing and had to leave; giving him a share of land (presumably the younger son got the expected one third; Deut. 21:17) was *designed* to keep him tied to family and village! As Derrett points out, 'He was not the younger son of an English landed family of the pre-1925 period, to whom the virtue of adventurousness was a necessity.'[42] Moreover, as the prodigal sells the land and it is lost to the family the potential support of its extended members is diminished. A lot of people would have interests at stake here.

We noted earlier that in peasant societies in which land is split among heirs the village pattern is normally one of networked nuclear families. Thus Jesus' hearers undoubtedly expected the younger son to marry locally, at least within the village and preferably within the extended family (endogamy), thereby forming a new nuclear family close by.[43] The land would

---

[39] As Bailey points out (*Poet and Peasant*: 166), the father has granted both possession and disposition of the property to the younger son—highly unusual in light of the father's right to the usufruct.

[40] Peristiany, 'Introduction': 14.

[41] I. H. Marshall argues that the term *sunagō* here means to 'turn into cash:' *The Gospel of Luke: A Commentary on the Greek Text*, New International Greek Text Commentary (Grand Rapids, MI: Eerdmans, 1978): 607. Also Joseph A. Fitzmyer, *The Gospel According to Luke X-XXIV*, Anchor Bible, 28 (New York: Doubleday, 1985): 1087, who cites Plutarch's use of it in this sense (*Cato Min.* 6.7§672c).

[42] Derrett, 'Law in the New Testament': 106.

[43] As Marshall, *Commentary*: 607, notes, the story implies that the young man was unmarried.

remain in or near the family and maintain all the needed networks. But the prodigal left instead, obviating this type of marriage arrangement.

The elder brother's accusation in verse 30 notwithstanding, the Greek text does not indicate *how* the younger son blew the money, only that he did so (*zōn asōtōs*, literally: living wastefully; the RSV, 'loose,' is misleading). The notice is not surprising. Space does not permit a full discussion of peasant behaviour when cut off from the restraining social networks of the village, but the prodigal's seemingly irrational behaviour is widely attested in social science literature.[44] Dislocated peasants are unfortunately in a situation where 'tradition is no longer a sufficient guide to life.'[45] Lacking experience with long-term views of managing capital, peasants who go to the cities usually live just as they do in the village: hand to mouth. Frequent stories of third-world peasants who migrate into modern cities and blow all their money illustrate the tragedy all too well. When short-term sources of money dry up, they are in serious trouble.

'So he went and joined himself to one of the citizens of that country, who sent him into his fields to feed swine. And he would gladly have fed on the pods that the swine ate; and no one gave him anything' (15:15–16). Traditional studies of the parable focus here on explanations of the 'pods' and the degradation involved in a Jewish person feeding swine. These items are significant, but have been explained often and need not be repeated here. The line above that gets less attention, but is equally important, is the notice that he 'joined himself' to a local citizen. Since ancient citizenship was normally in a city, usually the central place in a 'region,' we can assume the citizen is an urbanite. At a minimum, this citizen is a landowner capable of hiring wage labourers and thus he is very likely among the elite. It is from this sort of patron that the prodigal seeks aid.

Patronage, of course, pervades all levels of peasant societies.[46] Meager opportunities beyond basic survival are the usual peasant

[44] For insightful comment in this regard, see George M. Foster, 'Peasant Society and the Image of Limited Good,' in *Peasant Society*: 302–303.

[45] George M. Foster, 'Introduction: What is a Peasant?' in *Peasant Society*: 8.

[46] Such a review is available in Halvor Moxnes, 'Patron-Client Relations and the New Community in Luke-Acts,' in *The Social World of Luke-Acts: Models for Interpretation*, ed. Jerome H. Neyrey (Peabody, MA: Hendrickson, 1991): 241–68.

lot. Anything more, including help in times of trouble, comes from the largesse of patrons who broker resources to the peasant class.[47] The younger son here obviously knows the system and thus seeks aid by becoming the client of a local patron.

There is a certain poignancy to the notice of what the younger son has done here. To get a feel for this, it is worth quoting George Foster at length:

> The emotional dependence of the peasant on the city presents an especially poignant case. Peasants throughout history have admired the city and have copied many of the elements they have observed there. The city, with its glitter and opportunity, holds a fascination, like a candle for a moth. But at the same time, and for good cause, peasants hate and fear cities and the city dwellers who exercise control over them. Since time immemorial city people have alternately ridiculed, ignored, or exploited local country people, on whom they depend for food, for taxes, for military conscripts, for labour levies, and for market sales. Peasants know they need the city, as an outlet for their surplus production and as the source of many material and nonmaterial items they cannot themselves produce. Yet they recognise that the city is the source of their helplessness and humiliation, and in spite of patrons half trusted, the peasant knows he can never really count on a city man.[48]

It would be hard to imagine a more telling description of the position of the prodigal son!

'But when he came to himself he said, "How many of my father's hired servants have bread enough and to spare, but I perish here with hunger! I will arise and go to my father, and I will say to him, 'Father, I have sinned against heaven and before you; I am no longer worthy to be called your son; treat me as one of your hired servants'"' (15:17–19). Through most of Christian history these verses have been seen as the 'turning point' in the story—the moment of 'repentance' to traditional exegetes who imagine this to be a soteriological

---

[47] 'Patron-client relations, in which peasant villagers seek out more powerful people who may be city dwellers, wealthy hacienda owners, religious leaders, or other individuals with the power to aid, are a significant element of most peasant societies.' Foster, 'What is a Peasant?:' 9.

[48] Ibid.: 10.

tale.[49] However, careful reading suggests that this may not be the case at all.[50] As Scott makes clear the prodigal is really motivated by his stomach and is therefore not repentant in the truest sense.[51]

The critical issue is the meaning of the phrase, 'he came to himself.' Various attempts have been made to find Aramaic equivalents and/or rabbinic parallels for it. Some have claimed Hellenistic equivalents meaning to 'have second thoughts.'[52] But perhaps closer to the implications in the story is the suggestion of Dan O. Via that the prodigal is remembering his own past and thereby remembering who he is.[53]

If Via is right, and if this is indeed such a moment of self-recognition, then it is above all recognition of the family from which the prodigal derives his identity. Granted the envisioned return will only put him on the periphery of the family, nonetheless it will reconnect him with the family's social networks and place him in a social location in which he *knows how to operate.* The community's guiding hand, even if not full membership in the family, will be restored. He will no longer be among outsiders who exploit, ridicule or ignore him. Perhaps that is enough to hope for.

'And he arose and came to his father. But while he was yet at a distance, his father saw him and had compassion, and ran and embraced him and kissed him. And the son said to him, "Father, I have sinned against heaven and before you; I am no longer worthy to be called your son." But the father said to his servants, "Bring quickly the best robe, and put it on him; and put a ring

---

[49] Most notably Luise Schottroff, 'Das Gleichnis vom verlorenen Sohn,' *Zeitschrift für Theologie und Kirche*, 68/1 (1971): 27–52, but many others as well.

[50] Bailey, *Poet and Peasant*: 175–77, allows that the prodigal may have repented of blowing the money, but his principal argument is that the prodigal is simply cooking up a self-rescue scheme by which to pay back the father. Obviously, the theological axe being ground here is making a case for the prodigal's unwillingness to accept unmerited grace.

[51] Scott, *Hear Then the Parable*: 116. A bit earlier Günther Bornkamm took the same view: *Jesus of Nazareth*, trans. I. and F. McLuskey and J. Robinson (New York: Harper, 1960): 126. Marshall, *Commentary*: 609, cites M. Lam. 1:7 [53b]; SB I, 568, II, 215f.) 'When a son (in need in a strange land) goes barefoot, then he remembers the comfort of his father's house.'

[52] The evidence, or better the lack thereof, is carefully reviewed by Bailey, *Poet and Peasant*: 173–76.

[53] Dan O. Via, *The Parables: Their Literary and Existential Dimension* (Philadelphia: Fortress Press, 1967): 168.

on his hand, and shoes on his feet"' (15:20–22). Kenneth Bailey was probably the first to set this line fully in its proper social context. Especially important is that he (nearly alone) takes seriously the embedded (and indebted) position of the family in the village:

> The father also knows how the village (which certainly has told him he should not have granted the inheritance in the first place) will treat the boy on his arrival. The prodigal will be mocked by a crowd that will gather spontaneously as word flashes across the village telling of his return . . . he will be subject to taunt songs and many other types of verbal and perhaps even physical abuse.[54]

The son's return to the edge of the village thus precipitates a crisis. It also makes the subsequent actions of the father understandable. As Bailey points out, in the Mediterranean world *old men do not run.*[55] It is not only shameful (ankles show), it also indicates lack of control. They *certainly* do not run to meet or welcome anyone, and especially not their children. But if an emergency exists, perhaps it is another matter. This makes sense of the unique Greek term used here: *dramōn* means to 'exert oneself to the limit of one's powers.'[56] It implies straining to the utmost. Obviously the father acts in this way because the boy is in trouble. The villagers would be angry and the father's 'compassion' is well placed. Hence we can argue that the embrace and kiss are not first of all signs of welcome, they are signs of *protection.*

Of course much has been made of the actions of the father as expressions of incredible paternal love. Perhaps that is true, since a Mediterranean audience might have expected instead to see the father beat the son in public in order to signal his disapproval. But we must point out that the villagers here see both a son *and a father* of whom they would disapprove. They would fear the son's behaviour might infect their own sons, but would equally

---

[54] *Poet and Peasant:* 180–82 (181).

[55] Ibid.: 181. Bailey also cites Aristotle: 'Great men never run in public' (undocumented); and Sir. 19:30: 'A man's manner of walking tells you what he is.'

[56] W. F. Arndt and F. W. Gingrich, *A Greek-English Lexicon of the New Testament and other Early Christian Literature* (Chicago: University of Chicago Press, 1957): 833.

deplore the father's foolishness for having given in. Thus we must ask if more is going on here than simply an outpouring of paternal love.

Our contention is that the father's task is not only to reconcile his son to the family, but also to reconcile himself and his family to the village. The first step in that process has been taken when the father (1) protects the son and (2) publicly demonstrates his re-integration into the family with the robe, ring and sandals.[57] Bailey argues that the robe, ring and sandals would have signalled to the *servants* how the son is to be treated, and that the robe would have signalled the same to the *villagers*. That is probably true, but Bailey is almost certainly not correct in suggesting that the robe would 'assure' village reaction.[58] Unfortunately, for the village simply to acquiesce in the prodigal's return would not settle the matter.

The problem is that the *father and older son* have also offended the community and therefore something further is required in order to address *their* offences. In fact something must be done to re-establish confidence in the entire family by demonstrating its respect for and solidarity with the village. Only in this way can the father rescue not only his two sons but also himself and his extended family.

'"And bring the fatted calf and kill it, and let us eat and make merry; for this my son was dead, and is alive again; he was lost, and is found." And they began to make merry' (15:23–24). Here the father takes the necessary action to reconcile himself and his family with the village.[59] As Bailey correctly notes, 'the selection of a calf rather than a goat or a sheep means that most, if not all, the village will be present that evening.[60] To kill a calf is rare and expensive. Not to share it with neighbours would be to add insult to injury. But as we noted earlier, by spending on

[57] If it is the best robe in the house, it is probably the father's. If the ring is a signet ring as is often argued (Derrett, Plummer, Marshall, et al.), it is a sign of authority. Since slaves went barefoot, sandals may well have indicated free status (Marshall).

[58] Bailey, *Poet and Peasant*: 185.

[59] Scott, *Hear Then the Parable*: 118, argues that this making merry in the family is also designed to 'encompass the reader.' Perhaps, but the statement is premature. It skips the critical reconciliation with the village the father's party now provides.

[60] Bailey, *Poet and Peasant*:186.

elaborate feasts an individual gives back to the community and gains (or, in this case, re-gains) honour. A feast is a gesture of solidarity with and respect for those invited.

But there is also a huge risk here. What if the invitees refuse to come? If the father throws a party and the villagers do not come, they will have signalled their unwillingness to reconcile with the family. That is always a risk in such a situation and if it occurs the family will be worse off than they were before. By making the first move toward the village, therefore, the father risks a disastrous rejection. At this point listeners to the story would probably have been a bit on edge wondering what might happen next. But when the villagers do indeed show up, the hearer/reader would be much relieved that the desired reconciliation had succeeded.[61] The story would seem to be resolved.

'Now his elder son was in the field; and as he came and drew near to the house, he heard music and dancing. And he called one of the servants and asked what this meant. And he said to him, "Your brother has come, and your father has killed the fatted calf, because he has received him safe and sound." But he was angry and refused to go in' (15:25–28a). The second half of this parable has been disconcerting to nearly all who have read it. Up to this point the daring but generous efforts of the father have succeeded in rescuing his beleaguered family. The son has been reconciled to the father and the father and his sons to the village. The villagers have acquiesced in what is going on and all appears to be going well. The older son's refusal to come in, however, is totally unexpected. It is shocking. It is a public humiliation of the family and the father that would have taken any Middle-Eastern hearer/reader seriously aback.

The notice that the party has to be reported to the unknowing older son has put off some commentators who see this as an unrealistic situation. However, most commentators argue that it is simply a 'stage-managed' literary effect designed to set up a contrast between the two sons.[62] The first half of that explanation

---

[61] For an example of an attempt to throw a party in which the guests did not show up, see Luke 14:16–24, and chapter 11 below.

[62] Usually following Eta Linnemann, *Jesus of the Parables: Introduction and Exposition*, trans. from the 3rd German ed. by J. Sturdy (New York: Harper & Row, 1967): 10.

will probably satisfy any who recognise the art in storytelling. But the latter (traditional) notion that the story here contrasts the two sons requires a closer look.

The contrast here is not between the two sons at all. It is between the villagers and the older son. The contrast between the two sons took place earlier in the story when one asked for the inheritance, both took it, but only one left home. Now we propose to take our clue from what has just been said about the need to reconcile with the villagers and the fear that they might signal their disapproval by not showing up at the party. They do. But will the older son? There was never any question of the younger son showing up at the party. That is a given. The doubt centres on the villagers and the older son. The music and dancing signal that the villagers have indeed arrived and affirmed the reconciliation. The question then is whether the older son will follow suit.

After all, he is another of the aggrieved parties. The prodigal's loss of the money means the older brother will be the sole support of the father in his old age and likely of the prodigal as well. His interests have been damaged. Yet a reconciliation between the brothers is essential to the well-being of *all* members of the family and indeed to its relations with the larger community. If the younger son is to remain at home, a debilitating sibling rivalry would strain family interaction with outsiders—as anyone knows who has tried to stay neutral in a fight between a pair of friends. Whatever tensions remain inside the family belong there and not in public. But once again the public is drawn into the family quarrel.

Obviously the expected public role of the eldest son at a feast would be very conspicuous by his absence. Bailey reports that the current custom in the Middle East is for the oldest son to stand barefoot at the door and greet guests.[63] The present writer has experienced that same phenomenon on several occasions, notably on arriving for tea at the home of the sheik of Bethany in 1986. The oldest son introduced the father to everyone present and supervised the serving and entertainment. Whether such a role pertained in antiquity is difficult to say, but the older son's deliberate and public refusal

---

[63] Bailey, *Poet and Peasant* 194.

to come to the party leaves no doubt that he is trying to humiliate his father.[64]

'His father came out and entreated him, but he answered his father, "Lo, these many years I have served you, and I never disobeyed your command; yet you never gave me a kid, that I might make merry with my friends. But when this son of yours came, who has devoured your living with harlots, you killed for him the fatted calf!"' (15:28b–30) This is truly a remarkable scene. In the Middle East, old men do not entreat their sons. They order them. To beg is demeaning and indicates a lack of shame. The father did not seek out the younger son, but ran to protect him when he did return. Now his extraordinary behaviour in trying to keep his family together gets even more bizarre as he begs the older son to come in. It is safe to say that family reconciliation is a high priority with this father indeed.

Nonetheless, the tragedy of these lines in the story is three-fold. First, there is the fact that the father cannot convince his own son to do what the villagers did so readily. Instead, he goes in the opposite direction. As is often noted, the language of the older brother—'this son of yours'—suggests that he is attempting to dissociate himself from the rest of the family. That is what the younger son had done earlier, and here the parallel between the two sons is clear. Ibrahim Said puts it nicely: 'The difference between him and his younger brother was that the younger brother was estranged and rebellious while absent from the house, but the older son was estranged and rebellious in his heart while he was in the house.'[65] He then adds: 'The estrangement and rebellion of the younger son were evident . . . in his request to leave his father's house. The estrangement and rebellion of the older son were evident in his anger and his refusal to enter the house.'[66]

The issue, then, is plainly drawn. Who is really in and who is out? Who belongs and who does not? The villagers confirmed that the younger son was really in. He is re-accepted as a member

---

[64] Note that the elder son disregards the expected respectful address to his father; cf. 1 Tim. 5:1.
[65] Ibrahim Said, *Sharh Bisharat Luqa* (Beirut: Near East Council of Churches, 1970): 402. Translated and cited by Bailey, *Poet and Peasant*: 197.
[66] Said, *Luqa*: 403.

of both family and village. But at the end of the story the villagers publicly witness the fact that the older son is really out. He is completely disloyal. Moreover, the consequences of this would be no less devastating to the long-range prospects of the family and its place in the village than the earlier behaviour of the prodigal.

The second unfortunate display is the accusation of the older son toward his younger brother. He accuses his sibling of spending the inheritance on harlots, even though the story earlier left no such implication. He is mocking. He is cooking up a scurrilous explanation of events in the attempt to destroy his brother. This is what anthropologists call 'deviance labelling' —the attempt to pin a label on someone in order to undermine them in the public eye.[67] As Said puts it, 'He [the older son] volunteers this exaggeration in order to label his brother with this polluted accusation.'[68] If he can make the promiscuous label stick, he can destroy the younger brother's place in the family and probably in the village as well. The fear would be that down the road 'sons' of the prodigal might show up claiming family and village rights and chaos would ensue. If the older son's label sticks, therefore, the younger son would have to leave the village for good and no progeny of his could ever return.

The final discouraging comment of the older son is that the calf had been killed 'for him,' that is, for the younger brother. That is not precisely what is going on here. The calf is for the villagers, not the prodigal. It is a peace offering aimed at the community. At a secondary level it is also for the members of the prodigal's extended family who have been rescued by the actions of the father. They too have much to celebrate. Of course, if the older brother joins the party, it will also be for him because his place in the village has been restored as well. After all, he took his share of the inheritance in a manner of which the village would disapprove and thereby raised questions about his own familial loyalties. By claiming the calf was for his younger brother, then, the older son refuses to recognise the need to reconcile with the village and compounds the insult aimed at his father.

---

[67] For a full discussion of both the phenomenon and its prevalence in the gospels, see Bruce J. Malina and Jerome H. Neyrey, *Calling Jesus Names* (Sonoma, CA: Polebridge, 1988).

[68] Said, *Luqa*: 404, cited by Bailey, *Poet and Peasant*: 199.

'And he said to him, "Son, you are always with me, and all that is mine is yours. It was fitting to make merry and be glad, for this your brother was dead, and is alive; he was lost, and is found"' (15:31–32). Commentators have often noticed the term of endearment used here by the father (*teknon*:child; the vocative form indicates affection). Just as the father was compassionate toward his younger son, so he is here toward the elder. He acknowledges the son's place in the family and the fact that everything remaining belongs to him.[69]

The listening audience of course would not miss the father's playback of the older son's line ('this *son* of yours') with the critical substitution ('this *brother* of yours'). The two lines are otherwise identical in the Greek.[70] The comment that the prodigal 'was lost and is found' may well be evidence of the editorial hand of Luke, since it echoes the two parables earlier in chapter (15:6, 9). It nonetheless summarises beautifully the substance of what has happened here and provides a *family* rationale for why the older son should indeed participate.[71]

The lack of an ending to the parable has frustrated some readers. Yet it has inclined others to see in it an artful example of open-endedness that places the reader in the position of the older son: the father pleads and a decision must be made about whether or not to come to the party.[72] For the moment, however, we are content to leave the story as it is, wondering whether the older brother eventually did or did not come to the party.

---

[69] Many commentators have worried over an ambiguity in the Greek text here and translations differ. It is not clear who is supposed to rejoice. The vast majority opt for 'we' as opposed to 'you:' so the KJV, NAB, JB, TEV, NIV and the REB. The old RSV retains the ambiguity. The NRSV goes with the majority and reads, 'we.' But the choice is unnecessary. *Everyone* is supposed to be included in the celebration.

[70] Alfred Plummer, *A Critical and Exegetical Commentary on the Gospel According to S. Luke* (New York: Scribner, 1914): 379; Fitzmyer, *Luke* 1091–92; Tom Corlett, 'This Brother of Yours,' *Expository Times*, 100 (1989): 216.

[71] While most commentators treat the three parables of chapter 15 as a unit, Michael R. Austin argues that the literary connections between 15:11–32 and 16:1–8 are far more significant: 'The Hypocritical Son,' *Evangelical Quarterly*, 57 (1985): 307–15.

[72] For the parable's conclusion being an open-ended invitation see Bailey and Plummer. Fitzmyer thinks the issue inappropriate because it detracts from the Lukan story of a loving father.

Our final question has to do with why Jesus might have told this story about the chaotic life of a village family and the attempts of the father to reconcile things gone wrong. Obviously it is the kind of story any peasant could easily identify with and understand. It clearly commends the valiant struggles of the beleaguered, if somewhat foolish, father. It is a story which depends on the dynamics of real village life.

Hearers might initially have been scandalised at the behaviour of the father and the two sons, but perhaps grudgingly recognised that the older son at least stayed home. As the younger son woke up to his family identity, however, and as the father risked everything to restore the situation, they might quickly recognise that they judged father and prodigal a bit hastily. Ultimately, both recognised the gravity of the situation. The actions of the father to protect his son and then to reconcile the family to the village would likely have evoked admiration. The father's respect for the community would have been especially gratifying. Perhaps the erratic members of a community should not be judged too quickly.

Would stories about family reconciliation make any sense in the setting of Jesus? No doubt they would, especially to the quarrelsome, fictive kin-group (disciples, followers) Jesus gathered around himself (Luke 9:46–50, 11:23, 22:24–27, Gos. Thom 12; POxy 1224). In the face of the all too common family conflict in peasant societies (the ideal notwithstanding), this story affirms responsibility to both family and community. It even affirms generosity of spirit in the face of scurrilous behaviour. In the setting of Jesus that message seems plausible indeed.

If one takes a step back from the details of the story and thinks about what is going on as the plot unfolds, it is obvious that one of the key things being celebrated here is the return of a villager who had gone to the city, with tragic consequences. Since the non-elite populations of the cities came primarily from those separated from village families by debt, non-inheritance or family dispute, the experience of the prodigal would have been all too familiar to peasant hearers of Jesus. The story would celebrate the return of one of their own who had experienced the devastating impact of the city upon displaced peasants. Moreover, if Richard Horsley is correct that the social revolution of Jesus was aimed at the renewal of local community and the resolution of community conflict, the place of the story in the ministry of Jesus would be even clearer.[73] It would call into question the fatal attraction peasants felt toward the city and offer scepticism about reliance on elite institutions such as patronage. Above all it would celebrate the reconciliatory efforts of the father and force open the question of participation (the older son) in community reconciliation on the part of the hearer.

Like many of the stories of Jesus, this one features persons who break all the conventional rules of honour. After all, this is a foolish father who divides his estate while alive, runs to rescue a shameless son, begs another son bent on humiliating him in public. Like the story of a foolish shepherd who leaves ninety-nine sheep to rescue one, this one also suggests an improbable sort of kingdom in which prudence is not the highest value. With respect to Jesus that sort of comment has a familiar ring.

---

[73] Richard Horsley, *Jesus and the Spiral of Violence: Popular Jewish Resistance in Roman Palestine* (San Francisco: Harper & Row, 1987): 246–84.

10

The Shocking Prospect of Killing the Messiah

(Luke 20:9–19)

The Parable of the Wicked Tenants

J. C. O'NEILL

The Text in Translation

A man planted a vineyard, and leased it to tenants, and went to another country for a long time. When the season came, he sent a slave to the tenants in order that they might give him his share of the produce of the vineyard; but the tenants beat him, and sent him away empty-handed. Next he sent another slave; that one also they beat and insulted, and sent away empty-handed. And he sent still a third; this one also they wounded and threw out. Then the owner of the vineyard said, 'What shall I do? I will send my beloved son; perhaps they will respect him.' But when the tenants saw him, they discussed it among themselves and said, 'This is the heir; let us kill him so that the inheritance may be ours.' So they threw him out of the vineyard and killed him. What then will the owner of the vineyard do to them? He will come and destroy those tenants and give the vineyard to others.

In 1945 or 1946, some Egyptian peasant farmers, looking for fertiliser in the ruins of an ancient cemetery at Nag Hammadi in Upper Egypt, about fifty miles downstream from Luxor, discovered a jar containing papyri, among which was the Gospel of Thomas. Logion 65 of that Gospel gives a shorter version of the Parable of the Wicked Tenants found in the canonical Gospels at Matthew 21:33–46, Mark 12:1–12, Luke 20:9–19. The Gospel of Thomas Logion 65 reads:

A good man had a vineyard. He gave it to tenants that they might cultivate it and he might receive its fruit from them.

165

He sent his servant so that the tenants might give him the
fruit of the vineyard. They seized his servant; they beat him;
a little more and they would have killed him. The servant came
and told his master. His master said, 'Perhaps he did not pay
due honour to them [literally: he did not *know* them; see Matt
25:12, 1 Thess. 5:12 for know in this sense].' He sent another
servant. The tenants beat him as well. Then the owner sent
his son. He said, 'Perhaps they will respect my son.' Since the
tenants knew that he was the heir of the vineyard, they seized
him. They killed him. Let whoever has ears hear.

This parable, like the Gospel parables, had attached to it a
citation of Psalm 118:22: 'Jesus said, "Show me the stone which
the builders rejected. It is the cornerstone."' When we print
Luke's version parallel to the Gospel of Thomas, omitting only
the section about what the owner will do to the tenant farmers,
we discover an almost perfect match. The only substantial
difference is that the Gospel of Thomas does not have the sending of the third servant before the man sends his son.

TABLE I: PARABLE OF THE WICKED TENANTS IN LUKE AND THOMAS

Luke (omitting section Z, below)   Gospel of Thomas

Luke (omitting section Z, below)	Gospel of Thomas
A: A man planted a vineyard, and let it out to tenants.	A: A good man had a vineyard. He gave it to tenants that they might cultivate it and he might receive its fruit from them.
B: When the time came, he sent a servant to the tenants, that they should give him some of the fruit of the vineyard; but the tenants beat him, and sent him away empty-handed.	B: He sent his servant so that the tenants might give him the fruit of the vineyard. They seized his servant; they beat him; a little more and they would have killed him. His master said, 'Perhaps he did not pay due honour to them.'
C: And he sent another servant; him also they beat and treated shamefully, and sent him away empty-handed.	C: He sent another servant. The tenants beat him as well.

D: And he sent yet a third; this one they wounded and cast out.	
E: Then the owner of the vineyard said, 'What shall I do? I will send my beloved son; it may be they will respect him.'	E: Then the owner sent his son. He said, 'Perhaps they will respect my son.'
F: But when the tenants saw him, they said to themselves, 'This is the heir; let us kill him, that the inheritance may be ours.' And they cast him out of the vineyard and killed him.	F: Since the tenants knew that he was the heir of the vineyard, they seized him. They killed him.
	G: Let whoever has ears hear.

Here is Matthew's version, with the parallels from Mark's version, but in each case printing only the parts where there are no extensive parallels in the Gospel of Thomas.

TABLE II: PARABLE OF THE WICKED TENANTS IN MATTHEW AND MARK

Matthew	Mark
W: There was a householder who planted a vineyard, and set a hedge around it, and dug a wine press in it, and built a tower, and let it out to tenants, and went into another country.	W: A man planted a vineyard, and set a hedge around it, and dug a pit for the wine press, and built a tower, and let it out to tenants, and went into another country.
X: When the season of fruit drew near, he sent his servants to the tenants, to get his fruit; and the tenants took his servants and beat one, killed another, and stoned another.	
Y: Again he sent other servants, more than the first, and they did the same to them.	Y: And so with many others, some they beat and some they killed.

Matthew	*Mark*
Z: When therefore the owner of the vineyard comes, what will he do to those tenants?' They said to him, 'He will grievously ruin[1] those wicked men and let out the vineyard to other tenants who will give him the fruits in their seasons.'	Z: What will the owner of the vineyard do? He will come and ruin the tenants, and give the vineyard to others. [Luke 20:15b, 16: What then will the owner of the vineyard do to them? He will come and destroy those tenants, and give the vineyard to others.' When they hard this, they said, 'God forbid.']

The fact that Matthew's material not in the Gospel of Thomas makes a complete parable is striking. The actors here are only the absentee owner and the tenants, but those two sets of actors are sufficient to make a coherent story. Perhaps, then, this was another parable that had been combined with the parable represented more purely by Luke and most purely by the Gospel of Thomas.

The case for positing that this was once an independent parable is strengthened when we compare the material in Matthew not in Luke or the Gospel of Thomas with similar material in Mark. Notice, first, that Mark contains a section, Mark 12:5b, that has always struck commentators as superfluous: the reference to many other servants in addition to the three servants already sent and mistreated in various ways with increasing severity. Notice, next, that this material runs parallel to Matthew, for in Matthew both the sendings are of servants in the plural.

---

[1] I have modified the RSV translation at this point. The words usually translated *put them to a miserable death* are not quite as strong as that. The verb means *to ruin*, and the ruin often, in context, involves complete destruction. Here, however, no one would think that even a great landowner had the power of summary execution. The addition of the adverb *grievously* implies a lesser punishment than death, for death would not be likely to have degrees in this context. (J. Duncan M. Derrett, 'The Parable of the Wicked Vinedressers,' *Law in the New Testament* [London: Darton, Longman & Todd, 1970]: 286–312. At page 308, Derrett makes much the same point: the owner 'ejected the tenants (he was in no position to put them to death— the word *apolesei* by no means suggests this), ruined them, and put others in their room.')

The most likely conclusion is this. The Gospel of Thomas preserved a parable that was also available to the canonical Gospel collections. All three Synoptic Gospels reproduced other versions of this parable. There was also a second parable which all three canonical Evangelists took as variants of the first parable. Matthew's Gospel preserved this second parable in its entirety, choosing to replace the features of the original parable that I have marked B and C with the features I have marked X and Y from the second parable. Mark added to his version of the first parable two features that are not clearly in the Gospel of Thomas version (the reference to the delegation consisting of many servants, marked Y above, and the section about what the absent landlord would do to his tenants when he returned, marked Z above). Luke preserved only one feature of the second parable (the section I have marked Z, about what the absent landlord would do to his tenants when he returned). Only the old, over-simplified theory that our Gospel of Mark was the source for both the Gospel of Matthew and the Gospel of Luke has stood in the way of the conclusion now forced on us by the discovery of the Gospel of Thomas, namely, that Matthew, Mark, and Luke are using as sources two parables, and each of them is using them in a distinctive way, while the Gospel of Thomas had as his source only one of these two parables.[2] We do not need the hypothesis that the variations between our four versions are due to the editorial work of the compiler of each. Every difference between the four versions we possess can be explained as either different use of the available sources or as the sort of minor embellishment or variation that always arose as stories were told and retold by the original storyteller and subsequent storytellers.

Modern discussion of the canonical versions of the parable have been dominated by Jülicher's charge that the story so obviously referred allegorically to the death of Jesus that it could not have been told by him during his lifetime but must have been made up by some member of the early church. 'The whole thing, though expressed in the tone of voice of a prophet, is the view of history of a mediocrity who had lived through Jesus'

[2] See further J. C. O'Neill, 'The Lost Written Records of Jesus' Words and Deeds behind our Records,' *Journal of Theological Studies*, n.s. 42 (1991): 483–504.

crucifixion and still believed in him as the Son of God; every original feature, any finer psychological touches in the depiction of the vinedressers or the master, all poetic freshness is missing, and the parable itself breaks off in a quite unusual way in that those addressed understand it . . .' (referring to testimony in all three canonical Gospels that the leaders of Israel understood the parable as a reference to them [Matt. 21:45–46, Mark 12:12, Luke 20:19]).[3]

Dodd, whose treatment was largely followed by Jeremias, opposed Jülicher.[4] Dodd's reconstruction of the original story, made long before the discovery of the Gospel of Thomas, corresponded remarkably to its wording: 'He sent to the cultivators at the season a slave to receive from the cultivators (the amount due) from the produce of the vineyard; and they took and beat him and sent him away empty-handed. And again he sent to them another slave, and him they beheaded and outraged. He still had a favourite son. He sent him to them last of all.'[5]

Dodd and Jeremias and their numerous successors have made a good case for saying that the story is a story that could have happened, and a story that would enlist the sympathy of an audience at the time of Jesus. Both the parables that I have isolated are realistic, in the sense that tenants at the time could well have treated roughly and sent away empty-handed the owner of a vineyard's envoys who were sent to collect the agreed proportion of the crop each year when the harvest was ready. The first parable, which culminates in the owner's sending his only son and heir, is also realistic. It remains to notice some more recent defences of realism that perhaps throw new light on the setting of the parables.

---

[3] Adolf Jülicher, *Die Gleichnisreden Jesu*, 2nd part, *Auslegung der Gleichnisreden der drei ersten Evangelien* (Freiburg I.B, Leipzig, Tübingen: Mohr, 1899): 406.

[4] C. H. Dodd, *The Parables of the Kingdom*, 3rd ed. (London: Nisbet, 1936), 124–32; rev. ed. (London and Glasgow: Collins, 1961): 93–98. Joachim Jeremias, *Die Gleichnisse Jesu*, Abhandlungen zur Theologie des Alten und Neuen Testaments, 11 (Zürich: Zwingli Verlag, 1947): 45–49; 3rd ed. (1954); *The Parables of Jesus*, trans. S. H. Hooke (London: SCM Press, 1954): 55–60; 6th ed. (Zürich: Zwingli Verlag, 1962; London: SCM Press, 1963), 70–77; 10th ed. (Göttingen: Vandenhoeck & Ruprecht, 1984): 67–75.

[5] Dodd, 1st ed. (1935): 129; Fontana ed.(1961): 96.

In the second parable (Table II) the owner has just opened up a new vineyard. William R. Herzog II[6] has argued that the very opening up of a new vineyard could well have implied that the peasant farmers who were left to work the property were the former owners who had been dispossessed by the new owner. The tenants would then be ready to do anything to wrest back their property from him. If the three years of the story were the first three years of the new vineyard, then there would be precious little crop (no grapes, only vegetables grown between the rows of vines) with which to pay the owner his share, and every reason for the tenants to claim that their expenditure exceeded any income the owner might have thought was his due.

I think it unlikely that the story would hinge on the tenants' having been the previous owners, without the storyteller's having said so. Herzog further suggests that the story assumed that the peasant farmers had a legitimate grievance, although it taught also, according to this view, that resort to violence would be futile and lead to ruin. On the contrary, the whole point of the story was to enlist the sympathies of the hearers for the owner. The Gospel of Thomas specifically labels him a good man, and that fits the rest of the narrative.

Nevertheless, Herzog is right to emphasise that the tactic of denying the rent for two or three years in succession could raise the possibility of the tenants being able eventually to claim ownership. Derrett has argued that the sending of the son in the fourth year, as a member of the owner's household, perhaps invested with part-ownership of the property, would be a necessary step in defending the owner's ownership.[7] Whatever the truth of that assertion about Jewish law, it seems more important to accept Jeremias's suggestion that the tenants rightly supposed that the son was the heir, and then jumped to the false conclusion that the father was dead, and that by killing the heir, they could claim ownership of the property by virtue of possession. The sending of the son is a sign of the goodness of the owner.

Another feature of the Gospel of Thomas emphasises this point. In the Gospel of Thomas version of the return of the

---

[6] William R. Herzog II, *Parables as Subversive Speech: Jesus as Pedagogue of the Oppressed* (Louisville, Kentucky: Westminster/John Knox, 1994): 98–113.
[7] 'Wicked Vinedressers:' 286–312.

servant sent to collect the first year's rent the owner takes account of the possibility that his own servant did not treat the tenants with the respect due to them. Here is an owner who wants the agreed rent, it is true, but thinks that the tenants are to be treated properly. We must conclude that the eventual sending of his son in the first parable (Table I) is a sign of this generosity of mind. The hearers are meant to admire the owner and to be horrified at the reaction of the tenants—while fully understanding the temptation to which they succumbed. If the story really did break off with the death of the son, as it is best to assume, then the hearers were left with plenty to think about. As a story, it is a story of human ingratitude.

Both Dodd and Jeremias emphasised that, although the story was not an allegory made up by some nameless Christian after the death of Jesus, as Jülicher had supposed, it had a definite religious meaning on the lips of Jesus, and a religious meaning that regarded the owner of the vineyard as God and the son as at least a very important prophet. J. D. Crossan has tried to defend the religious value of the parable and its origin in the teaching of Jesus without allowing that the father referred, allegorically, to God and the son to Jesus.[8] He divides the Synoptic parables into two classes, genuine parables of Jesus which are stories that seek 'so to articulate the speaker's experience as to draw the hearer into a like encounter,' and parables made up by the early church which follow a didactic form that either is allegorical or is an example-story. If this parable is genuine, it has to work in the first way and not be an allegory.

Crossan rightly saw that the Isaiah reference and the story of the punishment of the tenants did not belong to one of the original parables. He then took this pared-down parable (my Table I) as a parable designed to shock the hearers into emulating the boldness of the tenants who saw their chance and took it. However, it seems to me that the story would still have allegorical features, for the opportunity to own the vineyard would correspond to the opportunity to become members of the kingdom of God, and the teacher would be recommending the hearers to follow the example of the tenants—save for the

---

[8] J. D. Crossan, 'The Wicked Husbandmen,' *Journal of Biblical Literature* 90 (1971): 451–65 (462).

wickedness. The parable could hardly be just a general proverb about striking when the iron is hot, to reinforce the lesson that nothing risked, nothing gained.

Crossan is right that all parables were told by an artist who could imagine important human experiences, like that of losing one of the ten coins, or of meeting as children with cold indifference from friends who would not join in playing weddings or funerals. The story was told to draw the hearers into like experiences. Nevertheless, the purpose of telling the story was not just to amuse or to convey general human wisdom. The purpose of all the parables seems to have been to teach the hearers to have in mind the life and death experience all would face on the Day of Judgement. The parable of the wicked husbandmen was certainly not exempt from the poetic features that Crossan stressed as the mark of genuine parables of Jesus. The chief poetic feature in this case was irony. The tenants rightly supposed that the son was the heir, and they guessed that the father was dead and that only the heir's continued life stood between them and the ownership of the vineyard. But the supreme irony lay, I would argue, in the possibility that the son was the Messiah and the owner God. If that was what was at stake, God cannot die and, as for the Messiah, although he can be killed, he cannot finally be overcome. The tenants in the story did not know for certain the true situation. Neither did the hearers who were aware of the possible divine significance of the set-up, not knowing for certain whether the Messiah had yet been born, nor, if he had, who he was.

Jülicher's charge that the story was allegorical was used to deny it to the corpus of the genuine parables of Jesus. Dodd and Jeremias and their successors have successfully shown that the parable was realistic. They did not feel obliged, in defending the realistic nature of the parable, to deny that it bore allegorical features on Jesus' lips.

There is no doubt that the great owner of Matthew 21:33 and the 'man' of all three canonical Gospels and the Gospel of Thomas could have been taken to stand for God. Any story about an owner of a vineyard would immediately summon up images of God and of Israel, God's own people, for the vineyard planted with vines or the vine itself is a commonplace reference to Israel. This allusion would have been as well known to the audience of

Parable 1 as to the audience of Parable 2, for they were all familiar with Psalm 80:8, 'Thou hast brought a vine out of Egypt,' and with the various allusions to the destruction that awaits the vine that disappoints the expectation of the owner who planted it (Isa. 27:2–3, 6; Jer. 2:21; Ezek. 15:6–7, 17:6–10, 19:10–14). Isaiah 5 is drawn upon explicitly in Parable 2, though not in the exact order of Isaiah, and with a different point, since this vineyard has produced good grapes, enough to sustain the reasonable expectation in the owner that rent was due (like the vineyard in the Song of Songs 8:11–12), not sour grapes as in Isaiah 5 and Jeremiah 2:21. Aaron A. Milavec has rightly drawn attention to this feature of the parable to show us that the parable was not directed against Israel as such, which in the parable is good, productive and to be preserved, but to the leaders of Israel, the tenant farmers.[9]

It is more controversial to argue, as I shall do, that the son must, in the hearer's understanding, have had to refer to the Messiah. Jeremias in the first edition of his book contented himself with saying:

> The introduction of the figure of the only son is the result, not of theological considerations, but of the inherent logic of the story. This does not exclude, but rather requires that by the slaying of the owner's son the parable may point to the actual situation, namely, the rejection of God's definite and final message.[10]

This sentence was repeated in the third edition but he added that the audience would not have had the idea that Jesus (whom Jeremias always insisted first told the story) was referring to the Messiah since 'the allegorical application of the "son" to the Son of God would have been entirely foreign to the minds of his audience.'[11] In the revised sixth edition, he said, more cautiously, that 'there can be no doubt that in the sending of the son Jesus

---

[9] Aaron A. Milavec, 'Mark's Parable of the Wicked Husbandmen as Reaffirming God's Predilection for Israel,' *Journal of Ecumenical Studies*, 26 (1989): 289–312; 'The Identity of "the son" and "the others:" Mark's Parable of the Wicked Husbandmen Reconsidered,' *Biblical Theology Bulletin*, 20 (1990): 30–37.

[10] J. Jeremias, *Die Gleichnisse Jesu* (Zürich: Zwingli Verlag, 1947): 48; *Parables of Jesus* (1954): 60.

[11] Idem, *Die Gleichnisse Jesu*, 3rd ed. (Zürich: Zwingli Verlag, 1954); *Parables of Jesus* (1954): 57.

himself had his own sending in mind, but for the mass of his hearers the Messianic significance of the son could not be taken for granted . . .'[12] By the tenth edition, he even allows that the hearers could have recognised that Jesus had his own sending in mind. After noting that the early church could not have made up an allegorical story without mentioning the resurrection, he continues: 'Yet in the situation of Jesus, to which we are accordingly driven back, the murder of the son would be a fitting climax for the hearers. They would have understood that Jesus in mentioning the son had himself in mind as the last of God's messengers.'[13] But Jeremias always insisted that *Son of God* was not a messianic term in pre-Christian Palestinian Judaism, and he was able to cite Kümmel in his support.[14] Jeremias dismissed the messianic use of the word *son* in 1 (Ethiopic) Enoch 105:2 as too late; in 4 Ezra (2 Esdras) 7:28–29; 13:32, 37, 52; 14:9 as referring to the Servant rather than to the Son; and he regarded 5 Ezra (2 Esdras) 2:47 as a Christian work. But we now have strong evidence from Qumran that *Son of God*, a title drawn from 2 Sam. 7:14 (1 Chron. 17:13); Psalm 2:7; 89:26–27, was well established at the time of Jesus (4Q Florilegium 2:11–12; 4Q 246). It is likely, then, that any mention of the son of the owner would also raise in the hearers' minds the possibility that the storyteller was talking about the Messiah.

This then raises the possibility that Jesus could speak of the Messiah as destined to die. Jeremias and many others have strenuously denied that the death of the Messiah was a notion that had occurred to any Jewish mind before the early church began to assert that their crucified leader was indeed the Messiah. However, if the parable is to work, it must, according to the preceding argument, have been perfectly possible for Jesus' audience to have contemplated the awful possibility that the 'tenants of the vineyard' could even put to death the Messiah, the Son of God. The parable is not teaching a new doctrine that the Messiah could be put to death; the parable only works as a

---

[12] Idem, *Die Gleichnisse Jesu*, 6th ed. (1962); *The Parables of Jesus*, (1963): 72–73.
[13] Idem, *Die Gleichnisse Jesu*, 10th ed. (1984): 70–71.
[14] 'Das Gleichnis von den bösen Weingärtnern (Mk 12, 1–9).' *Aux Sources de la Tradition Chrétienne, Mélanges offerts à M. Goguel.* Neuchâtel-Paris, 1950: 120–31. Reprinted in Werner Georg Kümmel, Heilsgeschehen und Geschichte. Gesammelte Aufsätze 1933–64. Edited by Erich Graesser, Otto Merk and Adolf Fritz. Marburg: N. G. Elwert Verlag, 1965: 207–17.

parable if the audience is perfectly familiar with the possibility that the Messiah could be killed, for the shock of the parable rests on the basis of the assumption that people who saw themselves as God's 'tenants' could act in such a shocking way as to think that they could get possession of the property by killing the very Son of the living God. The parable works because the hearers were forced to face this awful reading of their own situation. That implies that the hearers were perfectly familiar with a theology of the Messiah that held that he would first come as a mortal human being whose identity was hidden except to the eyes of faith.[15]

---

[15] See J. C. O'Neill, *Who Did Jesus Think He Was?* (Leiden: Brill, 1995).

11

Unexpected Banquet People
(Luke 14:16–24)

The Parable of the Great Feast

WILLARD M. SWARTLEY

The Text in Translation

Someone gave a great dinner and invited many. At the time
for the dinner he sent his slave to say to those who had been
invited, 'Come; for everything is ready now.' But they all alike
began to make excuses. The first said to him, 'I have bought
a piece of land, and I must go out and see it; please accept
my regrets.' Another said, 'I have bought five yoke of oxen,
and I am going to try them out; please accept my regrets.'
Another said, 'I have just been married, and therefore I
cannot come.' So the slave returned and reported this to his
master. Then the owner of the house became angry and said
to his slave, 'Go out at once into the streets and lanes of the
town and bring in the poor, the crippled, the blind, and the
lame.' And the slave said, 'Sir, what you ordered has been
done, and there is still room.' Then the master said to the
slave, 'Go out into the roads and lanes, and compel people
to come in, so that my house may be filled. For I tell you,
none of those who were invited will taste my dinner.'

This parable in its present three extant versions (Matt. 22:1–
14; Luke 14:16–24; Gospel of Thomas 64) demonstrates well
the pliability of the Jesus tradition in the service of different
writers and communities of faith. The main point in each appears
to be different: for Matthew, it is judgement upon those who
refused the banquet invitation; for Luke, inclusion of the
Gentiles represented by his distinctive third invitational call;
and for Thomas, admonition of those who allow business to
crowd out the feast of the kingdom. For purposes of comparison
the three versions may be set out in parallel form thus:

177

Matt. 22:1–14

Once more Jesus spoke to them in parables, saying: 'The kingdom of heaven may be compared to a king who gave a wedding banquet for his son. He sent his slaves to call those who had been invited to the wedding banquet, but they would not come. Again he sent other slaves, saying, "Tell those who have been invited: Look, I have prepared my dinner, my oxen and my fat calves have been slaughtered, and everything is ready; come to the wedding banquet." But they made light of it and went away, one to his farm, another to his business, while the rest seized his slaves, mistreated them, and killed them. The king was enraged. He sent his troops, destroyed those murderers, and burned their city. Then he said to his slaves, "The wedding is ready, but those invited were not worthy. Go therefore into the main streets, and invite everyone you find to the wedding banquet." Those slaves went out into the streets and gathered all whom they found, both good and bad; so the wedding hall was filled with guests. But when the king came in to see the guests, he noticed a man there who was not wearing a wedding robe, and he said to him, "Friend, how did you get in here without a wedding robe?" And he was speechless. Then the king said to the attendants, "Bind him hand and foot, and throw him into the outer darkness, where there will be weeping and gnashing of teeth. For many are called, but few are chosen."

Luke 14:16–24

Then Jesus said to him, 'Someone gave a great dinner and invited many. At the time for the dinner he sent his slave to say to those who had been invited, "Come; for everything is ready now." But they all alike began to make excuses. The first said to him, "I have bought a piece of land, and I must go out and see it; please accept my regrets." Another said, "I have bought five yoke of oxen, and I am going to try them out; please accept my regrets." Another said, "I have just been married, and therefore I cannot come." So the slave returned and reported this to his master. Then the owner of the house became angry and said to his slave, "Go out at once into the streets and lanes of the town and bring in the poor, the crippled, the blind, and the lame." And the slave said, "Sir, what you ordered has been done, and there is still room." Then the master said to the slave, "Go out into the roads and lanes, and compel people to come in, so that my house may be filled. For I tell you, none of those who were invited will taste my dinner."'

Gospel of Thomas 64

A man had guests, and when he had prepared the dinner, he sent his servant to summon the guests. He came to the first; he said to him. My master summons thee. He said: I have money with some merchants. They are coming to me in the evening. I will go and give them orders. I pray to be excused from the dinner. He went to another; he said to him: My master has summoned thee. He said to him: I have bought a house and they ask me for a day. I shall not have time. He came to another; he said to him: My master summons thee. He said to him: My friend is about to be married, and I am to hold a dinner. I shall not be able to come. I pray to be excused from the dinner. He went to another; he said to him: My master summons thee. He said to him: I have bought a village; I go to collect the rent. I shall not be able to come. I pray to be excused. The servant came; he said to his master: Those whom thou didst summon to the dinner have excused themselves. The master said to his servant: Go out to the road. Bring those whom thou shalt find, that they may dine. The buyers and the merchants [shall] not enter the places of my father.

(E. Hennecke trans., *New Testament Apocrypha*, London, 1963).

While all three versions portray a feast/dinner to which invited guests[1] refuse to come, basic differences appear in the three accounts. Both Miller and Stein begin their studies of this parable by noting these differences.[2] In Matthew the host is a king who throws a wedding feast for his son, but in Luke and Thomas the host is simply a man who hosts a banquet. Matthew's meal is a marriage feast (*gamos*), but in Luke and Thomas it is simply a banquet (*deipnon*). In Matthew servants (plural) are sent out, but in Luke and Thomas only one servant goes out to extend the invitations. In Matthew the first group receiving the invitation makes no excuses (only 'they would not come'); in Luke those receiving the invitation give three different excuses, while Thomas has the servant of the Master giving four invitations to separate people, with four excuses (merchants coming tonight to repay a loan; purchased a house; having to direct a wedding banquet(!); and bought a village). On the second sending, in Matthew some of those who refused made light of the invitation and went off, one to the farm and another to business, and the others mocked, persecuted, and killed the servants. In Luke and Thomas the servant is only politely refused. In Matthew the king (now *angered* as is the host in Luke, but not so stated in Thomas) then mobilises troops to destroy both those who murdered his servants and their city. None of this occurs in Luke or Thomas. Instead, Luke narrates a third call to still another group, with great care to distinguish it from the second group. Further, Luke emphasises that all the spaces are to be filled! Thomas narrates the first round of invitations and excuses in great detail but, the second invitation is brief, followed by a concluding moralism against the rich, with the *master* saying to the servant, 'Go out to the road. Bring those whom you will find, that they may dine. The buyers and the merchants [shall] not

[1] Most commentators point out that the Palestinian custom of inviting late afternoon dinner guests (for the second and last meal of the day) would have included an earlier invitation, and that this call to come to the dinner was the second—all is now ready—invitation, reminding the guests and calling them to come now. This information, based on the customs, is not in the parable, and strains the story, for it makes the refusals problematic. More significant, the designation, 'the guests,' indicates some long-standing invitation, thus identifying the first group as God's covenant people.
[2] John W. Miller, *Step By Step Through the Parables* (New York/Ramsey: Paulist, 1981): 109–10; Robert H. Stein, *An Introduction to the Parables of Jesus* (Philadelphia: Westminster, 1981): 83.

[enter] into the places (*topoi*) of my father.' Luke ends his story with a pronouncement, ' . . . none of those who were invited shall taste my banquet.' Matthew moves directly to a related parable, the guest without a wedding garment.

Scholars divide over which version is closest to Jesus' original, as Fitzmyer recounts.[3] None of the positions is totally satisfactory, even though the Gospel of Thomas appears less encumbered with obvious concerns of the later church (providing warrant for judgement upon the Jews and their city of Jerusalem, and empowering the church in its Gentile mission). But Thomas joins this parable to that of the rich fool (cf. Luke 12:16–20),[4] and thus manifests a redactional hand to show Jesus' critique of business and riches as hindrances to the demands of the kingdom. We might think this to be vintage Jesus, but this is clearly also the mark of the Lukan hand and *The Shepherd of Hermas* in the early second century, followed by numerous patristic writers. If one uses R. Bultmann's axiom 'neither Jewish nor later church' to determine the assured historical Jesus core, then Thomas' version is manifestly suspect as historical, for warnings against riches permeate Old Testament writings. In my judgement, this method of discounting on the basis of 'known Jewish or later church emphases' simply does not get us to Jesus. To assess the issue of 'earliest' among the three versions by another consideration, we note that Luke generally is strong on warnings against riches. Thus it is difficult to explain Luke's exclusion of the ending in Thomas if that version were the original. Rather than search for the assured minimum of the words of the historical Jesus, we do well rather to hear the voice of Jesus in the Gospels as the apostolic church's faithful witness to Jesus' teachings together with their appropriating them into the needs and circumstances of their times.

Nonetheless, as Jeremias observes, the core of teaching, derived from the Q-Sayings or oral tradition behind all three versions accentuates two points: (1) warning against spurning

---

[3] Joseph A. Fitzmyer, *The Gospel According to Luke X–XXIV*, Anchor Bible, vol. 28 (Garden City, NY: Doubleday, 1985): 1050–52. For an analysis of what portions of the Lukan version are from Luke and what from the tradition behind Luke, see Detley Dormeyer, 'Literarische und theologische Analyse der Parable Lukas 14, 15–24,' *BibLeb*, 15 (1974): 207–11.

[4] See Beavis, chapter 4 above, p. 57, and note 11.

the offer of the kingdom, directed originally against Jesus' Jewish hearers, the expected guests at the banquet, and (2) Jesus' offer of salvation to the tax collectors and sinners, those invited when the first declined.[5] But even this reflects 'salvation history' theology so much evident in Matthew and Luke. To point to parallel stories in the culture of the time, as Jeremias then does to establish historical plausibility,[6] only compounds the problem, for then anyone could have told the story. We must rather turn to another direction of inquiry to grasp adequately the meaning(s) of the parable.

John R. Donahue has pointed us in a productive direction by studying the parables in relation to the meaning they carry within the respective gospel traditions.[7] I have also developed Matthew's point of view in this section of his Gospel to show that emphases of the parable carry forward a larger narrative purpose[8] and to show that the Jewish religious leaders are under judgement because they did not respond to, but rather in hostility objected to, Jesus' invitations of salvation to them *and* to those marginalized from free worship of God. The immediate context in this section begins with the triumphal entry and the dramatic act in the temple court. Even there Matthew brings in a special note that prepares for the emphases in the parable of the feast. Jesus healed the blind and lame in the temple, and thereby disregarded David's prohibition in 2 Samuel 5:8, which forbade the blind and the lame to enter the temple. Now even for the 'blind and the lame'—referring perhaps to Israel's Jebusite enemies[9]—salvation has come, and they are welcomed into the

[5] Joachim Jeremias, *The Parables of Jesus* (6th ed. trans. S. H. Hooke (New York: Scribner's, 1963): 176–80.

[6] Jeremias, *Parables*: 178–79.

[7] John R. Donahue, *The Gospel in Parable: Metaphor, Narrative and Theology in the Synoptic Gospels* (Philadelphia: Fortress Press, 1988).

[8] Willard M. Swartley, *Israel's Scripture-Traditions and the Synoptic Gospels: Story Shaping Story* (Peabody, MA: Hendrickson, 1994): 172–76.

[9] Robert H. Gundry says that the context of 2 Sam. 5:8 indicates that David by the phrase, 'lame and the blind,' was referring to the Jebusites. Jesus' action of healing 'denies the Jews' false deduction from David's statement (cf. 1QSa 2:19–25; 1QM 7:4–5; 4QD^b/CD 15:15–17; m. Hag. 1:1),' in *Matthew: A Commentary on His Literary and Theological Art* (Grand Rapids: Eerdmans): 413. If Matthew's Jesus corrected the Jews' misunderstanding of 'blind and lame,' then he also reversed David's policy against the enemy: rather than exclude, Jesus welcomed and healed, i.e. transformed the symbol of enmity into a condition of shalom—they were welcomed to the holy place.

temple! The children acclaim: 'Hosanna to the Son of David.' But the chief priests and the scribes were indignant (21:15d). This indignation, in opposition to God's offer of salvation in Jesus, sets the atmosphere for all that follows until Jesus leaves the temple, never to return (24:1).

The subsequent extended narrative shows God's judgement upon those who refuse God's offer of salvation. Each segment of the narrative ends with a harsh word of judgement against those who indignantly resisted God's offer of salvation:

> **Ending 1:** Truly, I tell you, the tax collectors and the prostitutes are going into the kingdom of God ahead of you. For John came to you in the way of righteousness, and you did not believe him, but the tax collectors and the prostitutes believed him; and even when you saw it, you did not change your minds and believe him (21:31b–32).

> **Ending 2:** Have you never read in the scriptures: 'The stone which the builders rejected has become the cornerstone; this was the Lord's doing, and it is amazing in our eyes?' (21: 42)

> **Ending 3:** 'Go therefore into the main streets, and invite everyone you find to the wedding banquet' (22:9), and to the one without a wedding garment, 'Bind him hand and foot, and cast him into the outer darkness; where there will be weeping and gnashing of teeth. For many are called, but few are chosen' (22:13b–14).

These concluding words to Matthew's twin parable of the feast and the guest without a wedding garment reiterate the key points of this section on two complementary levels: *others* are now invited to the marriage feast and if one—one who still thinks he is entitled to manage the vineyard and the kingdom—shows up at the feast with no wedding garment because he says in his heart that this is not the time of God's *wedding* feast, he will be shut out into outer darkness.[10]

---

[10] In the communities receiving and using Matthew's Gospel, these parables—as well as the narrative more broadly—functioned on two levels: to explain Jesus' rejection by the Jewish leaders together with Israel's standing outside the Messianic community and to warn Christians against presumption upon their own standing. As John R. Donahue puts it, 'they summon Christians who are the heirs of Matthew, not merely to respond with promises of labour in the vineyard, but to bear fruit and to "put on Christ" by deeds of justice and charity' (*Gospel in Parable*. 96).

To understand Matthew's 'differences' from Luke or Thomas requires entering into Matthew's Gospel at a sustained narrative level. This is true not only of this parable, but also for all stories and teaching in any of the Gospels and extra-canonical writings as well. For, as Donahue notes, Thomas's version reflects certain gnostic interests, with which the Gospel has been associated: '"Businessmen and merchants will not enter" reflects the gnostic rejection of worldly activity, and the change of the excuse from the marriage to the hosting of a marriage feast may reflect gnostic rejection of marriage.'[11]

Beyond this observation it is not possible to observe Thomas's narrative flow of emphasis because Thomas, unlike the canonical Gospels, does not have narrative structure and development, but rather resembles the style of Proverbs, strings of sayings of Jesus linked sometimes by similar recurring 'hook-words.'

Luke's version must also be understood within his larger emphases. In Luke the parable occurs within the journey section that develops themes of 'journeying banquet guest and rejected prophet,' 'journey to peace and justice,' and 'journey to conquest and judgement of evil.'[12] Luke definitely likes banquets. His story overflows with three special features: banquets, peace, and forgiven sinners. Quite aptly, David Moessner titles his exposition of Luke's theology, *Lord of the Banquet*.[13] The journey narrative is strewn with banquets at almost every intersection: 10:38–42 in Mary and Martha's house; 11:37–54 in a Pharisee's house; 14:1ff. in the house of a leader of the Pharisees; 14:7–11 in a parable about a wedding banquet; 14:15 in the great banquet parable (our study here); 15:23–24 in the feast for the homecoming of the sinner; and 19:1–10 in the home of Zacchaeus, the tax collector (cf. also 22:7–27; 24:13–35). Luke uses the word *peace* fourteen times in his Gospel in places where Matthew has only one parallel.[14] And Luke abounds with depictions of sinners forgiven. All this means that Luke invites us to see Jesus through the glasses of gift, grace, and celebration.

[11] Donahue, *Gospel in Parable*: 93.

[12] Swartley, *Scripture Traditions*: 133–44.

[13] David P. Moessner, *Lord of the Banquet: The Literary and Theological Significance of the Lukan Travel Narratives* (Minneapolis: Fortress Press, 1989)

[14] Willard M. Swartley, 'Politics and Peace (*Eirene*) in Luke's Gospel,' *Political Issues in Luke-Acts*, eds Richard J. Cassidy and Philip J. Scharper (Maryknoll, NY: Orbis Books, 1983): 25ff.

This parable's immediate context sets the banquet stage, in that 14:1–6 is a miracle occurring in a banquet context. Then in verses 7–14, Jesus gives instructions on proper conduct when invited to a banquet and whom to invite when giving a banquet, the same 'four-group' that recurs in the banquet parable (v. 21): 'the poor, the cripples, the lame and the blind' (v. 13).[15] Verse 14 speaks then of blessing for those who act in these ways, for they 'will be repaid at the resurrection of the just.' Immediately following the parable, in 14:25–35, come the hardest demands for discipleship that we find anywhere in the Gospels. They speak about hating—and this must certainly be hyperbole—father, mother, wife, children, brother, and sister, even life itself, in order to be Jesus' disciple. Next is the call to count the cost and to consider whether we are willing to commit to this way. To further shock, the section ends with the bold statement, 'none of you can be my disciple if you do not give up all your possessions' (14:33). Then follows a serious warning that if we are not the kind of salt that makes a difference, we are good for neither the land nor the manure heap, but must be thrown out. Rather, we are to be an influence for good in this world, as fertiliser for the land.[16] Hence, the larger literary context of the parable in Luke indicates that the extensive emphasis on banqueting is not devoid of costly discipleship. The two go hand in hand in Luke.

Verse 15 provides the transition from 14:1–14 to the banquet parable, thematically and theologically. An anonymous dinner guest connects the banquet theme to the 'kingdom of God' and thus sets the discourse within the messianic banquet theme associated with the coming of the kingdom (see esp. Isa. 25:6). As I demonstrate at length elsewhere,[17] Deuteronomic themes and structure shape Luke's journey narrative, and this parable bears this feature also.

There is a remarkable parallel between the reasons for exemption from male participation in Israel's holy war in Deuteronomy 20:5 and the excuses in Luke's parable of the great

[15] John Navone points out this and other Lukan 'dyptych' formations within this section and the larger Gospel, 'The Parable of the Banquet,' *Biblical Theology* 1, 14 (1964): 923–29.
[16] See Shillington, 'The Land,' chapter 1 above, pp. 9–11.
[17] Swartley, *Scripture Traditions*: 126–53.

banquet.[18] The excuses of the guests invited first to the banquet
echo the same reasons why male Israelites were exempted from
responding to the call to Holy War in the Deuteronomy text, as
follows:

1. Built a new house
2. Planted a vineyard
3. Engaged to a woman

The parallelism is indeed striking. The first are property
excuses; the second, work excuse—the oxen tilled the vineyard;
and the third, marital obligation. As Donahue observes, Luke's
portrayal of Jesus departs from the standard Jewish eschatological
anticipations in that 'he omits those violent elements . . .
normally associated with the eschatological banquet.'[19] Stressing
non-violence and peace, Luke's Jesus takes the parable into a
second dimension in which substitute guests are invited: the
poor, the crippled, and the lame—precisely those who in the
Qumran literature (1QM 7:4–6; 1QSa 2:5–10) were excluded
from the expected messianic banquet.[20] Even after these ritually
unclean people are gathered into the feast, a third invitation
compels more to come from the highways and hedges. Thus Luke
accentuates the inclusiveness of the kingdom banquet. And in
this echo of the earlier war tradition, the human enemy has
disappeared.

There is also a structural *inclusio* for this parable, between the
exclamation in verse 15, 'Blessed is anyone who will eat bread in
the kingdom of God,' and the concluding words, 'for I tell you,
none of those who were invited will eat of my banquet' (v. 24)!
It is clear who will *not eat,* but who *will eat?* In Luke the second
and third groups will eat of the banquet. The second group
consists of those who, as numerous commentators have rightly

[18] Donahue develops this point at length in *Gospel in Parable*: 140-46. I. Howard
Marshall notes this resemblance, but does not think it close enough to merit
consideration, *The Gospel of Luke: A Commentary on the Greek Text*, New
International Greek Text Commentary (Grand Rapids, MI: Eerdmans, 1978):
588. But when this matter is assessed in light of Luke's larger imitation of
Deuteronomy in his Journey narrative, as I have shown (Swartley, *Scripture
Traditions*: 130–32, 151–53), intended parallelism is apparent.
[19] Donahue, *Gospel in Parable*: 142.
[20] Ibid.: 144.

said, are those judged unfit for access to the holy in the Pharisaic tradition's understanding of Torah requirements (on this point, Matthew agrees). But who is the third group? David Bosch, in his dissertation, has argued persuasively that Luke signals Gentile inclusion here, for the servant goes out of the city into the country, denoted by 'the highways and byways' (*tas hodous kai phragmous*).[21] Gnilka argues the same,[22] and Wilson contends that this point in Luke is to be joined, on the basis of 24:27, to the themes of the Holy Spirit initiative and fulfilment of prophecy.[23] Indeed, these are at the core of Luke's narrative purpose.

Braun, in his study of Luke 14, questions this line of widely accepted interpretation and seeks to reconstruct the significance of these three groups against the context of Greco-Roman views on social classes. Rather than limit the second group to urban (note the use of *polis*: city in v. 21c) 'outcast Jews,' those who did not meet the demands of Pharisaic purity, he argues rather for socio-economic class structure as the key to understanding these differing groups. He contends: that some level of business transaction is present in all the excuses of the first group; that the second group likely consists of the 'filth and dregs' of urban society, those living in slum huts or tenements; and that the third group, peasants in the countryside, were those scorned by the urban-dwelling elite (the first group of guests).[24] Thus, in Braun's study, the heart of this story[25] is the conversion of the householder, the one hosting the banquet. When his invited elite

[21] David Bosch, *Die Heidenmission in der Zukunftsschau Jesu; eine Untersuchung zur Eschatologie der synoptischen Evangelien*, Abhandlungen zur Theologie des Alten und Neuen Testaments, 36 (Zurich: Zwingli Verlag, 1959): 124–31.

[22] Joachim Gnilka, *Die Verstockung Israels: Isaias 6, 9–10 in der Theologie der Synoptiker*, Studien zum Alten und Neuen Testament (Munchen: Käsel Verlag, 1961): 132–33.

[23] S. G. Wilson *The Gentiles and the Gentile Mission in Luke-Acts* (Cambridge: Cambridge University Press, 1973): 52–4, 57.

[24] Willi Braun, *Feasting and Social Rhetoric in Luke 14*, Society for New Testament Studies Monograph Series, 85 (Cambridge: Cambridge University Press, 1995): 73–97.

[25] Braun takes up at length the question of *form* for this story and the larger 14:1–24 unit. He notes that the text does not call the householder story a parable, that the miracle in vv. 1–6 does not emphasise the miracle as such, but the characterisation of the one healed (having dropsy, which he suggests to be symbolic of Jesus' critics, having a 'craving desire' [pp. 22–42]), that vv. 1–24 are a unified extended argument, and that the householder story is best understood as an elaborated argumentation based upon key *chreia* declarations (short memorable sayings; vv. 3, 5, 11, 15, 24 [pp. 145–75]).

urban guests boycotted his invitation, likely because of some social impropriety on the host's part, he experienced the shame of peer rejection. The host, questing for honour in throwing a great banquet, was demeaned, his generosity rejected. Thus the householder was forced to undergo a conversion in socio-economic values. He had to rethink his basic social and class identity, alignments, and commitments.[26] While Braun's contribution adds richness to the socio-economic dimensions of the story, it fails to assess the function of the story in its larger Lukan narrative purpose, the very point Donahue rightly suggests is the most fruitful in parable study. Braun thus misses the salvation-historical, theological, and eschatological significance of the story. The emphasis in the *inclusio* on eating 'the bread of the kingdom' and 'my banquet' signals surely the expected eschatological meal, and thus points to the messianic feast expected in the end-time, celebrating triumph over sin and evil (Isa. 25:6f., 55.1f., 65:11f., Deut.12:4–7; 1 Enoch 62:14; 2 Enoch 42:5; *Midr Esth* 1.4). While Navone holds that here the feast is a fulfilment of the Old Testament banquet prophecies,[27] others emphasise a relation between this feast and the Feast it signifies yet to come.[28] On this case there exists a tension between the frame of the parable and the story itself, a tension that binds together the present and future. If one does not come to the feast that *now* already had been prepared in Jesus' offer, one will not be eligible to eat the bread of the coming messianic feast. Further, the invitation to the feast depends not on human effort or achievement, but solely on the invitation and grace of the host Jesus.[29]

As with all Jesus' parables, many levels of meaning are potentially freed forth. Mary Ann Tolbert speaks of polyvalent meaning in the parables.[30] Eta Linnemann identifies numerous

[26] Braun, *Feasting*: 98–131.
[27] Navone, 'The Parable:' 926.
[28] Bosch correlates Luke's third call with the book of Acts, showing how the mission of the church stands between the parable in Jesus' day and the consummation of the kingdom. He suggests that the three invitations in Luke may be influenced by the Acts 1:8 pattern: Jerusalem Judea and Samaria, and the ends of the earth (*Heidenmission*: 129–30).
[29] Otto Glombitza stresses this point, 'Das Grosse Abendmahl,' *Novum Testamentum*, 5 (1962): 10–16.
[30] Mary Ann Tolbert, *Perspectives on the Parables: An Approach to Multiple Interpretations* (Philadelphia: Fortress Press, 1979).

levels of meaning the parable conveyed in its original Jesus and Gospel settings. She holds that its original emphases fell on the *now* of the banquet invitation. *Now is* the time of the kingdom, 'Today is the acceptable time' (2 Cor. 6:2)—here Jeremias asks us to see the note of joy in the parable, 'Everything is now ready!',[31] but the Pharisees spurned the opportunity, failing to see what had come to their doorstep. Haenchen underscores and extends this latter point, saying that the parable also declares that the door is now shut to those who refused to come, and thus the outsiders, the 'tax collectors and sinners,' as well as the Gentiles, are welcomed into the kingdom.[32] Similarly, Dormeyer says that Luke's use of the parable stresses both judgement upon the Pharisees for refusing the invitation and calls the readers into mission, for the 'sending out' (*apostellō*) of the servant(s) sounds the note of the gospel-mission, sending out the apostles to call people into the kingdom.[33] But later in the church's understanding, Linnemann says, the parable's meaning focused on the conflict between earthly cares and the heavenly kingdom call. Still later, the parable answered the question why those invited (God's covenant people) were not worthy to be at the banquet. Answer? Because they refused: they excluded themselves.[34] Again, in another period, it provided warrant for the mission to the Gentiles.[35] S. Brown points to this parable to stress that the 'call' (*kaleō*) of Jesus is not *verbum efficax*. It can be refused.[36]

The same dimensions of appropriation are fitting today as well. Miller combines several of these in his application, saying:

> Our parable sounds a warning. 'You may *think you* have said yes to God. But what if you are like those . . . who were invited to a banquet, accepted it, but then when the meal was actually

---

[31] Jeremias, *Parables*: 180.

[32] Ernst Haenchen, 'Das Gleichnis vom grossen Mahl,' in *Die Bibel und Wir* (Tübingen: Mohr [Siebeck], 1968): 151–53.

[33] Dormeyer, 'Literarische:' 217–19.

[34] Eta Linnemann, *Jesus of the Parables; Introduction and Exposition* (New York: Harper & Row, 1967): 91. Linnemann holds that the excuses were meant originally as delays—it doesn't suit now—not refusals. But most commentators regard the excuses as refusals. Marshall explicitly rejects Linnemann's proposal. *Luke*: 590–91.

[35] Linnemann, *Jesus*: 158–67.

[36] Schuyler Brown, *Apostasy and Perseverance in the Theology of Luke*, Analecta biblica (Rome: Pontifical Biblical Institute, 1969): 90.

ready, were too snobbish and too busy to attend? What if others whom you now despise take your place? Therefore, take care, you polite, self-righteous Pharisee. Take care that in your aloof busyness with fields and oxen and wives [Luke], with money, houses, wedding feasts, and capital investments [Thomas], with farms and commerce [Matthew], you do not miss out on what God is now doing. If you do, tax collectors and harlots might indeed find their way into the kingdom of God before you.'[37]

T. W. Manson[38] has pointed out that this parable contains two essential truths: that no one can enter God's kingdom without an invitation and that no one is excluded except by his or her own choice. Further, we cannot save ourselves, but we are culpable for our own lostness and judgement. In my own appropriation of the parable,[39] I have connected the parable to trends in the church today:

In striking ways this parable is re-enacted in our world today. Western cultural people who have the Christian tradition and have received the invitation to the kingdom banquet are going after money and family security and are making and dodging wars, while the so-called second and third world peoples are coming to the feast. We see the results of these choices in what people consider important: minimal or no church involvement but many self-help agendas; dwindling support for church-wide institutions and their programs but larger investments for personal security for the future; and fewer people from . . . congregations choosing to prepare for pastoral ministry and church leadership but choosing instead more secure and lucrative vocations. But the point of the parable is: others will respond and the kingdom mission will go forward. Thus, we can expect that more and more the growing churches, mission programs, and seminaries will be increasingly populated by the two-thirds world peoples. . . .

Now perhaps the fault lies with the church and its institutions: we have lost the celebrative, the banquet aspect

[37] Miller, *Step By Step*: 111–12.
[38] T. W. Manson, *The Sayings of Jesus as Recorded In the Gospels according to St. Matthew and St. Luke Arranged with Introduction and Comment* (London: SCM Press, 1971): 130.
[39] Willard M. Swartley. 'What Does It Mean To Be Ready for the Celebration?' *Gospel Herald* (Oct. 4, 1994): 7–8.

of the gospel with its central feature of welcoming the repentant with forgiveness and grace. Or, perhaps the cause goes even deeper: because we have chosen other priorities we have lost our capacity to discern the time and nature of the banquet. We can no longer hear the call of the kingdom ... [to the banquet]. We are becoming ... the salt that has lost its fertilising power.

Index of Authors

Index of Scripture References

Index of Ancient Sources